Adobe®
Adobe® After Effects® CC

CLASSROOM IN A BOOK®
The official training workbook from Adobe Systems

ISBN-13: 978-0-321-92960-0
ISBN-10:   0-321-92960-8

9 8 7 6 5 4 3 2

WHERE ARE THE LESSON FILES?

Purchasing this Classroom in a Book gives you access to the lesson files that you'll need to complete the exercises in the book, as well as other content to help you learn more about Adobe software and use it with greater efficiency and ease. The diagram below represents the contents of the lesson files directory, which should help you locate the files you need. Please see the Getting Started section for full download instructions.

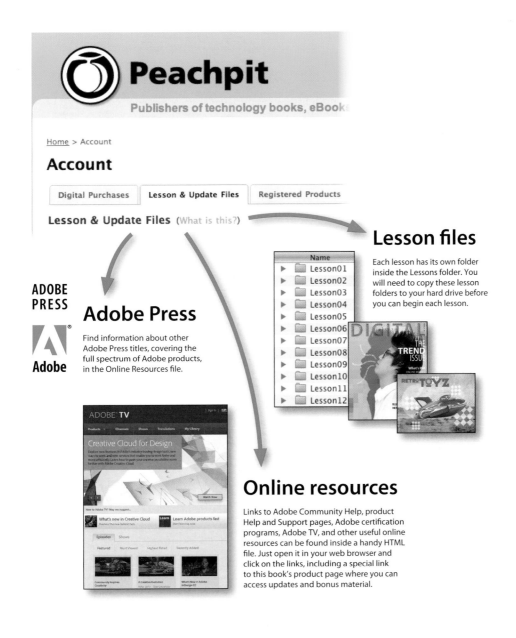

Adobe Press

Find information about other Adobe Press titles, covering the full spectrum of Adobe products, in the Online Resources file.

Lesson files

Each lesson has its own folder inside the Lessons folder. You will need to copy these lesson folders to your hard drive before you can begin each lesson.

Online resources

Links to Adobe Community Help, product Help and Support pages, Adobe certification programs, Adobe TV, and other useful online resources can be found inside a handy HTML file. Just open it in your web browser and click on the links, including a special link to this book's product page where you can access updates and bonus material.

CONTENTS

GETTING STARTED

Adobe After Effects CC provides a comprehensive set of 2D and 3D tools for compositing, animation, and effects that motion-graphics professionals, visual effects artists, web designers, and film and video professionals need. After Effects is widely used for digital post-production of film, video, DVD, and the web. You can composite layers in various ways, apply and combine sophisticated visual and audio effects, and animate both objects and effects.

About Classroom in a Book

Adobe After Effects CC Classroom in a Book is part of the official training series for Adobe graphics and publishing software, developed with the support of Adobe product experts. The lessons are designed to let you learn at your own pace. If you're new to Adobe After Effects, you'll learn the fundamental concepts and features you'll need to master the program. And if you've been using Adobe After Effects for a while, you'll find that Classroom in a Book teaches many advanced features, including tips and techniques for using the latest version.

Although each lesson provides step-by-step instructions for creating a specific project, there's room for exploration and experimentation. You can follow the book from start to finish, or do only the lessons that match your interests and needs. Each lesson concludes with a review section summarizing what you've covered.

Prerequisites

Before beginning to use *Adobe After Effects CC Classroom in a Book*, make sure that your system is set up correctly and that you've installed the required software and hardware. You should have a working knowledge of your computer and operating system. You should know how to use the mouse and standard menus and commands, and also how to open, save, and close files. If you need to review these techniques, see the printed or online documentation included with your Microsoft® Windows® or Apple® Mac® OS software.

To complete the lessons in this book, you'll need to have both Adobe After Effects CC and Adobe Bridge CC installed.

Installing After Effects and Bridge

You must purchase the Adobe After Effects CC software separately. For system requirements and complete instructions on installing the software, visit www.adobe.com/support. Note that After Effects CC requires a 64-bit operating system and OpenGL 2.0 support. You must also have Apple QuickTime 7.6.6 or later installed on your system.

Many of the lessons in this book use Adobe Bridge. After Effects and Bridge use separate installers. You must install these applications from Adobe Creative Cloud onto your hard disk. Follow the onscreen instructions.

Optimizing performance

Creating movies is memory-intensive work for a desktop computer. After Effects CC requires a minimum of 4GB of RAM. The more RAM that is available to After Effects, the faster the application will work for you. For information about optimizing memory, cache, and other settings for After Effects, see "Improve performance" in After Effects Help.

Restoring default preferences

The preferences files control the way the After Effects user interface appears on your screen. The instructions in this book assume that you see the default interface when they describe the appearance of tools, options, windows, panels, and so forth. Therefore, it's a good idea to restore the default preferences, especially if you are new to After Effects.

Each time you quit After Effects, the panel positions and certain command settings are recorded in the preferences files. To restore the original default settings, press Ctrl+Alt+Shift (Windows) or Command+Option+Shift (Mac OS) while starting After Effects. (After Effects creates new preferences files if they don't already exist the next time you start the program.)

Restoring the default preferences can be especially helpful if someone has already customized After Effects on your computer. If your copy of After Effects hasn't been used yet, these files won't exist, so this procedure is unnecessary.

Important: If you want to save the current settings, you can rename a preferences file instead of deleting it. When you are ready to restore those settings, change the name back, and make sure that the file is located in the correct preferences folder.

1 Locate the After Effects preferences folder on your computer:

   • **For Windows:** .../Users/*<user name>*/AppData/Roaming/Adobe/
     AfterEffects/12.0.

   • **For Mac OS:** .../Users/*<user name>*/Library/Preferences/Adobe/
     After Effects/12.0

2 Rename any preferences files you want to preserve, and then restart After Effects.

Accessing the Classroom in a Book files

The lessons in *Adobe After Effects CC Classroom in a Book* use specific source files, such as image files created in Adobe Photoshop® and Adobe Illustrator®, audio files, and prepared QuickTime movies. To complete the lessons in this book, you need to download the lesson files from peachpit.com. You can download the files for individual lessons, or download them all in a single file.

Your Account page is also where you'll find any updates to the chapters or to the lesson files. Look on the Lesson & Update Files tab to access the most current content.

To access the Classroom in a Book files, do the following:

1 On a Mac or PC, go to www.peachpit.com/redeem, and enter the code found at the back of your book.

2 If you do not have a Peachpit.com account, create one when you're prompted to do so.

3 Click the Lesson & Update Files tab on your Account page. This tab lists downloadable files.

4 Click the lesson file links to download them to your computer.

5 Create a new folder on your hard disk, and name it **Lessons**. Then, drag the lesson files you downloaded into the Lessons folder on your hard disk.

● Note: In Mac OS 10.7 and later, the user library folder is hidden by default. To see it, in the Finder, choose Go > Go To Folder. In the Go To Folder dialog box, type **~/Library**, and then click Go.

● Note: As you complete each lesson, you will preserve the start files. In case you overwrite them, you can restore the original files by downloading the corresponding lesson files from your Account page at peachpit.com.

When you begin each lesson, you will navigate to the folder with that lesson number, where you will find all of the assets, sample movies, and other project files you need to complete the lesson.

If you have limited storage space on your computer, you can download each lesson folder individually as you need it, and delete it afterward if desired. You do not have to save any finished project if you don't want to, or if you have limited hard disk space.

About copying the sample movies and projects

You will create and render one or more QuickTime movies in some lessons in this book. The files in the Sample_Movie folders are examples that you can use to see the end results of each lesson and to compare them with your own results.

The files in the End_Project_File folders are samples of the completed project for each lesson. Use these files for reference if you want to compare your work in progress with the project files used to generate the sample movies. These end-project files vary in size from relatively small to a couple of megabytes, so you can either download them all now if you have ample storage space, or download just the end-project file for each lesson as needed, and then delete it when you finish that lesson.

How to use these lessons

Each lesson in this book provides step-by-step instructions for creating one or more specific elements of a real-world project. The lessons build on each other in terms of concepts and skills, so the best way to learn from this book is to proceed through the lessons in sequential order. In this book, some techniques and processes are explained and described in detail only the first few times you perform them.

Many aspects of the After Effects application can be controlled by multiple techniques, such as a menu command, a button, dragging, and a keyboard shortcut. Only one or two of the methods are described in any given procedure, so that you can learn different ways of working even when the task is one you've done before.

The organization of the lessons is also design-oriented rather than feature-oriented. That means, for example, that you'll work with layers and effects on real-world design projects over several lessons, rather than in just one lesson.

Additional resources

Adobe After Effects CC Classroom in a Book is not meant to replace documentation that comes with the program or to be a comprehensive reference for every feature. Only the commands and options used in the lessons are explained in this book. For comprehensive information about program features and tutorials, refer to these resources:

- **Adobe After Effects Help and Support:** www.adobe.com/support/aftereffects is where you can find and browse Help and Support content on Adobe.com.

- **Adobe Creative Cloud Learning:** helpx.adobe.com/creative-cloud/tutorials.html provides inspiration, key techniques, cross-product workflows, and updates on new features. The Creative Cloud Learn page is available only to Creative Cloud members.

- **Adobe Forums:** forums.adobe.com lets you tap into peer-to-peer discussions, questions, and answers about Adobe products.

- **Adobe TV:** tv.adobe.com is an online video resource for expert instruction and inspiration about Adobe products, including a How To channel to get you started with your product.

- **Adobe Design Center:** www.adobe.com/designcenter offers thoughtful articles on design and design issues, a gallery showcasing the work of top-notch designers, tutorials, and more.

- **Resources for educators:** www.adobe.com/education and edex.adobe.com offer a treasure trove of information for instructors who teach classes on Adobe software. Find solutions for education at all levels, including free curricula that use an integrated approach to teaching Adobe software and can be used to prepare for the Adobe Certified Associate exams.

Also check out these useful links:

- **Adobe Marketplace & Exchange:** www.adobe.com/cfusion/exchange is a central resource for finding tools, services, extensions, code samples, and more to supplement and extend your Adobe products.

- **Adobe After Effects CC product home page:** www.adobe.com/products/aftereffects

- **Adobe Labs:** labs.adobe.com gives you access to early builds of cutting-edge technology as well as forums where you can interact with both the Adobe development teams building that technology and other like-minded members of the community.

Adobe certification

The Adobe training and certification programs are designed to help Adobe customers improve and promote their product-proficiency skills. There are four levels of certification:

- Adobe Certified Associate (ACA)
- Adobe Certified Expert (ACE)
- Adobe Certified Instructor (ACI)
- Adobe Authorized Training Center (AATC)

The Adobe Certified Associate (ACA) credential certifies that individuals have the entry-level skills to plan, design, build, and maintain effective communications using different forms of digital media.

The Adobe Certified Expert program is a way for expert users to upgrade their credentials. You can use Adobe certification as a catalyst for getting a raise, finding a job, or promoting your expertise.

If you are an ACE-level instructor, the Adobe Certified Instructor program takes your skills to the next level and gives you access to a wide range of Adobe resources.

Adobe Authorized Training Centers offer instructor-led courses and training on Adobe products, employing only Adobe Certified Instructors. A directory of AATCs is available at partners.adobe.com.

For information on the Adobe Certified programs, visit www.adobe.com/support/certification/main.html.

1 GETTING TO KNOW THE WORKFLOW

Lesson overview

In this lesson, you'll learn how to do the following:

- Create a project and import footage.

- Create compositions and arrange layers.

- Navigate the Adobe After Effects interface.

- Use the Project, Composition, and Timeline panels.

- Apply basic keyframes and effects.

- Preview your work using standard and RAM previews.

- Customize the workspace.

- Adjust preferences related to the user interface.

- Find additional resources for using After Effects.

 This lesson will take about an hour to complete. Download the Lesson01 project files from the Lesson & Update Files tab on your Account page at www.peachpit.com, if you haven't already done so. As you work on this lesson, you'll preserve the start files. If you need to restore the start files, download them from your Account page.

Whether you use After Effects to animate a simple DVD title sequence or to create complex special effects, you generally follow the same basic workflow. The After Effects interface facilitates your work and adapts to each stage of production.

Getting started

A basic After Effects workflow follows six steps: importing and organizing footage, creating compositions and arranging layers, adding effects, animating elements, previewing your work, and rendering and outputting the final composition so that it can be viewed by others. In this lesson, you will create a simple animated video using this workflow, and along the way, you'll learn your way around the After Effects interface.

First, you'll preview the final movie to see what you'll create in this lesson.

1 Make sure the following files are in the AECC_CIB/Lessons/Lesson01 folder on your hard disk, or download them from your Account page at www.peachpit.com now:

   • In the Assets folder: bgwtext.psd, dancers.mov, gc_adobe_dance.mp3, kaleidoscope_waveforms.mov, pulsating_radial_waves.mov

   • In the Sample_Movie folder: Lesson01.mov

2 Open and play the Lesson01.mov sample movie to see what you will create in this lesson. When you are done, quit QuickTime Player. You may delete this sample movie from your hard disk if you have limited storage space.

Creating a project and importing footage

▶ **Tip:** Restoring default preferences can be tricky in Windows, especially if you're working on a fast system. Press the keys after you double-click the application icon but before After Effects begins to list the files it's activating.

When you begin each lesson of this book, it's a good idea to restore the default preferences for After Effects. (See "Restoring default preferences" on page 2.) You can do this with a simple keyboard shortcut.

1 Start After Effects, and then immediately hold down Ctrl+Alt+Shift (Windows) or Command+Option+Shift (Mac OS) to restore default preferences settings. When prompted, click OK to delete your preferences.

2 Click Close to close the Welcome screen.

After Effects opens to display an empty, untitled project.

An After Effects project is a single file that stores references to all the footage you use in that project. It also contains *compositions*, which are the individual containers used to combine footage, apply effects, and, ultimately, drive the output.

When you begin a project, often the first thing you'll do is add footage to it.

▶ **Tip:** To quickly maximize a panel, position the pointer over it and press the accent grave (`) key— the unshifted character under the tilde (~) on standard US keyboards. Press the ` key again to return the panel to its original size.

3 Choose File > Import > File.

4 Navigate to the Assets folder in your AECC_CIB/Lessons/Lesson01 folder. Shift-click to select the dancers.mov, gc_adobe_dance.mp3, kaleidoscope_waveforms.mov, and pulsating_radial_waves.mov files (all the files except bgwtext.psd). Then click Import or Open.

About the After Effects work area

After Effects offers a flexible, customizable work area. The main window of the program is called the *application window*. Panels are organized in this window in an arrangement called a *workspace*. The default workspace contains groups of panels as well as panels that stand alone, as shown below.

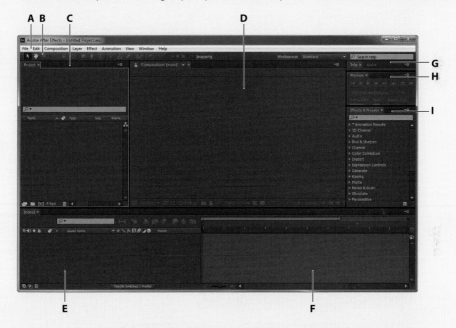

*A. Application window B. Tools panel C. Project panel D. Composition panel E. Timeline panel
F. Time graph G. Grouped panels (Info and Audio) H. Preview panel I. Effects & Presets panel*

You customize a workspace by dragging the panels into the configuration that best suits your working style. You can drag panels to new locations, move panels into or out of a group, place panels alongside each other, and undock a panel so that it floats in a new window above the application window. As you rearrange panels, the other panels resize automatically to fit the window.

When you drag a panel by its tab to relocate it, the area where you can drop it—called a *drop zone*—becomes highlighted. The drop zone determines where and how the panel is inserted into the workspace. Dragging a panel to a drop zone either docks it or groups it.

If you drop a panel along the edge of another panel, group, or window, it will dock next to the existing group, resizing all groups to accommodate the new panel.

If you drop a panel in the middle of another panel or group, or along the tab area of a panel, it will be added to the existing group and be placed at the top of the stack. Grouping a panel does not resize other groups.

You can also open a panel in a floating window. To do so, select the panel, and then choose Undock Panel or Undock Frame from the panel menu. Or, drag the panel or group outside the application window.

A *footage item* is the basic unit in an After Effects project. You can import many types of footage items, including moving-image files, still-image files, still-image sequences, audio files, layered files from Adobe Photoshop and Adobe Illustrator, other After Effects projects, and projects created in Adobe Premiere® Pro. You can import footage items at any time.

As you import assets, After Effects reports its progress in the Info panel.

Because one of the footage items for this project is a multilayer Photoshop file, you'll import it separately as a composition.

▶ **Tip:** You can also choose File > Import > Multiple Files to select files located in different folders, or drag and drop files from Explorer or the Finder. You can use Adobe Bridge to search for, manage, preview, and import footage.

5 Double-click in the lower area of the Project panel to open the Import File dialog box.

6 Navigate to the Lesson01/Assets folder again, and select the bgwtext.psd file. Choose Composition from the Import As menu, and then click Import or Open.

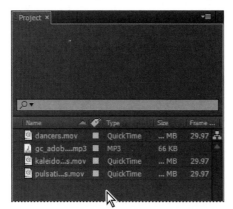

After Effects opens an additional dialog box with options for the file you're importing.

7   In the bgwtext.psd dialog box, choose Composition from the Import Kind menu to import the layered Photoshop file as a composition. Select Editable Layer Styles in the Layer Options area, and then click OK. The footage items appear in the Project panel.

8   In the Project panel, click to select different footage items. Notice that a thumbnail preview appears at the top of the Project panel. You can also see the file type and size, as well as other information about each item, in the Project panel columns.

When you import files, After Effects doesn't copy the video and audio data itself into your project. Instead, each footage item in the Project panel contains a reference link to the source files. When After Effects needs to retrieve image or audio data, it reads it from the source file. This keeps the project file small, and allows you to update source files in another application without modifying the project.

If you move a file or if After Effects can't access its location, it will report that the file is missing. To find missing files, choose File > Dependencies > Find Missing Footage. You can also type **Missing Footage** into the Search box in the Project panel to look for the missing assets.

To save time and minimize the size and complexity of a project, import a footage item once, and then use it multiple times in a composition. In some cases, you may need to import a source file more than once, such as if you want to use it at two different frame rates.

After you've imported footage, it's a good time to save the project.

9   Choose File > Save. In the Save As dialog box, navigate to the AECC_CIB/ Lessons/Lesson01/Finished_Project folder. Name the project **Lesson01_ Finished.aep**, and then click Save.

Creating a composition and arranging layers

The next step of the workflow is to create a composition. You create all animation, layering, and effects in a composition. An After Effects composition has both spatial dimensions and a temporal dimension (time).

Compositions include one or more layers, arranged in the Composition panel and in the Timeline panel. Any item that you add to a composition—such as a still image, moving-image file, audio file, light layer, camera layer, or even another composition—becomes a new layer. Simple projects may include only one composition, while elaborate projects may include several compositions to organize large amounts of footage or intricate effects sequences.

To create a composition, you'll drag the footage items into the Timeline panel, and After Effects will create layers for them.

1   In the Project panel, Ctrl-click (Windows) or Command-click (Mac OS) to select the bgwtext composition as well as the dancers, gc_adobe_dance, kaleidoscope_waveforms, and pulsating_radial_waves footage items.

2   Drag the selected footage items into the Timeline panel. The New Composition From Selection dialog box appears.

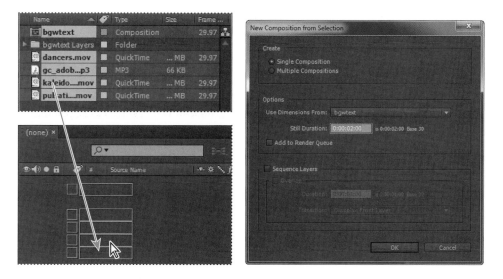

After Effects bases the dimensions of the new composition on the selected footage. In this example, all of the footage is sized identically, so you can accept the default settings.

3 Click OK to create the new composition.

The footage items appear as layers in the Timeline panel, and After Effects displays the composition, named bgwtext 2, in the Composition panel.

About layers

Layers are the components you use to build a composition. Any item that you add to a composition—such as a still image, moving-image file, audio file, light layer, camera layer, or even another composition—becomes a new layer. Without layers, a composition consists only of an empty frame.

Using layers, you can work with specific footage items in a composition without affecting any other footage. For example, you can move, rotate, and draw masks for one layer without disturbing any other layers in the composition, or you can use the same footage in more than one layer and use it differently in each instance. In general, the layer order in the Timeline panel corresponds to the stacking order in the Composition panel.

When you add a footage item to a composition, the footage becomes the source for a new layer. A composition can have any number of layers, and you can also include a composition as a layer in another composition, which is called *nesting*.

Some of the assets are longer than others, but you want them all to appear only as long as the dancers are on the screen. You'll change the length of the entire composition to 1:15 to match the dancers.

4 Choose Composition > Composition Settings.

5 In the Composition Settings dialog box, type **1:15** for the Duration, and then click OK.

The Timeline panel displays the same duration for each of the layers.

In this composition, there are five footage items, and therefore five layers in the Timeline panel. Depending on the order in which the elements were selected when you imported them, your layer stack may differ from the one shown on the previous page. The layers need to be in a specific order as you add effects and animations, however, so you'll rearrange them now.

6   Click an empty area of the Timeline panel to deselect the layers, and then drag bgwtext to the bottom of the layer stack if it is not already there. Drag the other four layers so that they're in the order shown in the figure.

● **Note:** You may need to click a blank area of the Timeline panel or press F2 to deselect layers before you can select an individual layer.

From this point forward in the workflow, you should be thinking about layers, not footage items. You'll change the column title accordingly.

7   Click the Source Name column title in the Timeline panel to change it to Layer Name.

8   Choose File > Save to save your project so far.

About the Tools panel

As soon as you create a composition, the tools in the Tools panel in the upper left corner of the After Effects application window become available. After Effects includes tools that enable you to modify elements of your composition. Some of these tools—the Selection tool and the Hand tool, for example—will be familiar to you if you use other Adobe applications, such as Photoshop. Others will be new. The following image identifies the tools in the Tools panel for your reference.

A. Selection *B.* Hand *C.* Zoom *D.* Rotation *E.* Camera tools *F.* Pan Behind *G.* Mask and Shape tools *H.* Pen tools *I.* Type tools *J.* Brush *K.* Clone Stamp *L.* Eraser *M.* Roto Brush *N.* Puppet tools

When you hover the pointer over any button in the Tools panel, a tool tip identifies the tool and its keyboard shortcut. A small triangle in the lower right corner of the button indicates that one or more additional tools are hidden behind it. Click and hold the button to display the hidden tools, and then select the tool you want to use.

Adding effects and modifying layer properties

● **Note:** This exercise is just the tip of the iceberg. You will learn more about effects and animation presets in Lesson 2, "Creating a Basic Animation Using Effects and Presets," and throughout the rest of this book.

Now that your composition is set up, you can start having fun—applying effects, making transformations, and adding animation. You can add any combination of effects and modify any of a layer's properties, such as size, placement, and opacity. Using effects, you can alter a layer's appearance or sound, and even generate visual elements from scratch. The easiest way to start is to apply any of the hundreds of effects included with After Effects.

Preparing the layers

You'll apply the effects to duplicates of selected layers—the dancers layer and the kaleidoscope_waveforms layer. Working with duplicates lets you apply an effect to one layer and then use it in conjunction with the unmodified original.

1 Select the first layer, dancers.mov, in the Timeline panel, and then choose Edit > Duplicate. A new layer with the same name appears at the top of the stack, so the first two layers are now both named dancers.mov.

▶ **Tip:** You can make the Layer Name column wider in order to see the full layer name, if you need to.

2 Select the second layer, and rename it to avoid confusion: Press Enter (Windows) or Return (Mac OS) to make the name editable, and type **dancers_with_effects.mov**. Then press Enter or Return again to accept the new name.

▶ **Tip:** Use the keyboard shortcut Ctrl+D (Windows) or Command+D (Mac OS) to copy the layers quickly.

3 Select the kaleidoscope_wave-forms layer, and make two duplicates. Rename the duplicates **kaleidoscope_left.mov** and **kaleidoscope_right.mov**.

4 Drag if necessary to rearrange the layers in the Timeline panel so that they're in the order shown.

Adding a Radial Blur effect

The Radial Blur effect creates blurs around a specific point in a layer, simulating the effects of a zooming or rotating camera. You'll add a Radial Blur effect to the dancers.

1 Select the dancers_with_effects layer in the Timeline panel. Notice that layer handles appear around the layer in the Composition panel.

● **Note:** If you double-click a layer in the Timeline panel, it appears in the Layer panel. To return to the Composition panel, click the Composition tab.

2 In the Effects & Presets panel at the right side of the application window, type **radial blur** in the search box.

After Effects searches for effects and presets that contain the letters you type, and displays the results interactively. Before you have finished typing, the Radial Blur effect—located in the Blur & Sharpen category—appears in the panel.

3　Drag the Radial Blur effect onto the dancers_with_effects layer in the Timeline panel. After Effects applies the effect and automatically opens the Effect Controls panel in the upper left area of the workspace.

Now you'll customize the settings.

4　In the Effect Controls panel, choose Zoom from the Type menu.

▶ Tip: You can also type the x and y values directly into the coordinate fields in the Effect Controls panel, or you can position the pointer over the fields to see the double-arrow icon (↔), and then drag right or left to increase or decrease the values, respectively. Dragging to change values is sometimes called *scrubbing*.

5　In the Composition panel, move the center point of the blur lower by dragging the center cross-hair (⊕) down until it's at the horizon line. As you drag the cross-hair, the Center value updates in the Effect Controls panel. The left and right values are x and y coordinates, respectively. Center the blur at approximately 325, 335.

6　Click the number next to Amount, type **200**, and press Enter or Return.

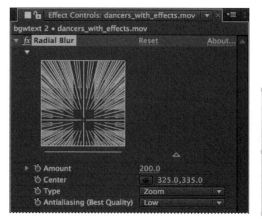

Adding an exposure effect

To punch up the brightness of this layer, you will apply the Exposure color-correction effect. This effect lets you make tonal adjustments to footage. It simulates the result of modifying the exposure setting (in f-stops) of the camera that captured the image.

1 Click the *x* in the search box in the Effects & Presets panel to clear it, and then locate the Exposure effect by doing one of the following:

- Type **Exposure** in the search box.

- Click the triangle next to Color Correction to expand the list of color-correction effects in alphabetical order.

2 Drag the Exposure effect in the Color Correction category onto the dancers_with_effects layer name in the Timeline panel. After Effects adds the Exposure settings to the Effect Controls panel under the Radial Blur effect.

3 In the Effect Controls panel, click the triangle next to the Radial Blur effect to collapse those settings so that you can see the Exposure settings more easily.

4 For Master Exposure, enter **1.60**. This will make everything brighter in the layer to simulate an overexposed image.

▶ **Tip:** Make sure to select the Exposure effect in the Color Correction category, not the Exposure animation preset in the Lights And Optical category.

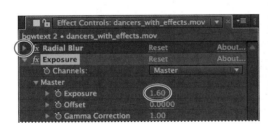

Transforming layer properties

The dancers look smashing, so you can turn your attention to the kaleidoscope waveforms that are part of the background. You'll reposition the copies you created earlier to create an edgy effect.

1 Select the kaleidoscope_left layer (layer 5) in the Timeline panel.

2 Click the triangle to the left of the layer number to expand the layer, and then expand the layer's Transform properties: Anchor Point, Position, Scale, Rotation, and Opacity.

▶ **Tip:** With any layer selected in the Timeline panel, you can display any single Transform property by pressing a keyboard shortcut: P displays Position; A displays Anchor Point; S displays Scale; R displays Rotation; T displays Opacity.

3 If you can't see the properties, scroll down the Timeline panel using the scroll bar at the right side of the panel. Better yet, select the kaleidoscope_left layer name again and press P. This keyboard shortcut displays only the Position property, which is the only property you want to change for this exercise.

You'll move this layer to the left about 200 pixels.

4 Change the x coordinate for the Position property to **160**. Leave the y coordinate at 243.

5   Select the kaleidoscope_right layer (layer 6), and press P to display its Position property. You will move this layer to the right.

6   Change the x coordinate for the kaleidoscope_right Position property to **560**. Leave the y coordinate at 243. Now you can see the three waveforms—left, center, and right—in the Composition panel, hanging like a beaded light curtain.

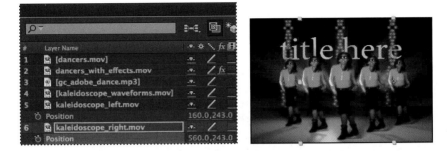

To contrast the left and right waveforms with the center waveform, you will reduce their opacity.

7   Select the kaleidoscope_left layer in the Timeline panel, and press T to reveal its Opacity property. Set it to **30%**.

8   Select the kaleidoscope_right layer in the Timeline panel, press T to reveal its Opacity property, and set it to **30%**.

Tip: To change the Opacity property for multiple layers at once, select the layers, press T, and change the property for one of the selected layers.

9   Choose File > Save to save your work so far.

Animating the composition

So far, you've started a project, created a composition, imported footage, and applied some effects. It all looks great, but how about some movement? You've applied only static effects.

In After Effects, you can change any combination of a layer's properties over time using conventional keyframing, expressions, or keyframe assistants. You'll explore many of these methods throughout the lessons of this book. For this exercise, you will animate the Position property of a text layer using keyframes, and then use an animation preset so that the letters appear to rain down on the screen.

Preparing the text composition

For this exercise, you'll work with a separate composition—the one you imported from a layered Photoshop file.

● **Note:** If the Project tab isn't visible, choose Window > Project to open the Project panel.

1 Select the Project tab to display the Project panel, and then double-click the bgwtext composition to open it as a composition in its own Timeline panel.

This composition is the layered Photoshop file you imported. Two layers—Title Here and Background—appear in the Timeline panel. The Title Here layer contains placeholder text that was created in Photoshop.

About the Timeline panel

Use the Timeline panel to animate layer properties and set In and Out points for a layer. (In and Out points are the points at which a layer begins and ends in the composition.) Many of the Timeline panel controls are organized in columns of related functions. By default, the Timeline panel contains a number of columns and controls, as shown in the following figure:

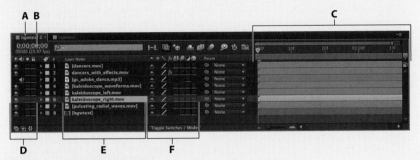

A. Composition name B. Current time C. Time graph/Graph Editor area
D. Audio/Video Switches column E. Source Name/Layer Name column F. Layer switches

Understanding the time graph

The time graph portion of the Timeline panel (the right side) contains a time ruler, markers to indicate specific times, and duration bars for the layers in your composition.

Before delving too deeply into animation, it will help to understand at least some of these controls. The duration of a composition, a layer, or a footage item is represented visually in the time graph. On the time ruler, the current-time indicator marks the frame you are viewing or editing, and the frame appears in the Composition panel.

The work area start and end brackets indicate the part of the composition that will be rendered for previews or final output. When you work on a composition, you may want to render only a portion of it by specifying a segment of the composition time ruler as a work area.

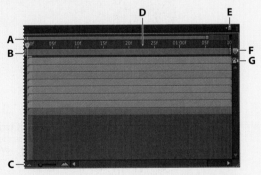

A. Time navigator start and end brackets B. Work area start and end brackets C. Time zoom slider D. Time ruler E. Timeline panel menu F. Composition marker bin G. Composition button

A composition's current time appears in the upper left corner of the Timeline panel. To move to a different time, drag the current-time indicator in the time ruler or click the current-time field in the Timeline panel or Composition panel, type a new time, and click OK.

For more information about the Timeline panel, see After Effects Help.

At the top of the Composition panel is the Composition Navigator bar, which displays the relationship between the main composition (bgwtext 2) and the current composition (bgwtext), which is nested within the main composition.

You can nest multiple compositions within each other; the Composition Navigator bar displays the entire composition path. Arrows between the composition names indicate the direction in which information flows.

Before you can replace the text, you need to make the layer editable.

Note: If you see a warning about missing fonts or layer dependencies, click OK.

2 Select the Title Here layer (layer 1) in the Timeline panel, and then choose Layer > Convert To Editable Text.

A T icon appears next to the layer name in the Timeline panel, indicating that it is now an editable text layer. The layer is also selected in the Composition panel, ready for you to edit.

Animating text with animation presets

You'll start by replacing the placeholder text with real text. Then you'll animate it.

Note: After Effects offers robust character and paragraph formatting controls, but the default settings—whatever typeface appears when you type—should be fine for this project. You'll learn more about type in Lesson 3, "Animating Text."

1 Select the Horizontal Type tool (T) in the Tools panel, and drag over the placeholder text in the Composition panel to select it. Then type **AQUO**.

2 Select the Title Here layer in the Timeline panel again, and make sure you're at the first frame of the animation by doing one of the following:

- Drag the current-time indicator all the way to the left of the time ruler, to 0:00.

- Press the Home key on your keyboard.

3 Select the Effects & Presets tab to display the panel. Then type **bubble** in the search box.

4 Select the Zoom-Bubble effect in the Transitions-Movement category, and drag it onto the AQUO text in the Composition panel.

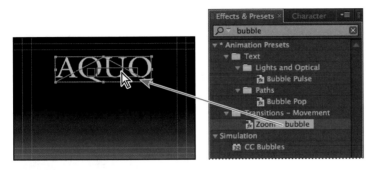

After Effects adds the effect, and displays its settings in the Effect Controls panel. You can change effect settings in this panel or in the Timeline panel. You'll add keyframes in the Timeline panel.

About timecode and duration

The primary concept related to time is *duration*, or length. Each footage item, layer, and composition in a project has its own duration, which is reflected in the beginning and ending times displayed in the time rulers in the Composition, Layer, and Timeline panels.

The way you view and specify time in After Effects depends on the display style, or unit of measure, that you use to describe time. By default, After Effects displays time in Society of Motion Picture and Television Engineers (SMPTE) timecode: hours, minutes, seconds, and frames. Note that the figures are separated by semicolons in the After Effects interface, representing drop-frame timecode (which adjusts for the real-time frame rate), but this book uses a colon to represent non-drop-frame timecode.

To learn when and how to change to another system of time display, such as frames, or feet and frames of film, see After Effects Help.

5   In the Timeline panel, expand the Title Here layer, and then expand Effects > Zoom-bubble to reveal the Transition Completion setting.

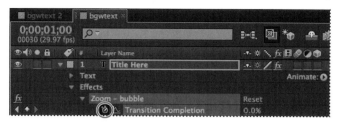

● **Note:** Don't select the Transition Completion property, as that will select both keyframes, and you want to change only the value of the second one.

The stopwatch icon (⏱) next to Transition Completion is selected, and the value is 0%. A diamond appears in the Transition Completion bar for the layer in the time graph, indicating the keyframe that After Effects created when you added the effect.

6   Go to 1:00 in the timeline by clicking the Current Time field in the Timeline panel and typing **100**, or by dragging the current-time indicator to 1:00.

7   Change the Transition Completion value to **100%**.

Even though this is a simple animation, you'll learn good animation practices right away by adding ease-in controls using the Easy Ease feature. Easing into (and out of) animations keeps the motion from appearing to be too sudden or robotic.

▶ **Tip:** To see greater detail in the Timeline panel, move the time zoom slider at the bottom of the panel.

8   Right-click or Control-click the keyframe at 1:00, and choose Keyframe Assistant > Easy Ease In.

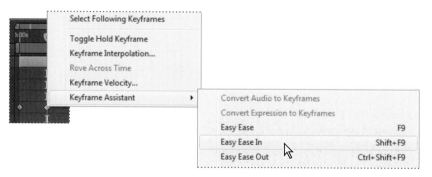

Keyframes are used to create and control animation, effects, audio properties, and many other kinds of changes that occur over time. A keyframe marks the point in time where you specify a value, such as spatial position, opacity, or audio volume. Values between keyframes are *interpolated*. When you use keyframes to create a change over time, you must use at least two keyframes—one for the state at the beginning of the change, and one for the state at the end of the change.

9   Manually preview the effect by moving the current-time indicator from 0 to 1:00.

Changing preset settings in the Effect Controls panel

You'll add another animation preset to the type layer, but this time, you'll adjust its settings in the Effect Controls panel.

1 Go to the beginning of the time ruler by doing one of the following:

   • Drag the current-time indicator to the left in the time ruler so that it's positioned at 0:00.

   • Click the Current Time field in the Timeline panel or Composition panel, and type **00**. If you clicked in the Current Time field in the Composition panel, click OK to close the Go To Time dialog box.

2 Type **channel blur** in the search box in the Effects & Presets panel.

3 Drag the Channel Blur effect onto the type in the Composition panel. After Effects adds the Channel Blur effect to the Timeline panel and displays its settings in the Effect Controls panel.

4 In the Effect Controls panel, click the triangles next to Zoom-bubble, Spherize, and Transform to hide their settings so you can focus on the Channel Blur settings.

5 Set the Red Blurriness, Green Blurriness, Blue Blurriness, and Alpha Blurriness values to **50**.

6 Click the stopwatch icon next to each of the settings you changed to create initial keyframes.

7 From the Blur Dimensions menu, choose Vertical.

8 Go to 1:00 in the timeline.

9 Change the values as follows:

- Red Blurriness: **75**

- Green Blurriness: **25**

- Blue Blurriness: **0**

- Alpha Blurriness: **0**

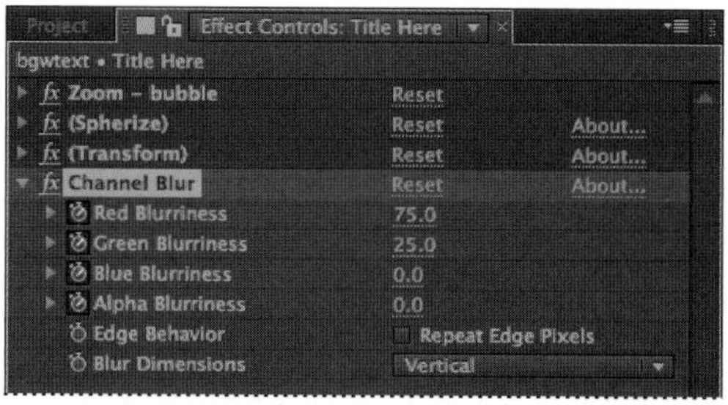

The blue lines at the top, bottom, and sides of the Composition panel indicate title-safe and action-safe zones. Television sets enlarge a video image and allow some portion of its outer edges to be cut off by the edge of the screen. This is known as *overscan*. The amount of overscan is not consistent between television sets, so you should keep important parts of a video image, such as action or titles, within margins called *safe zones*. Keep your text inside the inner blue guides to ensure that it is in the title-safe zone, and keep important scene elements inside the outer blue guides to ensure that they are in the action-safe zone.

Previewing your work

You're probably eager to see the results of your work. After Effects provides several methods for previewing compositions, including standard preview, RAM preview, and manual preview. (For a list of manual preview controls, see After Effects Help.) All three methods are accessible through the Preview panel, which appears on the right side of the application window in the Standard workspace.

Using standard preview

Standard preview (commonly called a *spacebar preview*) plays the composition from the current-time indicator to the end of the composition. Standard previews usually play more slowly than real time. They are useful when your composition is simple or in its early stages and doesn't require additional memory for displaying complex animations, effects, 3D layers, cameras, and lights. You'll use it now to preview the text animation.

1   In the Bgwtext Timeline panel, collapse the Title Here layer, and deselect both layers.

2   Make sure that the Video switch (⊙) is selected for the layers that you want to preview—in this case, the Title Here and Background layers.

3   Press the Home key to go to the beginning of the time ruler.

▶ **Tip:** Click the pasteboard of the Composition panel if you want to hide the motion path for this preview.

4   Do one of the following:

• Click the Play/Pause button (▶) in the Preview panel.

• Press the spacebar.

5   To stop the standard preview, do one of the following:

• Click the Play/Pause button in the Preview panel.

• Press the spacebar.

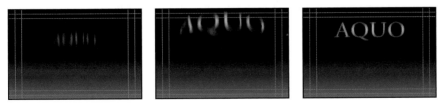

Using RAM preview

RAM preview allocates enough RAM to play the preview (with audio) as fast as the system allows, up to the frame rate of the composition. Use RAM preview to play footage in the Timeline, Layer, or Footage panel. The number of frames played depends on the amount of RAM available to the application.

In the Timeline panel, RAM preview plays either the span of time you specify as the work area, or from the beginning of the time ruler. In the Layer and Footage panels, RAM preview plays only untrimmed footage. Before you preview, check which frames are designated as the work area.

You'll preview the entire composition—the animated text plus graphic effects—using a RAM preview.

1 Click the Bgwtext 2 tab in the Timeline panel to bring it forward.

2 Make sure that the Video switch (●) is turned on for all of the layers in the composition, and press F2 to deselect all layers.

3 Drag the current-time indicator to the beginning of the time ruler, or press the Home key.

▶ **Tip:** You can interrupt the caching process at any time by pressing the spacebar, and the RAM preview will play back only the frames that have been cached to that point.

4 Click the RAM Preview button (▙▶) in the Preview panel, or choose Composition > Preview > RAM Preview.

A green progress bar indicates which frames are cached to RAM. When all of the frames in the work area are cached, the RAM preview plays back in real time.

5 To stop the RAM preview, press the spacebar.

The more detail and precision you want to see, the more RAM is required for RAM preview. You can control the amount of detail shown in either the standard or RAM preview by changing the resolution, magnification, and preview quality of your composition. You can also limit the number of layers previewed by turning off the Video switch for certain layers, or limit the number of frames previewed by adjusting the composition's work area.

6 Choose File > Save to save your project.

Optimizing performance in After Effects

How you configure After Effects and your computer determines how quickly After Effects renders projects. Complex compositions can require a large amount of memory to render, and the rendered movies can take a large amount of disk space to store. Refer to "Improve Performance" in After Effects Help for tips that can help you configure your system, After Effects preferences, and your projects for better performance.

Rendering and exporting your composition

When you're finished with your masterpiece—as you are now—you can render and export it at the quality settings you choose, and create movies in the formats that you specify. You will learn more about exporting compositions in subsequent lessons, especially in Lesson 14, "Rendering and Outputting."

Customizing workspaces

In the course of this project, you may have resized or repositioned some panels, or opened new ones. As you modify a workspace, After Effects saves those modifications, so the next time you open the project, the most recent version of a workspace is used. However, you can choose to restore the original workspace at any time by choosing Window > Workspace > Reset "Standard."

Alternatively, if you find yourself frequently using panels that aren't part of the Standard workspace, or if you like to resize or group panels for different types of projects, you can save time by customizing the workspace to suit your needs. You can save any workspace configuration, or use any of the preset workspaces that come with After Effects. These predefined workspaces are suitable for different types of workflows, such as animation or effects work.

Using predefined workspaces

Take a minute to explore the predefined workspaces in After Effects.

1   If you closed the Lesson01_Finished.aep project, open it—or any other project—
    to explore the workspaces.

2   Choose Window > Workspace > Animation.

After Effects opens the following panels at the right side of the application window:
Info and Audio (grouped), Preview, Smoother, Wiggler, Motion Sketch, and Effects
& Presets.

You can also change workspaces using the Workspace menu at the top of the application window.

3   Choose Paint from the Workspace menu at the top of the application window,
    next to the Search Help box.

The Paint and Brushes panels open. The Composition panel is replaced by the
Layer panel, for easy access to the tools and controls you need to paint in your
compositions.

Saving a custom workspace

You can save any workspace, at any time, as a custom workspace. Once saved, new and edited workspaces appear in the Window > Workspace submenu and in the Workspace menu at the top of the application window. If a project with a custom workspace is opened on a system other than the one on which it was created, After Effects looks for a workspace with a matching name. If After Effects finds a match (and the monitor configuration matches), it uses that workspace; if it can't find a match (or the monitor configuration doesn't match), it opens the project using the current local workspace.

1   Close the Paint and Brushes panels by clicking the small *x* next to the panel names.

2   Choose Window > Effects & Presets to open that panel, and then drag it into a group with the Preview panel.

3   Choose Window > Workspace > New Workspace. Enter a name for the workspace and click OK to save it, or click Cancel if you don't want to save it.

4   Choose Standard from the Workspace menu.

Controlling the brightness of the user interface

You can brighten or darken the After Effects user interface. Changing the brightness preference affects panels, windows, and dialog boxes.

1   Choose Edit > Preferences > Appearance (Windows) or After Effects > Preferences > Appearance (Mac OS).

2 Drag the Brightness slider to the left or right, and notice how the screen changes.

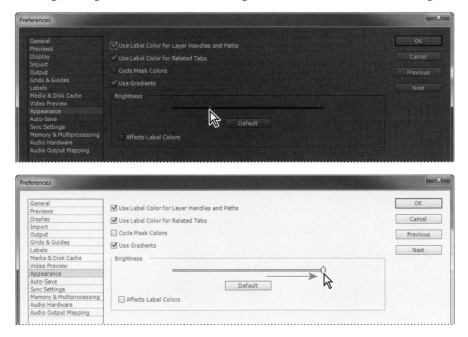

3 Click OK to save the new brightness setting or Cancel to leave your preferences unchanged. You can click Default to restore the default brightness setting.

Finding resources for using After Effects

For complete and up-to-date information about using After Effects panels, tools, and other application features, visit the Adobe website. To search for information in After Effects Help and support documents, as well as on other websites relevant to After Effects users, simply enter a search term in the Search Help box in the upper right corner of the application window. You can narrow the results to view only Adobe Help and support documents.

For additional resources, such as tips and techniques and the latest product information, check out the After Effects Help And Support page at www.adobe.com/support/aftereffects.

Review questions

1 What are the basic components of the After Effects workflow?

2 What is a composition?

3 How can you find missing footage?

4 Describe three ways to preview your work in After Effects.

5 How can you customize an After Effects workspace?

Review answers

1 Most After Effects workflows include these steps: importing and organizing footage, creating compositions and arranging layers, adding effects, animating elements, previewing your work, and rendering and exporting the final composition.

2 A composition is where you create all animation, layering, and effects. An After Effects composition has both spatial and temporal (time) dimensions. Compositions include one or more layers—video, audio, still images—arranged in the Composition panel and in the Timeline panel. Simple projects may include only one composition, while elaborate projects may include several compositions to organize large amounts of footage or intricate effects sequences.

3 To locate missing footage, choose File > Dependencies > Find Missing Footage. Or type **Missing Footage** into the Search field in the Properties panel.

4 You can manually preview your work in After Effects by moving the current-time indicator, or you can view either a standard or RAM preview. A standard preview plays your composition from the current-time indicator to the end of the composition, usually more slowly than real time. A RAM preview allocates enough RAM to play the preview (with audio) as fast as the system allows, up to the frame rate of the composition.

5 You can customize an After Effects workspace by dragging the panels into the configuration that best suits your working style. You can drag panels to new locations, move panels into or out of groups, place panels alongside each other, and undock a panel so that it floats above the application window. As you rearrange panels, the other panels resize automatically to fit the application window. You can save custom workspaces by choosing Window > Workspace > New Workspace.

2 CREATING A BASIC ANIMATION USING EFFECTS AND PRESETS

Lesson overview

In this lesson, you'll learn how to do the following:

- Use Adobe Bridge to preview and import footage items.
- Work with the layers of an imported Adobe Illustrator file.
- Apply drop-shadow and emboss effects.
- Apply a text animation preset.
- Adjust the time range of a text animation preset.
- Precompose layers.
- Apply a dissolve transition effect.
- Adjust the transparency of a layer.
- Render an animation for broadcast use.

 This lesson will take about an hour to complete. Download the Lesson02 project files from the Lesson & Update Files tab on your Account page at www.peachpit.com, if you haven't already done so. As you work on this lesson, you'll preserve the start files. If you need to restore the start files, download them from your Account page.

PROJECT: ANIMATED LOGO

Hit the ground running with a variety of effects and animation presets in After Effects. You can use them to create great-looking animations quickly and easily.

Getting started

In this lesson, you will become more familiar with the Adobe After Effects project workflow. You'll learn new ways to accomplish basic tasks as you create a simple identification graphic for a fictional travel show called "Travel Europe" on the fictional Destinations cable network. You will animate the travel show ID so that it fades to become a watermark that can appear in the lower right corner of the screen during other TV programs. Then you'll export the ID for use in broadcast output.

First, take a look at the final project files to see what you'll be doing.

1 Make sure the following files are in the AECC_CIB/Lessons/Lesson02 folder on your hard disk, or download them from your Account page at www.peachpit.com now:

   • In the Assets folder: destinations_logo.ai, parthenon.jpg

   • In the Sample_Movie folder: Lesson02.mov

2 Open and play the Lesson02.mov sample movie to see what you will create in this lesson. When you are done, quit QuickTime Player. You may delete this sample movie from your hard disk if you have limited storage space.

When you begin the lesson, restore the default application settings for After Effects. See "Restoring default preferences" on page 2.

3 Start After Effects, and then immediately hold down Ctrl+Alt+Shift (Windows) or Command+Option+Shift (Mac OS) to restore default preferences settings. When prompted, click OK to delete your preferences.

4 Click Close to close the Welcome screen.

After Effects opens to display a blank, untitled project.

5 Choose File > Save As > Save As.

6 In the Save As dialog box, navigate to the AECC_CIB/Lessons/Lesson02/ Finished_Project folder.

7 Name the project **Lesson02_Finished.aep**, and then click Save.

Importing footage using Adobe Bridge

In Lesson 1, you chose File > Import > File to import footage. However, After Effects offers another, more powerful and flexible way to import footage for a composition: Adobe Bridge. You can use Adobe Bridge to organize, browse, and locate the assets you need to create content for print, web, television, DVD, film, and mobile devices. Adobe Bridge keeps native Adobe files (such as PSD and PDF files) as well as non-Adobe application files available for easy access. You can drag assets into your layouts, projects, and compositions as needed; preview your assets; and even add metadata (file information) to assets to make files easier to locate.

Adobe Bridge is not automatically installed with After Effects CC. You'll need to download and install it separately. If Bridge is not installed, you'll be prompted to install it when you choose File > Browse In Bridge.

In this exercise, you will jump to Adobe Bridge to import the still image that will serve as the background of your composition.

1　Choose File > Browse In Bridge. If you receive a message about enabling an extension to Adobe Bridge, click Yes.

Adobe Bridge opens, displaying a collection of panels, menus, and buttons.

2　Click the Folders tab in the upper left corner of Adobe Bridge.

3　In the Folders panel, navigate to the AECC_CIB/Lessons/Lesson02/Assets folder. Click the arrows to open nested folders. You can also double-click folder thumbnail icons in the Content panel.

The Content panel updates interactively. For example, when you select the Assets folder in the Folders panel, thumbnail previews of the folder's contents appear in the Content panel. Adobe Bridge displays previews of image files such as those in PSD, TIFF, and JPEG formats, as well as Illustrator vector files, multipage Adobe PDF files, QuickTime movie files, and more.

▶ **Tip:** To open Adobe Bridge directly, choose Adobe Bridge from the Start menu (Windows) or double-click the Adobe Bridge icon in the Applications /Adobe Bridge folder (Mac OS).

● **Note:** We're using the Essentials workspace, which is the default workspace in Bridge.

▶ Tip: To prioritize different information in Adobe Bridge, change the workspace: Choose Window > Workspace, and then select a workspace. See Adobe Bridge Help to learn about customizing Adobe Bridge.

4   Drag the thumbnail slider at the bottom of the Adobe Bridge window to enlarge the thumbnail previews.

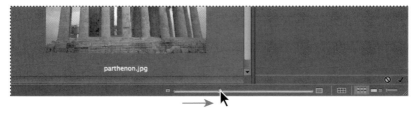

5   Select the parthenon.jpg file in the Content panel, and notice that it appears in the Preview panel as well. Information about the file, including its creation date, bit depth, and file size, appears in the Metadata panel.

6   Double-click the parthenon.jpg thumbnail in the Content panel to place the file in your After Effects project. Alternatively, you can drag the thumbnail into the Project panel in After Effects.

Adobe Bridge returns you to After Effects when you place the file. You can close Adobe Bridge if you'd like. You won't be using it again during this lesson.

Creating a new composition

Following the After Effects workflow you learned in Lesson 1, the next step to building the travel show ID is to create a new composition. In Lesson 1, you created the composition based on footage items that were selected in the Project panel. You can also create an empty composition, and then add your footage items to it.

1   Create a new composition by doing one of the following:

- Click the Create A New Composition button (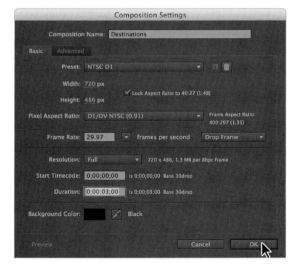) at the bottom of the Project panel.

- Choose Composition > New Composition.

- Press Ctrl+N (Windows) or Command+N (Mac OS).

2   In the Composition Settings dialog box, do the following:

- Name the composition **Destinations**.

- Choose NTSC D1 from the Preset pop-up menu. NTSC D1 is the resolution for standard-definition television in the United States and some other countries. This preset automatically sets the width, height, pixel aspect ratio, and frame rate for the composition to NTSC standards.

- In the Duration field, type **300** to specify 3 seconds.

- Click OK.

After Effects displays an empty composition named Destinations in the Composition panel and in the Timeline panel. Now, you'll add the background.

3 Drag the parthenon.jpg footage item from the Project panel to the Timeline panel to add it to the Destinations composition.

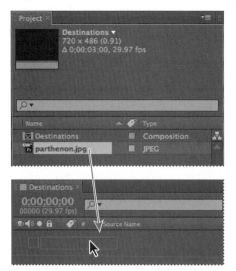

▶ **Tip:** The keyboard shortcut for fitting a layer to a composition is Ctrl+Alt+F (Windows) or Command+Option+F (Mac OS).

4 With the parthenon layer selected in the Timeline panel, choose Layer > Transform > Fit To Comp to scale the background image to the dimensions of the composition.

Importing the foreground element

Your background is now in place. The foreground object you'll use is a layered vector graphic that was created in Illustrator.

1 Choose File > Import > File.

2 In the Import File dialog box, select the destinations_logo.ai file in the AECC_CIB/Lessons/Lesson02/Assets folder. (The file appears as destinations_logo if you've hidden file extensions in Windows.)

3 Select Composition from the Import As menu, and then click Import or Open.

The Illustrator file is added to the Project panel as a composition named destinations_logo. A folder named destinations_logo Layers also appears. This folder contains the three individual layers of the Illustrator file. Click the triangle to open the folder and see its contents if you'd like.

4 Drag the destinations_logo composition file from the Project panel into the Timeline panel above the parthenon layer.

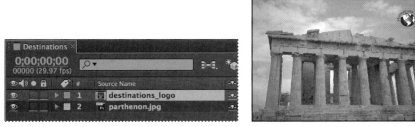

You should now see both the background image and the logo in the Composition panel and in the Timeline panel.

Working with imported Illustrator layers

The destinations_logo graphic was created in Illustrator; your job in After Effects is to add text and animate it. To work with the layers of the Illustrator file independently of the background footage, you'll open the destinations_logo composition in its own Timeline and Composition panels.

1 Double-click the destinations_logo composition in the Project panel. The composition opens in its own Timeline and Composition panels.

2 Select the Horizontal Type tool (T) in the Tools panel, and click in the center of the Composition panel.

3 Type **TRAVEL EUROPE**, all capital letters, and then select all of the text you just entered.

Note: If the Character panel isn't open, choose Window > Character.

4 In the Character panel, select a sans serif typeface such as Myriad Pro, and change the font size to **24** pixels. Click the eyedropper in the Character panel, and click on the rotated "Destinations" text on the logo to select the green color. After Effects applies it to the text you typed. Leave all other options in the Character panel at their defaults.

Note: If the Paragraph panel isn't open, choose Window > Paragraph.

5 In the Paragraph panel, click the Right Align Text button (≣). Leave all other options in the Paragraph panel at their defaults. You'll learn more about working with text in Lesson 3, "Animating Text."

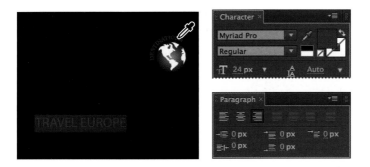

6 Select the Selection tool (➤), and then drag the text in the Composition panel to position it as it appears in the following figure. Notice that when you switch to the Selection tool, the generic Text 1 layer name in the Timeline panel changes to TRAVEL EUROPE, the text you typed.

▶ **Tip:** Choose View > Show Grid to make the nonprinting grid visible to help you position objects. Choose View > Show Grid again to hide the grid later.

Applying and controlling effects

You can apply or remove an effect at any time. Once you've applied effects to a layer, you can temporarily turn off one or all of the effects in the layer to concentrate on another aspect of your composition. Effects that are turned off do not appear in the Composition panel, and typically aren't included when the layer is previewed or rendered.

By default, when you apply an effect to a layer, the effect is active for the duration of the layer. However, you can make an effect start and stop at specific times, or make the effect more or less intense over time. You'll learn more about creating animation using keyframes or expressions in Lesson 5, "Animating a Multimedia Presentation," and Lesson 6, "Animating Layers."

You can apply and edit effects on adjustment layers just as you do with other layers. Note, however, that when you apply an effect to an adjustment layer, the effect is applied to all layers below it in the Timeline panel.

Effects can also be saved, browsed, and applied as animation presets.

Applying effects to a layer

Now you will return to the main composition, Destinations, and apply an effect to the destinations_logo layer. This will apply the effect to all of the layers nested in the destinations_logo composition.

1 Click the Destinations tab in the Timeline panel, and then select the destinations_logo layer.

The effect you create next will be applied only to the logo elements, not to the background image of the Parthenon.

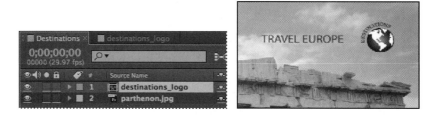

2 Choose Effect > Perspective > Drop Shadow.

A soft-edged shadow appears behind the nested layers of the destinations_logo layer—the logo graphic, the rotated type, and the words *travel Europe*—in the Composition panel. You can customize the effect using the Effect Controls panel, which appears in front of the Project panel when you apply an effect.

3 In the Effect Controls panel, reduce the drop shadow's Distance to **3** and increase its Softness to **4**. You can set these values by clicking the field and typing the number, or by dragging the orange, underlined value.

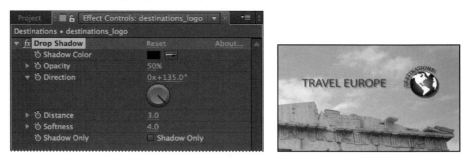

The drop shadow is nice, but the logo will stand out even more if you apply an emboss effect. You can use either the Effect menu or the Effects & Presets panel to locate and apply effects.

4 Click the Effects & Presets tab to bring that panel forward. Then click the triangle next to Stylize to expand the category.

5   With the destinations_logo layer selected in the Timeline panel, drag the Color Emboss effect into the Composition panel.

The Color Emboss effect sharpens the edges of objects in the layer without suppressing the original colors. The Effect Controls panel displays the Color Emboss effect and its settings below the Drop Shadow effect.

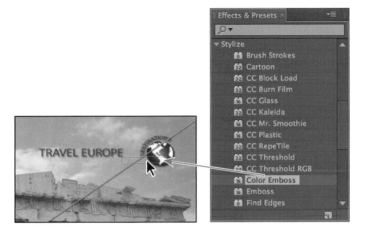

6   Choose File > Save to save your work.

Applying an animation preset

You've positioned the logo and applied some effects to it. It's time to add some animation! You will learn several ways to animate text in Lesson 3; for now, you'll use a simple animation preset that will fade the words *travel Europe* onto the screen next to the logo. You'll need to work in the destinations_logo composition so that you can apply the animation to only the TRAVEL EUROPE text layer.

1   Click the destinations_logo tab in the Timeline panel, and select the TRAVEL EUROPE layer.

2   Move the current-time indicator to 1:10, which is the point at which you want the text to start fading in.

3   In the Effects & Presets panel, choose Animation Presets > Text > Blurs.

4 Drag the Bullet Train animation preset onto the TRAVEL EUROPE layer in the Timeline panel or over the words *travel Europe* in the Composition panel. Don't worry about the text disappearing—you're looking at the first frame of the animation, which happens to be blank.

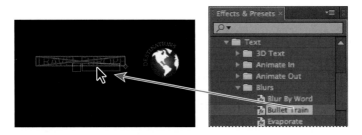

5 Click a blank area of the Timeline panel to deselect the TRAVEL EUROPE layer, and then drag the current-time indicator to 2:00 to manually preview the text animation. The text appears, letter by letter, until the words *travel Europe* are fully onscreen at 2:00.

Precomposing layers for a new animation

The travel show ID is coming along nicely, and you're probably eager to preview the complete animation. Before you do, however, you'll add a dissolve to all of the logo elements except the words *travel Europe*. To do this, you need to precompose the other three layers of the destinations_logo composition: rotated type, Globe logo, and crop area.

Precomposing is a way to nest layers within a composition. Precomposing moves the layers to a new composition. This new composition takes the place of the selected layers. When you want to change the order in which layer components are rendered, precomposing is a quick way to create intermediate levels of nesting in an existing hierarchy.

1 Shift-click to select the rotated type, Globe logo, and crop area layers in the destinations_logo Timeline panel.

2 Choose Layer > Pre-compose.

3 In the Pre-compose dialog box, name the new composition **Dissolve_logo**. Make sure the Move All Attributes Into The New Composition option is selected. Then click OK.

The three layers are replaced in the destinations_logo Timeline panel with a single layer, Dissolve_logo. This new, precomposed layer contains the three layers that you selected in step 1. You can apply the dissolve effect to it without affecting the TRAVEL EUROPE text layer and its Bullet Train animation.

4 Make sure the Dissolve_logo layer is selected in the Timeline panel, and press the Home key or drag the current-time indicator to go to 0:00.

5 In the Effects & Presets panel, choose Animation Presets > Transitions – Dissolves, and then drag the Dissolve – Vapor animation preset onto the Dissolve_logo layer in the Timeline panel or onto the Composition panel.

▶ **Tip:** To locate the Dissolve – Vapor preset quickly, type **vap** in the search box in the Effects & Presets panel.

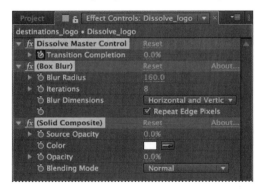

The Dissolve – Vapor animation preset includes three components—a master dissolve, a box blur, and a solid composite, all of which appear in the Effect Controls panel. The default settings are fine for this project.

6 Choose File > Save.

Previewing the effects

It's time to preview all of the effects together.

1   Click the Destinations tab in the Timeline panel to switch to the main composition. Press the Home key or drag the current-time indicator to make sure you're at the beginning of the time ruler.

2   Make sure the Video switch (👁) is selected for both layers in the Destinations Timeline panel.

3   Click the Play button (▶) in the Preview panel, or press the spacebar, to watch the preview. Press the spacebar to stop playback at any time.

Adding transparency

Many TV stations display logos semitransparently in the corner of the frame to emphasize the brand. You'll reduce the opacity of the ID so that it can be used this way.

1   Still in the Destinations Timeline panel, go to 2:24.

2   Select the destinations_logo layer, and press T to display its Opacity property. By default, the Opacity is 100%—fully opaque. Click the stopwatch icon (⏱) to set an Opacity keyframe at this point in time.

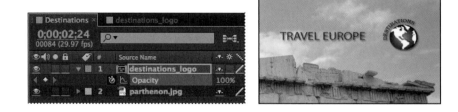

3 Press the End key or drag the current-time indicator to go to the end of the time ruler (2:29), and change the Opacity to **40%**. After Effects adds a keyframe.

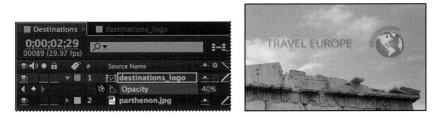

The logo appears, the words *travel Europe* fly in, and it all fades to 40% opacity.

4 Watch a preview of your composition by clicking the Play button in the Preview panel, by pressing the spacebar, or by pressing 0 on your numeric keypad. Press the spacebar to stop playback when you're done.

5 Choose File > Save to save your project.

Rendering the composition

You're ready to prepare your travel show ID for output. When you create output, the layers of a composition and each layer's masks, effects, and properties are rendered frame by frame into one or more output files or, in the case of an image sequence, into a series of consecutive files.

Making a movie from your final composition can take a few minutes or many hours, depending on the composition's frame size, quality, complexity, and compression method. When you place your composition in the Render Queue, it becomes a render item that uses the render settings assigned to it.

After Effects provides a variety of formats and compression types for rendering output; the format you choose depends on the medium from which you'll play your final output or on the requirements of your hardware, such as a video-editing system.

● **Note:** For more about output formats and rendering, see Lesson 14, "Rendering and Outputting."

You'll render and export the composition so that it can be broadcast on television.

1 Do one of the following to add the composition to the Render Queue:

- Select the Destinations composition in the Project panel, and then choose Composition > Add To Render Queue. The Render Queue panel opens automatically.

- Choose Window > Render Queue to open the Render Queue panel, and then drag the Destinations composition from the Project panel onto the Render Queue panel.

2 Choose Maximize Frame from the Render Queue panel menu so that the panel fills the application window.

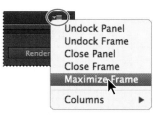

3 Click the triangle to expand the Render Settings options. By default, After Effects renders compositions with Best Quality and Full Resolution. The default settings are fine for this project.

4 Click the triangle to expand the Output Module options. By default, After Effects uses lossless compression to encode the rendered composition into a movie file, which is fine for this project. But you need to identify where to save the file.

5 Click the underlined words *Not Yet Specified* next to the Output To pop-up menu.

6   In the Output Movie To dialog box, accept the default movie name (Destinations), select the AECC_CIB/Lessons/Lesson02/Finished_Project folder for the location, and then click Save.

7   Back in the Render Queue panel, click the Render button.

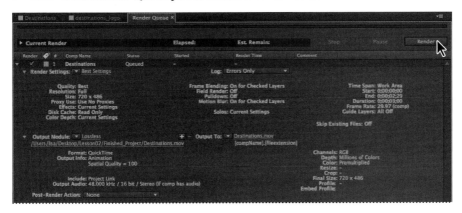

After Effects displays a progress bar in the Render Queue panel as it encodes the file, and issues an audio alert when all items in the Render Queue have been rendered and encoded.

8   When the movie is complete, choose Restore Frame Size from the Render Queue panel menu to restore your workspace.

9   If you want to see your final product, double-click the Destinations.avi or Destinations.mov file in the AECC_CIB/Lessons/Lesson02/Finished_Project folder to open it in Windows Media Player or QuickTime, and then play the file.

10 Close the project file, and then quit After Effects.

Congratulations. You've created a travel show ID suitable for broadcast.

Review questions

1 How do you use Adobe Bridge to preview and import files?

2 What is *precomposing*?

3 How do you customize an effect?

4 How do you modify the transparency of a layer in a composition?

Review answers

1 Choose File > Browse In Bridge to jump from After Effects to Adobe Bridge. If Bridge isn't installed, you'll be prompted to download and install it. In Bridge, you can search for and preview image assets. When you locate the asset you want to use in an After Effects project, double-click it or drag it to the Project panel.

2 *Precomposing* is a way to nest layers within a composition. Precomposing moves the layers to a new composition, which takes the place of the selected layers. When you want to change the order in which layer components are rendered, precomposing is a quick way to create intermediate levels of nesting in an existing hierarchy.

3 After you apply an effect to a layer in a composition, you can customize its properties in the Effect Controls panel. This panel opens automatically when you apply the effect, or you can open it at any time by selecting the layer with the effect and choosing Window > Effect Controls.

4 To modify the transparency of a layer, reduce its opacity. Select the layer in the Timeline panel, press T to reveal its Opacity property, and enter a value lower than 100%.

3 ANIMATING TEXT

Lesson overview

In this lesson, you'll learn how to do the following:

- Create and animate text layers.

- Stylize text using the Character and Paragraph panels.

- Apply and customize text animation presets.

- Preview animation presets in Adobe Bridge.

- Animate text using keyframes.

- Animate layers using parenting.

- Edit and animate imported Adobe Photoshop text.

- Use a text animator group to animate selected characters on a layer.

- Apply a text animation to a graphic object.

 This lesson will take approximately 2 hours to complete. Download the Lesson03 project files from the Lesson & Update Files tab on your Account page at www.peachpit.com, if you haven't already done so. As you work on this lesson, you'll preserve the start files. If you need to restore the start files, download them from your Account page.

PROJECT: MOVIE TITLE SEQUENCE

Your type doesn't need to sit still while your audience is reading it. In this lesson, you'll learn several ways to animate type in After Effects, including timesaving methods unique to text layers.

Getting started

Adobe After Effects offers many ways to animate text. You can animate text layers by manually creating keyframes in the Timeline panel, using animation presets, or using expressions. You can even animate individual characters or words in a text layer. In this lesson, you'll employ several different animation techniques, including some that are unique to text, while you design the opening title credits for an animated documentary called *Road Trip*.

As in other projects, you'll begin by previewing the movie you're creating, and then you'll open After Effects.

1   Make sure the following files are in the AECC_CIB/Lessons/Lesson03 folder on your hard disk, or download them from your Account page at www.peachpit.com now:

   • In the Assets folder: background_movie.mov, car.ai, compass.swf, credits.psd

   • In the Sample_Movie folder: Lesson03.mov

2   Open and play the Lesson03.mov sample movie to see the title credits you will create in this lesson. When you're done, quit QuickTime Player. You may delete this sample movie from your hard disk if you have limited storage space.

As you start the application, restore the default settings for After Effects. See "Restoring default preferences" on page 2.

3   Start After Effects, and then immediately hold down Ctrl+Alt+Shift (Windows) or Command+Option+Shift (Mac OS) to restore default preferences settings. When prompted, click OK to delete your preferences.

4   Click Close to close the Welcome screen.

After Effects opens to display a blank, untitled project.

5   Choose File > Save As > Save As, and navigate to the AECC_CIB/Lessons/Lesson03/Finished_Project folder.

6   Name the project **Lesson03_Finished.aep**, and then click Save.

Importing the footage

You need to import two footage items to begin this lesson.

1   Double-click an empty area of the Project panel to open the Import File dialog box.

2   Navigate to the AECC_CIB/Lessons/Lesson03/Assets folder on your hard disk, Ctrl-click (Windows) or Command-click (Mac OS) to select both the background_movie.mov and compass.swf files, and then click Import or Open.

After Effects can import several file formats including Adobe Photoshop and Adobe Illustrator files, as well as QuickTime and AVI movies. This makes After Effects an incredibly powerful application for compositing and motion graphics work.

Creating the composition

Now, you'll create the composition.

1 Press Ctrl+N (Windows) or Command+N (Mac OS) to create a new composition.

2 In the Composition Settings dialog box, name the composition **Road_Trip_ Title_Sequence**, select NTSC DV from the Preset menu, and set the Duration to **10:00**, which is the length of the background movie. Then click OK.

3 Drag the background_movie.mov and compass.swf footage items from the Project panel to the Timeline panel. Arrange the layers so that compass.swf is above background_movie.mov in the layer stack.

4 Choose File > Save.

You're ready to add the title text to the composition.

About text layers

In After Effects, you can add text with flexibility and precision. You can create and edit text directly on the screen in the Composition panel, and quickly change the font, style, size, and color of the text. You can add horizontal or vertical text anywhere in a composition. The Tools, Character, and Paragraph panels contain a wide range of text controls. You can apply changes to individual characters and set formatting options for entire paragraphs, including alignment, justification, and word-wrapping. In addition to all of these style features, After Effects provides tools for easily animating specific characters and properties, such as text opacity and hue.

After Effects uses two types of text: point text and paragraph text. Use *point text* to enter a single word or line of characters; use *paragraph text* to enter and format text as one or more paragraphs.

In many ways, text layers are just like any other layers in After Effects. You can apply effects and expressions to text layers, animate them, designate them as 3D layers, and edit the 3D text while viewing it in multiple views. As with layers imported from Illustrator, text layers are continuously rasterized, so when you scale the layer or resize the text, it retains crisp, resolution-independent edges. The main differences between text layers and other layers are that you cannot open a text layer in its own Layer panel, and you can animate the text in a text layer using special text animator properties and selectors.

Creating and formatting point text

When you enter point text, each line of text is independent—the length of a line increases or decreases as you edit the text, but it doesn't wrap to the next line. The text you enter appears in a new text layer. The small line through the I-beam marks the position of the text baseline.

● **Note:** If you press Enter or Return on the regular keyboard instead of on the numeric keypad, you'll begin a new paragraph.

1 In the Tools panel, select the Horizontal Type tool (T).

2 Click anywhere in the Composition panel, and type **Road Trip**. Then press Enter on the numeric keypad to exit text-editing mode and to select the text layer in the Composition panel. Or, you can select the layer name to exit text-editing mode.

Using the Character panel

The Character panel provides options for formatting characters. If text is high-lighted, changes you make in the Character panel affect only the highlighted text. If no text is highlighted, changes you make in the Character panel affect the selected text layers and the text layers' selected Source Text keyframes, if any exist. If no text is highlighted and no text layers are selected, the changes you make in the Character panel become the new defaults for the next text entry.

1   Choose Window > Workspace > Text to display only those panels you need while working with text.

2   Select the Road Trip text layer in the Timeline panel.

3   In the Character panel, choose Myriad Pro from the Font Family menu. If you don't have Myriad Pro, then choose another heavy sans serif typeface, such as Verdana.

4   Choose Bold from the Font Style menu. If Bold isn't available, click the Faux Bold button (**T**) in the lower left corner of the panel.

5   Set the Font Size to **90** pixels.

6   Leave all other options at their default settings.

▶ **Tip:** To open the panels individually, choose Window > Character or Window > Paragraph. To open both panels, select the Horizontal Type tool, and then click the Toggle The Character And Paragraph Panels button in the Tools panel.

▶ **Tip:** To select a font quickly, begin typing its name in the Font Family box. The Font Family menu jumps to the first font on your system that matches the letters you've typed. If a type layer is selected, the text in the Composition panel takes on the newly selected font.

Using the Paragraph panel

Use the Paragraph panel to set options that apply to an entire paragraph, such as alignment, indentation, and leading. For point text, each line is a separate paragraph. You can use the Paragraph panel to set formatting options for a single paragraph, multiple paragraphs, or all paragraphs in a text layer. You just need to make one adjustment in the Paragraph panel for this composition's title text.

1 In the Paragraph panel, click the Center Text button (≡). This aligns horizontal text to the center of the layer, not to the center of the composition.

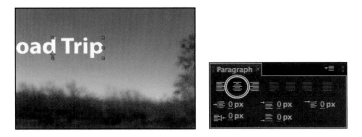

2 Leave all other options at their default settings.

Positioning the type

To precisely position layers, such as the text layer you're working on now, you can display rulers, guides, and grids in the Composition panel. These visual reference tools don't appear in the final rendered movie.

1 Make sure the Road Trip text layer is selected in the Timeline panel.

2 Choose Layer > Transform > Fit To Comp Width. This scales the layer to fit to the width of the composition.

Now you can position the text layer using a grid.

3 Choose View > Show Grid and then View > Snap To Grid.

4   Using the Selection tool (↖), drag the text up in the Composition panel until the base of the letters sits on the horizontal gridline in the center of the composition. Press Shift after you start dragging to constrain the movement and help you position the text.

5   When the layer is in position, choose View > Show Grid again to hide the grid.

This project isn't destined for broadcast TV, so it's okay that the title extends beyond the title-safe and action-safe areas of the composition at the beginning of the animation.

6   Choose Standard from the Workspace menu at the top of the application window to return to the Standard workspace, and then choose File > Save to save your project.

Using a text animation preset

Now you're ready to animate the title. The easiest way to do that is to use one of the many animation presets that come with After Effects. After applying an animation preset, you can customize it and save it to use again in other projects.

1   Press the Home key or go to 0:00 to make sure the current-time indicator is at the beginning of the time ruler. After Effects applies animation presets from the current time.

2   Select the Road Trip text layer.

Browsing animation presets

● **Note:** If Bridge isn't installed, you'll be prompted to install it when you choose Browse In Bridge. For more information, see page 2.

You already applied an animation preset in Lesson 2, "Creating a Basic Animation Using Effects and Presets." But what if you're not sure which animation preset you want to use? To help you choose the right animation preset for your projects, you can preview them in Adobe Bridge.

1   Choose Animation > Browse Presets. Adobe Bridge opens, displaying the contents of the After Effects Presets folder.

2   In the Content panel, double-click the Text folder, and then the Blurs folder.

3   Click to select the first preset, Blur By Word. Adobe Bridge plays a sample of the animation in the Preview panel.

4   Select a few other presets, and watch them in the Preview panel.

5   Preview the Evaporate preset, and then double-click its thumbnail preview. Alternatively, you can right-click (Windows) or Control-click (Mac OS) the thumbnail and choose Place In After Effects. After Effects applies the preset to the selected layer, which is the Road Trip layer.

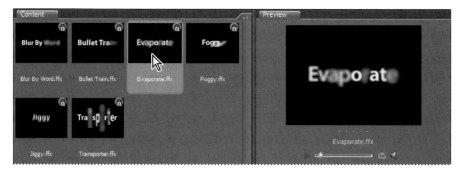

● **Note:** Leave Adobe Bridge open in the background. You'll use it again later in the lesson.

Nothing appears to change in the composition. This is because at 0:00, the first frame of the animation, the letters haven't yet evaporated.

Previewing a range of frames

Now, preview the animation. Although the composition is 10 seconds long, you need to preview only the first few seconds, since that is where the text animation occurs.

1   In the Timeline panel, move the current-time indicator to 3:00, and press N to set the end bracket of the work area.

2   Press 0 on the numeric keypad, or click the RAM Preview button (▶) in the Preview panel, to watch a RAM preview of the animation.

The letters appear to evaporate into the background. It looks great—but you want the letters to fade in and remain onscreen, not disappear. So you will customize the preset to suit your needs.

3   Press the spacebar to stop the preview, and then press the Home key to move the current-time indicator back to 0:00.

Customizing an animation preset

After you apply an animation preset to a layer, all of its properties and keyframes are listed in the Timeline panel. You'll use those properties to customize the preset.

1   Select the Road Trip text layer in the Timeline panel, and press U. The U key, sometimes referred to as the *Überkey*, is a valuable keyboard shortcut that reveals all the animated properties of a layer.

2   Click the Offset property name to select both of its keyframes. The Offset property specifies how much to offset the start and end of the selection.

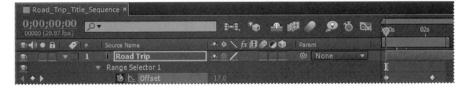

3   Choose Animation > Keyframe Assistant > Time-Reverse Keyframes. This command switches the order of the two Offset keyframes so that the letters are invisible at the beginning of the composition, and then emerge into view.

4   Drag the current-time indicator from 0:00 to 3:00 to manually preview the edited animation. The letters now fade into, rather than disappear from, the composition.

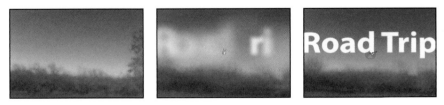

▶ **Tip:** If you press U twice (UU), After Effects displays all modified properties for the layer, instead of only the animated properties. Press the U key again to hide all the layer's properties.

5   Press U to hide the layer's properties.

6   Press the End key to move the current-time indicator to the end of the time ruler, and then press N to set the end bracket of the work area.

7   Choose File > Save to save your project.

Animating with scale keyframes

The text layer was scaled to more than 200% when you applied the Fit To Comp command to it earlier in this lesson. Now, you'll animate the layer's scale so that the type gradually shrinks down to its original size.

1   In the Timeline panel, move the current-time indicator to 3:00.

2   Select the Road Trip text layer, and press the S key to reveal its Scale property.

3   Click the stopwatch icon (⏱) to add a Scale keyframe at the current time (3:00).

4   Move the current-time indicator to 5:00.

5   Reduce the layer's Scale values to **100, 100%**. After Effects adds a new Scale keyframe at the current time.

Previewing the scale animation

Now you'll preview the change.

1   Move the current-time indicator to 5:10, and press N to set the end of the work area. The scale animation ends shortly before 5:10.

▶ **Tip:** You can experiment with text scale animation presets that are included with After Effects. They're located in the Presets/ Text/Scale folder in the After Effects CC folder on your hard drive.

2   Watch a RAM preview of the animation from 0:00 to 5:10. The movie title fades in and then scales to a smaller size.

3   Press the spacebar to stop playback after you've viewed the animation.

Adding Easy Ease

The beginning and end of the scale animation are rather abrupt. In nature, nothing comes to an absolute stop. Instead, objects ease into and out of starting and stopping points.

1   Right-click (Windows) or Control-click (Mac OS) the Scale keyframe at 3:00, and choose Keyframe Assistant > Easy Ease Out. The keyframe becomes a left-pointing icon.

2   Right-click (Windows) or Control-click (Mac OS) the Scale keyframe at 5:00, and choose Keyframe Assistant > Easy Ease In. The keyframe becomes a right-pointing icon.

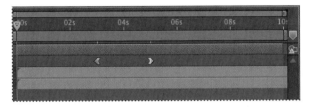

3   Watch another RAM preview. Press the spacebar to stop it when you're done.

4   Choose File > Save.

Animating using parenting

The next task is to make it appear as if the virtual camera is zooming away from the composition. The text scale animation you just applied gets you halfway there, but you need to animate the scale of the compass as well. You could manually animate the compass layer, but it's easier to take advantage of parenting relationships in After Effects.

1   Press the Home key or drag the current-time indicator to the beginning of the time ruler.

2   In the Timeline panel, click the Parent pop-up menu for the compass layer, and choose 1. Road Trip. This sets the Road Trip text layer as the parent of the compass layer, which in turn becomes the child layer.

As the child layer, the compass layer inherits the Scale keyframes of its parent layer (Road Trip). Not only is this a quick way to animate the compass, but it also ensures that the compass scales at the same rate and by the same amount as the text layer.

● **Note:** When you move the compass layer, its parent becomes 2. Road Trip, because Road Trip is now the second layer.

3　In the Timeline panel, move the compass layer above the Road Trip text layer.

4　Move the current-time indicator to 9:29, so you can clearly see the compasss in the Composition panel.

5　In the Composition panel, drag the compass so that its anchor point is over the dot in the letter *i* in the word *trip*. Alternatively, you can select the compass layer in the Timeline panel and press P to reveal its Position property. Then enter **122, −60**.

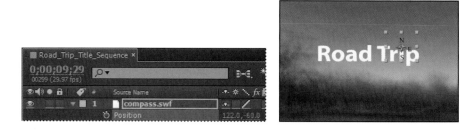

6　Move the current-time indicator from 3:00 to 5:00 to manually preview the scaling. Both the text and the compass scale down in size, so that it appears that the camera is moving away from the scene.

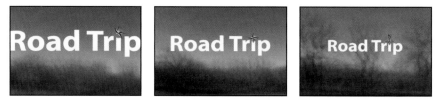

7　Press the Home key to return to 0:00, and drag the work area end bracket to the end of the time ruler.

8　Select the Road Trip layer in the Timeline panel, and press S to hide its Scale property. If you entered Position values for the compass, select the compass layer, and press P to hide the Position property, too. Then choose File > Save.

About parent and child layers

Parenting assigns one layer's transformations to another layer, called a *child layer*. Creating a parenting relationship between layers synchronizes the changes in the parent layer with the corresponding transformation values of the child layers, except opacity. For example, if a parent layer moves 5 pixels to the right of its starting position, then the child layer also moves 5 pixels to the right of its starting position. A layer can have only one parent, but a layer can be a parent to any number of 2D or 3D layers within the same composition. Parenting layers is useful for creating complex animations such as linking the movements of a marionette or depicting the orbits of planets in the solar system.

For more on parent and child layers, see After Effects Help.

Animating imported Photoshop text

If all text animations involved just two short words, such as *road trip,* life would be easy. But in the real world, you may often have to work with longer blocks of text, and they can be tedious to enter manually. Fortunately, After Effects lets you import text from Photoshop or Illustrator. You can preserve text layers, edit them, and animate them in After Effects.

Importing text

Some of the remaining text for this composition is in a layered Photoshop file, which you'll import now.

1 Double-click an empty area in the Project panel to open the Import File dialog box.

2 Select the credits.psd file in the AECC_CIB/Lessons/Lesson03/Assets folder. Choose Composition – Retain Layer Sizes from the Import As menu, and then click Import or Open.

3 In the Credits.psd dialog box, select Editable Layer Styles, and click OK.

After Effects can import Photoshop layer styles, retaining the appearance of the layers you're importing. The imported file is added as a composition to the Project panel; its layers are added in a separate folder.

4 Drag the credits composition from the Project panel into the Timeline panel, placing it at the top of the layer stack.

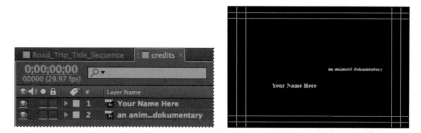

Because you imported the credits.psd file as a composition with layers intact, you can work on it in its own Timeline panel, editing and animating its layers independently.

Editing imported text

The text you imported isn't currently editable in After Effects. You'll change that so that you can control the type and apply animations. And if you have a sharp eye, you've noticed some typos in the imported text. So, first you'll clean up the type.

1 Double-click the credits composition in the Project panel to open it in its own Timeline panel.

2 Shift-click to select both layers in the credits Timeline panel, and choose Layer > Convert To Editable Text. (Click OK if you see a warning about missing fonts.) Now the text layers can be edited, and you can fix the typos.

3   Deselect both layers, and then double-click layer 2 in the Timeline panel
    to select the text and automatically switch to the Horizontal Type tool (T).

4   Type an *e* between the *t* and *d* in the word *animated.* Then change the
    k to a *c* in *documentary.*

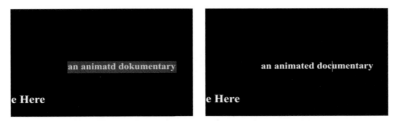

● **Note:** The layer
name does not change
in the Timeline panel
when you correct the
spelling in the layer. This
is because the original
layer name was created
in Photoshop. To
change a layer's name,
select it in the Timeline
panel, press Enter or
Return, type the new
name, and press Enter
or Return again.

5   Switch to the Selection tool (▶) to exit text-editing mode.

6   Shift-click to select both layers in the Timeline panel.

7   If the Character panel isn't open, choose Window > Character to open it.

8   Choose the same typeface you used for the words *Road Trip.* (We used Myriad
    Pro.) Leave all other settings as they are.

9   Click an empty area of the Timeline panel to deselect both layers. Then select
    layer 2 again.

10 In the Character panel, click the Fill Color box. Then, in the Text Color dialog
    box, select a shade of green, and click OK. We used R=66, G=82, B=42.

Animating the subtitle

You want the letters of the subtitle—*an animated documentary*—to fade onscreen from left to right under the movie title. The easiest way to do this is to use another text animation preset.

1 Go to 5:00 in the timeline. At that point, the title and the compass have finished scaling to their final size.

2 Select the subtitle layer (layer 2) in the Timeline panel.

3 Press Ctrl+Alt+Shift+O (Windows) or Command+Option+Shift+O (Mac OS) to jump to Adobe Bridge.

4 Navigate to the Presets/Text/Animate In folder.

5 Select the Fade Up Characters animation preset, and watch it in the Preview panel. This effect works well to reveal the text gradually.

6 Double-click the Fade Up Characters preset to apply it to the subtitle layer in After Effects.

7 With the subtitle layer selected in the Timeline panel, press UU to see the properties modified by the animation preset. You should see two keyframes for Range Selector 1 Start: one at 5:00, and one at 7:00.

You still have a lot of animation to do in this composition, so you will speed up the effect by 1 second.

8 Go to 6:00, and then drag the second Range Selector 1 Start keyframe to 6:00.

9 Drag the current-time indicator across the time ruler between 5:00 and 6:00 to see the letters fade in.

10 When you're done, select the subtitle layer, and press U to hide the modified properties. Then choose File > Save to save your work.

Animating text using a path animation preset

You've seen how versatile and convenient text animation presets can be. You'll use another type of text animation preset to animate the words *directed by* along a motion path. After Effects includes several animation presets that animate text along a prebuilt path. These presets also provide placeholder text when you apply them, so in this exercise, you will enter and format your text *after* you apply the animation preset.

1 Select the Road_Trip_Title_Sequence tab in the Timeline panel.

2 Deselect all layers, and then go to 5:00.

3 Press Ctrl+Alt+Shift+O (Windows) or Command+Option+Shift+O (Mac OS) to jump to Adobe Bridge.

4 Navigate to the Presets/Text/Paths folder.

5 Double-click the Pipes animation preset. Adobe Bridge returns you to After Effects, where the preset automatically creates a new layer, pipes, with a predefined path that zigzags across the composition. The text on the path is obscured by the movie title. You'll fix that soon.

Customizing the preset path

First, you need to change the placeholder word *pipes* to *directed by*. Then you'll adjust the path itself.

1 In the Timeline panel, go to 6:05, when the word *pipes* is visible—and horizontal—onscreen.

2 Double-click the pipes layer in the Timeline panel. After Effects switches to the Horizontal Type tool (T) and selects the word *pipes* in the Composition panel.

3 Type **directed by** to replace the word *pipes*. Press Enter on the numeric keypad or select the layer name when you're done. After Effects updates the Timeline panel with the new layer name.

4 In the Character panel, do the following:

- Set the Font Family to Minion Pro or another serif typeface.
- Set the Font Style to Regular.
- Set the Font Size to **20** pixels.
- Leave all other settings at their defaults.

5 Drag the current-time indicator across the time ruler between 5:00 and 8:00 to see how the words *directed by* move onscreen—and then offscreen.

You'll fix the text so that it stays onscreen, but now is a good time to adjust the position of the path in the composition so that it doesn't interfere with the movie title.

6 Using the Selection tool (✱), double-click the yellow motion path in the Composition panel.

7 Drag the path down and slightly to the left, until the words *Road Trip* are centered in the top curve and *Your Name Here* is within the lower curve. You may find it easiest to use the arrow keys.

8 Press Enter or Return to accept the change.

Later in the lesson, you'll attach a car graphic to the path so it appears to be pulling the text. But first, you'll finish animating the credits.

9 Select the directed by layer in the Timeline panel, and hide its properties. Then choose File > Save to save your work.

Animating type tracking

Next, you'll animate the appearance of the director's name in the composition using a text animation tracking preset. By animating tracking, you can make words seem to expand outward as they appear onscreen from a central point.

Customizing placeholder text

Currently, the director's name is simply a layer with placeholder text—*Your Name Here*. Before you animate it, change it to your own name.

1   Switch to the credits timeline in the Timeline panel, and select the Your Name Here layer.

2   Select the Horizontal Type tool (T), and then replace *Your Name Here* in the Composition panel with your own name. Use a first, middle, and last name so that you have a nice long string of text to animate. Click the layer name when you're done.

● **Note:** It doesn't matter where the current-time indicator is located when you edit the text of this layer. Currently, the text is onscreen for the duration of the composition. That will change once you animate it.

● **Note:** Again, the layer name doesn't change, because it was named in Photoshop.

Applying a tracking preset

Now you will animate the director's name with a tracking preset so that it starts to appear onscreen shortly after the words *directed by* reach the center of the composition.

1   Go to 7:10.

2   Select the Your Name Here layer in the Timeline panel.

3   Jump to Adobe Bridge, and go to the Presets/Text/Tracking folder. Double-click the Increase Tracking preset to apply it to the Your Name Here layer in After Effects.

4   Drag the current-time indicator across the time ruler between 7:10 and 9:10 to manually preview the tracking animation.

▶ **Tip:** If you're tired of jumping to Adobe Bridge and don't care to preview the preset, simply type **Increase Tracking** in the search box of the Effects & Presets panel. Then double-click the effect to apply it to the selected layer in the Timeline panel.

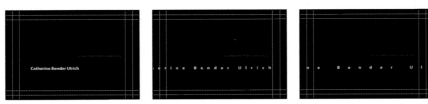

Customizing the tracking animation preset

The text expands, but you want the letters to be so close initially that they're on top of each other, and then to expand to a reasonable, readable distance apart. The animation should also occur faster. You'll adjust the Tracking Amount to achieve both goals.

1   Select the Your Name Here layer in the Timeline panel, and press UU to reveal the properties that were modified.

2   Go to 7:10.

3   Under Animator 1, change the Tracking Amount to −**5** so that the letters are squeezed together.

4   Click the Go To Next Keyframe arrow (▶) for the Tracking Amount property, and then change the value to **0**.

5   Drag the current-time indicator across the time ruler between 7:10 and 8:10. The letters expand as they appear onscreen, and stop animating at the last keyframe.

Animating text opacity

You'll take the animation of the director's name a little further by having it fade onscreen as the letters expand. To do this, you'll animate the layer's Opacity property.

1   Select the Your Name Here layer in the credits timeline.

2   Press T to reveal only the layer's Opacity property.

3   Go to 7:10, and set the Opacity to **0%**. Then click the stopwatch icon (⏱) to set an Opacity keyframe.

4   Go to 7:20, and set the Opacity to **100%**. After Effects adds a second keyframe. Now the letters of the director's name should fade in as they expand onscreen.

5   Drag the current-time indicator across the time ruler between 7:10 and 8:10 to see the letters of the director's name fade in as they spread out.

6   Right-click (Windows) or Control-click (Mac OS) the ending Opacity keyframe, and choose Keyframe Assistant > Easy Ease In.

7   Choose File > Save.

Using a text animator group

Text animator groups let you animate individual letters within a block of text in a layer. You'll use a text animator group to animate only the characters in your middle name without affecting the tracking and opacity animation of the other names in the layer.

1   In the Timeline panel, go to 8:10.

2   Hide the Opacity property for the Your Name Here layer. Then expand the layer to see its Text property group name.

About text animator groups

A text animator group includes one or more *selectors* and one or more *animator properties*. A selector is like a mask—it specifies which characters or section of a text layer you want an animator property to affect. Using a selector, you can define a percentage of the text, specific characters in the text, or a specific range of text.

Using a combination of animator properties and selectors, you can create complex text animations that would otherwise require painstaking keyframing. Most text animations require you to animate only the selector values—not the property values. Consequently, text animators use a small number of keyframes even for complex animations.

For more about text animator groups, see After Effects Help.

3 Next to the Text property name, click the Animate pop-up menu, and choose Skew. A property group named Animator 2 appears in the layer's Text properties.

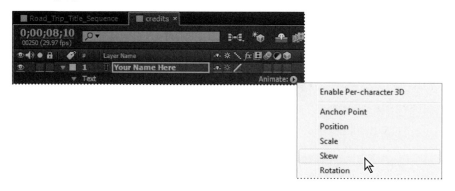

4 Select Animator 2, press Enter or Return, and rename it **Skew Animator**. Then press Enter or Return again to accept the new name.

Now you're ready to define the range of letters that you want to skew.

5 Expand the Skew Animator's Range Selector 1 properties.

Each animator group includes a default range selector. Range selectors constrain the animation to particular letters in the text layer. You can add additional selectors to an animator group, or apply multiple animator properties to the same range selector.

6 While watching the Composition panel, drag the Skew Animator's Range Selector 1 Start value up (to the right) until the left selector indicator (▌) is just before the first letter of your middle name (the *B* in *Bender*, in this example).

7 Drag the Skew Animator's Range Selector 1 End value down (to the left) until its indicator (▌) is just after the last letter of your middle name (the *r* in *Bender*, in this example) in the Composition panel.

Now, any properties that you animate with the Skew Animator will affect only the middle name that you selected.

Skewing the range of text

Now, make that middle name shake and shimmy by setting Skew keyframes.

1 Drag the Skew Animator's Skew value left and right, and notice that only the middle name sways. The other names in the line of text remain steady.

2 Set the Skew Animator's Skew value to **0**.

3 Go to 8:05, and click the stopwatch icon (⏱) for Skew to add a keyframe to the property.

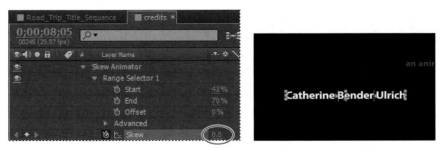

4   Go to 8:08, and set the Skew value to **50**. After Effects adds a keyframe.

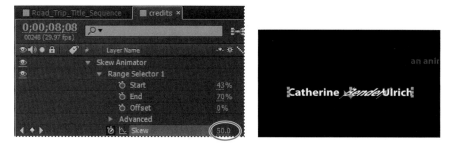

5   Go to 8:15, and change the Skew value to **−50**. After Effects adds another keyframe.

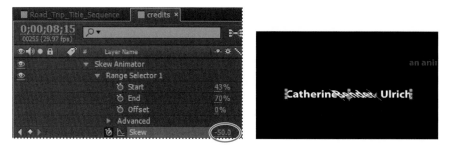

6   Go to 8:20, and change the Skew value to **0** to set the final keyframe.

▶ **Tip:** To quickly remove all text animators from a text layer, select the layer in the Timeline panel, and choose Animation > Remove All Text Animators. To remove only one animator, select its name in the Timeline panel, and press Delete.

7   Click the Skew property name to select all of the Skew keyframes. Then choose Animation > Keyframe Assistant > Easy Ease. This adds an Easy Ease to all keyframes.

8   Drag the current-time indicator across the time ruler from 7:10 to 8:20 to see how the director's name fades in and expands onscreen, and the middle name rocks side to side while the other names are unaffected.

9   Hide the properties for the Your Name Here layer in the Timeline panel.

10 Select the Road_Trip_Title_Sequence tab to open its timeline.

11 Press End, or move the current-time indicator to 9:29. Then press N to set the end bracket for the work area at the end of the composition.

12 Press Home, or go to 0:00, and then play a RAM preview of the entire composition.

13 Press the spacebar to stop playback, and then choose File > Save to save your work.

Cleaning up the path animation

Currently, the words *directed by* fade in and out as they wind along the Pipes path preset. You'll modify the text properties so that the words are opaque for the entire animation and come to rest just above your name.

1 With the directed by layer selected in the Timeline panel, press U to display the animated properties for the layer.

2 Click the stopwatch icon (🕓) for the Range Selector 1 Offset property to delete all of its keyframes.

3 Depending on where the current-time indicator is located in the time ruler, the resulting value for Range Selector 1 Offset may or may not be set to 0%. Set it to **0%** if it is not.

Now, *directed by* will be visible throughout the composition. Next, you'll modify the First Margin property to make the text stop animating above your name.

4 Select and delete the last keyframe for the First Margin property in the Timeline panel. Because the middle keyframe (now the last keyframe) is set to Easy Ease, the words *directed by* come gently to rest above your name.

5   Go to 6:14, and change the First Margin value to **685**.

You also need to adjust the path shape so that it starts and ends off the screen.

6   Using the Selection tool (▶) in the Composition panel, Shift-drag the control point at the top of the S-shaped curve to the right and off the screen. Drag it well off the screen so the car won't be visible.

7   Click the control point at the end of the S-shaped curve, and Shift-drag the control point off the left side of the screen, so that the car won't be visible.

● **Note:** Depending on how far you move the beginning and ending control points of the path, you may need to change the First Margin value again to reposition the text.

8   Preview the animation from about 5:00 to 9:00 to see the corrected path.

9   If the text doesn't stop directly above your name, adjust the First Margin value of the final keyframe.

10 Hide the properties for the directed by layer in the Timeline panel, and then choose File > Save.

Animating a nontext layer along a motion path

To cap off this project, you'll use a mask from a text layer to animate a nontext layer. Specifically, you'll use the mask shape for the *directed by* path to create a motion path for a car graphic so that it appears to be pulling the text. First, you'll import the car graphic and add it to your composition.

1   Double-click an empty area in the Project panel to open the Import File dialog box.

2   In the AECC_CIB/Lessons/Lesson03/Assets folder, select the car.ai file, choose
    Composition – Retain Layer Sizes from the Import As menu, and then click
    Import or Open.

3   Drag the car composition from the Project panel to the top of the layer stack
    in the Road_Trip_Title_Sequence Timeline panel.

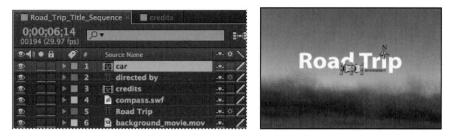

Copying the mask shape

Now you're ready to copy the mask shape from the path of the directed by layer
to the car layer.

1   Go to 5:00.

2   Select the directed by layer in the Timeline panel, and press M to display
    its Mask Path property.

3   Click the Mask Path property to select it, and then choose Edit > Copy.

4   Select the car layer, and then press P to display its Position property.

5   Click the Position property name to select it, and then choose Edit > Paste.

After Effects copies the Position keyframes from the directed by layer to the car layer.

Orienting the object

Unfortunately, the car is flying backward, but that's easy to fix.

1 With the car layer selected in the Timeline panel, choose Layer > Transform > Auto-Orient.

2 In the Auto-Orientation dialog box, select Orient Along Path, and then click OK.

Now the car is facing forward as it flies.

3 Select the car layer in the Timeline panel, and press P to hide its Position property.

Coordinating the text and object timing

Next, you need to coordinate the timing of the car's motion with the words *directed by* so that the words correctly trail behind the car.

1 Select the directed by layer, and press U to display its Path Options in the Timeline panel.

2 Go to 5:18, and change the First Margin value to **373**. After Effects adds a keyframe, and the text moves behind the car.

3 Go to 5:25, and change the First Margin value to **559**.

4 Go to 4:24, and drag the first First Margin keyframe (the left-pointing arrow) to that position.

5 Manually preview the corrected path animation by dragging the current-time indicator across the time ruler from about 4:20 to 7:10. The words follow the car and come to rest above your name, while the car continues to fly along the path and off the screen.

6 Hide the properties for the directed by layer, and then press the Home key or move the current-time indicator to the beginning of the time ruler.

Adding motion blur

Motion blur is the blur that occurs as an object moves. You'll apply motion blur to finesse the composition and make the movement look more natural.

1   In the Timeline panel, click the Motion Blur switch (⌀) for each layer *except* the background_movie and credits layers.

Now, apply motion blur to the layers in the credits composition.

2   Switch to the credits Timeline panel, and enable motion blur for both layers.

3   Switch back to the Road_Trip_Title_Sequence Timeline panel, and select the Motion Blur switch for the credits layer. Then click the Enable Motion Blur button (⌀) at the top of the Timeline panel so that you can see the motion blur in the Composition panel.

4   View a RAM preview of the entire, completed animation.

5   Choose File > Save.

Give yourself a pat on the back. You just completed some hard-core text animations. If you'd like to export the composition as a movie file, see Lesson 14, "Rendering and Outputting," for instructions.

Review questions

1   What are some similarities and differences between text layers and other types of layers in After Effects?

2   How can you preview a text animation preset?

3   How can you assign one layer's transformations to another layer?

4   What are text animator groups?

Review answers

1   In many ways, text layers are just like any other layer in After Effects. You can apply effects and expressions to text layers, animate them, designate them as 3D layers, and edit the 3D text while viewing it in multiple views. However, text layers are like shape layers in that you can't open them in their own Layer panels, and in that they are synthetic layers that consist entirely of vector graphics. You can animate the text in a text layer using special text animator properties and selectors.

2   You can preview text animation presets in Adobe Bridge by choosing Animation > Browse Presets. Adobe Bridge opens and displays the contents of the After Effects Presets folder. Navigate to folders containing categories of text animation presets, such as Blurs or Paths, and watch samples in the Preview panel. Then double-click a preset to add it to the currently selected layer in the After Effects Timeline panel.

3   You can use parenting relationships in After Effects to assign one layer's transformations to another layer (except opacity transformations). When a layer is made a parent to another layer, the other layer is called the *child layer*. Creating a parenting relationship between layers synchronizes the changes in the parent layer with corresponding transformation values of the child layers.

4   Text animator groups enable you to animate the properties of individual characters in a text layer over time. Text animator groups contain one or more *selectors*, which are like masks: They let you specify which characters or section of a text layer you want an animator property to affect. Using a selector, you can define a percentage of the text, specific characters in the text, or a specific range of text.

4 WORKING WITH SHAPE LAYERS

Lesson overview

In this lesson, you'll learn how to do the following:

- Create custom shapes.

- Customize a shape's fill and stroke.

- Use path operations to transform shapes.

- Animate shapes.

- Repeat shapes.

- Snap layers into alignment.

- Explore design options with the Brainstorm feature.

- Add a Cartoon effect to a video layer for a distinctive look.

- Use an expression to animate properties in time with audio.

This lesson will take approximately an hour to complete. Download the Lesson04 project files from the Lesson & Update Files tab on your Account page at www.peachpit.com, if you haven't already done so. As you work on this lesson, you'll preserve the start files. If you need to restore the start files, download them from your Account page.

PROJECT: DJ PROMO CLIP

Shape layers make it easy to create expressive
backgrounds and intriguing results. You can animate
shapes, apply animation presets, and add Repeaters
to intensify their impact.

Getting started

Shape layers are created automatically when you draw a shape with any of the drawing tools. You can customize and transform an individual shape or its entire layer to create interesting results. In this lesson, you will use shape layers to build a dynamic background for the introduction of a reality series called *DJ Quad Master*. You'll also use the Cartoon effect to change the overall look of the video. This effect can be processor-intensive. You may choose to skip the Cartoon effect exercise; if you do, you'll be able to finish the project, but it won't match the sample movie.

First, you'll preview the final movie and set up the project.

1 Make sure the following files are in the AECC_CIB/Lessons/Lesson04 folder on your hard disk, or download them from your Account page at www.peachpit.com now:

   • In the Assets folder: DJ.mov, gc_adobe_dj.mp3

   • In the Sample_Movie folder: Lesson04.mov

2 Open and play the Lesson04.mov sample movie to see what you will create in this lesson. When you are done, quit QuickTime Player. You may delete this sample movie from your hard disk if you have limited storage space.

As you start After Effects, restore the default application settings. See "Restoring default preferences" on page 2.

3 Start After Effects, and then immediately hold down Ctrl+Alt+Shift (Windows) or Command+Option+Shift (Mac OS) to restore default preferences settings. When prompted, click OK to delete your preferences.

4 Click Close to close the Welcome screen.

After Effects opens to display a blank, untitled project.

5 Choose File > Save As > Save As, and then navigate to the AECC_CIB/Lessons/Lesson04/Finished_Project folder.

6 Name the project **Lesson04_Finished.aep**, and then click Save.

Creating the composition

Next, you'll import the files you need and create the composition.

1 Double-click an empty area of the Project panel to open the Import File dialog box.

2 Navigate to the AECC_CIB/Lessons/Lesson04/Assets folder on your hard disk, Shift-click to select the DJ.mov and gc_adobe_dj.mp3 files, and then click Import or Open.

3 Choose File > New > New Folder to create a new folder in the Project panel.

4 Name the folder **Assets**, press Enter or Return to accept the name, and then drag the footage items you imported into the Assets folder. Then expand the folder so you can see its contents.

5 Press Ctrl+N (Windows) or Command+N (Mac OS) to create a new composition.

6 In the Composition Settings dialog box, name the composition **Shapes Background**, select the NTSC DV preset, and set the Duration to **10:00**. Then click OK.

> **Tip:** To specify 10 seconds, type **10.** in the Duration box. The period indicates that there are no units in that position. To specify 10 minutes, type **10..** in the box.

After Effects opens the new composition in the Timeline and Composition panels.

Adding a shape layer

One advantage of using a shape layer, rather than a solid layer, is that you can use the Fill option to create a linear or radial gradient. You'll use the Rectangle tool to create a gradient background for the composition.

About shapes

After Effects includes five shape tools: Rectangle, Rounded Rectangle, Ellipse, Polygon, and Star. When you draw a shape directly in the Composition panel, After Effects adds a new shape layer to the composition. You can apply stroke and fill settings to a shape, modify its path, and apply animation presets. Shape attributes are all represented in the Timeline panel, and you can animate each setting over time.

The same drawing tools can create both shapes and masks. Masks are applied to layers to hide or reveal areas of an image, while shapes have their own layers. When you select a drawing tool, you can specify whether the tool draws a shape or a mask.

Drawing a shape

You'll begin by drawing the rectangle that will contain the gradient fill.

1 Select the Rectangle tool (▢).

2 Choose 50% from the Magnification Ratio pop-up menu at the bottom of the Composition panel so that you can see the entire composition.

3 Click just outside the upper left corner of the composition, and drag the tool to the area just outside the bottom right corner, so that a rectangle covers the entire composition.

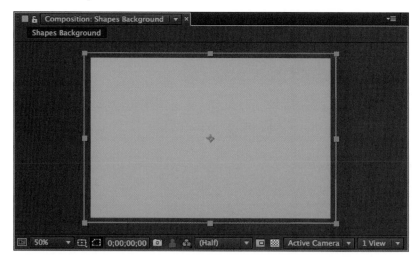

The shape appears in the Composition panel, and After Effects adds a shape layer named Shape Layer 1 to the Timeline panel.

Applying a gradient fill

You can change the color of a shape by modifying its Fill settings in the Tools panel. Clicking the word *Fill* opens the Fill Options dialog box, where you can select the kind of fill, its blending mode, and its opacity. Clicking the Fill Color box opens the Adobe Color Picker if the fill is solid, or the Gradient Editor if the fill is a gradient.

1 Click the word *Fill* to open the Fill Options dialog box.

2 Select the Radial Gradient option (◻), and click OK.

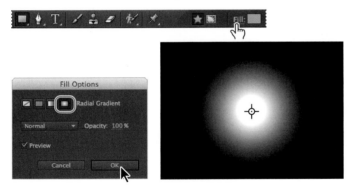

3 Click the Fill Color box (next to the word *Fill*) to open the Gradient Editor.

4 Select the white color stop (the left color stop below the gradient ramp), and select a light blue color. (We used R=100, G=185, B=240.)

5 Select the black color stop (the right color stop below the gradient ramp), and select a dark blue color. (We used R=10, G=25, B=150.)

6 Click OK to apply the new gradient colors.

Modifying gradient settings

The gradient is a little small, and it falls off quickly. You'll adjust the settings for the shape layer to expand the gradient.

1 In the Timeline panel, expand Shape Layer 1 > Contents > Rectangle 1 > Gradient Fill 1, if it isn't already visible.

2 Change the Start Point to **0, 225** and the End Point to **0, 740**.

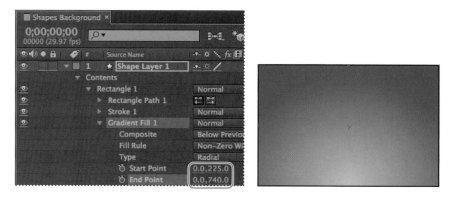

Now the gradient originates at the bottom of the screen and falls off near the top and edges of the composition.

3 Hide the Shape Layer 1 properties.

4 Select the layer name (Shape Layer 1), press Enter or Return, and type **Background**. Press Enter or Return again to accept the new layer name.

5 Click the Lock column (🔒) for the Background layer so that you don't accidentally select it.

Creating custom shapes

Though there are only five shape tools, you can modify the paths you draw to create a wide variety of shapes. The Polygon tool, in particular, gives you great flexibility. You'll use it to create rotating sun shapes in the background.

Drawing a polygon

By default, the Polygon tool draws a shape using the settings of the last shape drawn with that tool. However, by adjusting the points, position, rotation, outer radius, outer roundness, and other values, you can dramatically alter the initial shape. You'll modify a simple polygon to create a much more interesting shape.

1   Select the Polygon tool (⬡), which is hidden behind the Rectangle tool (◻).

2   Drag a polygon shape in the Composition panel.

▶ **Tip:** While you're dragging the shape, you can press the spacebar to reposition the shape in the Composition panel.

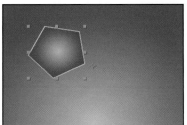

3   In the Timeline panel, expand Shape Layer 1 > Contents > Polystar 1 > Polystar Path 1.

4   Change the Points to **6**, the Rotation to **0** degrees, and the Outer Radius to **150**.

5   Change the Outer Roundness to **−500%**.

▶ **Tip:** You can change settings to values below 0 and above 100% for more dramatic results.

6   Hide the Polystar Path 1 properties.

7 Click the word *Fill* in the Tools panel to open the Fill Options dialog box. Select the Solid Color icon (■), and then click OK.

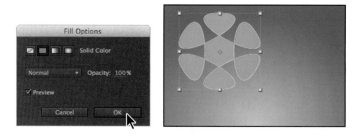

8 Click the Fill Color box, and select a bright yellow. (We used R= 250, G=250, B=0.) Click OK.

9 Click the Stroke Color box, and select a bright gray. (We used R=230, G=230, B=230.) Click OK.

10 Change the Stroke Width in the Tools panel to **5** pixels to emphasize the stroke.

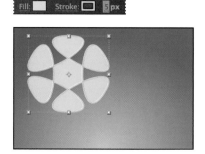

Twisting a shape

The Twist path operation rotates a path more sharply in the center than at the edges. Positive values twist clockwise; negative values twist counterclockwise. You'll use the Twist path operation to give the shape a little more definition.

1 In the Timeline panel, open the Add pop-up menu next to Contents in the Shape Layer 1 layer, and choose Twist.

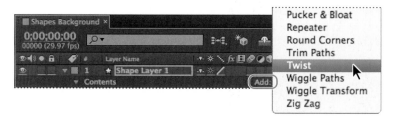

2 Expand Twist 1.

3 Change the Angle to **160**.

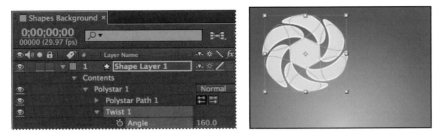

4 Hide the Polystar 1 properties.

5 Choose File > Save to save your work so far.

Repeating a shape

You've created the basic shape, but you need many copies of it to fill the composition. You could duplicate the shape manually, but instead, you'll use the Repeater path operation to create multiple rows of suns.

1 Select Shape Layer 1.

You're selecting the layer because you want to add the Repeater to the entire shape group, not just an individual shape.

2 Open the Add pop-up menu, and then choose Repeater.

3 Expand Repeater 1.

4 Change the number of copies to **5**.

The Repeater creates four copies of the shape, overlapping each other. You'll separate them next.

5 Expand Transform: Repeater 1.

6 Change the Position to **345,0**. The first value represents the x axis. To move the shapes closer together, use a smaller value for the x axis; to move them farther apart, use a larger value.

● **Note:** There are multiple Transform properties in the Timeline panel, applying to different path operators. Make sure you're selecting the appropriate Transform property for the object or layer you want to affect. In this case, you want to affect only the Repeater.

Now the shapes are farther apart. But you can't see them all at the same time. To move all of the shapes, you need to move the entire shape layer.

7 Hide the Transform: Repeater 1 properties.

8 Select Shape Layer 1, and then press P to display the Position property for the layer. Change the Position to **−50, 65**.

The shape layer is now in the upper left corner of the composition. You'll scale the layer and then add more rows.

Note: Because the horizontal and vertical values are linked, both values change when you change one.

9 Select Shape Layer 1, and then press S to display the Scale property for the layer. Change the Scale value to **50%**.

10 Press S to hide the Scale property for the layer.

11 Expand Shape Layer 1 > Contents.

12 Select Shape Layer 1, and then choose Repeater from the Add pop-up menu.

13 Expand Repeater 2 > Transform: Repeater 2.

14 Change the Position to **0, 385** so that there is vertical space between the rows.

15 Hide the Repeater 2 properties.

Rotating shapes

The suns should rotate on the background. You'll animate the Rotation property for the original shape; changes will automatically apply to the duplicated shapes.

1   In the Timeline panel, expand Shape Layer 1 > Contents > Polystar 1 > Transform: Polystar 1.

2   Press the Home key or drag the current-time indicator to the beginning of the timeline.

3   Click the stopwatch (⏱) next to the Rotation property to create an initial keyframe for the layer.

4   Press the End key, or drag the current-time indicator to the end of the timeline.

5   Change the Rotation to **3x+0** degrees. This setting causes the shape to rotate three times in 10 seconds.

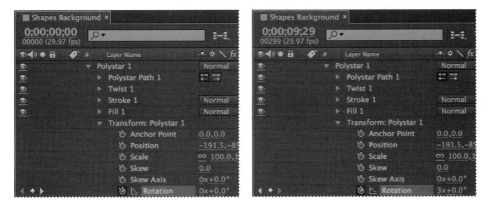

6   Hide the properties for Shape Layer 1.

7   Drag the current-time indicator across the timeline to preview the rotation.

Blending shapes with the background

The rotating suns look good, but they contrast with the background too much. You want the character in the main video file to be the focus of attention. You'll change the blending mode and opacity for the shape layer to make the background more subtle.

1   Click Toggle Switches/Modes at the bottom of the Timeline panel.

2   Choose Overlay from the Mode pop-up menu for the Shape Layer 1 layer.

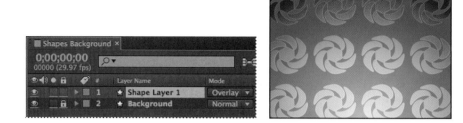

3   Select Shape Layer 1, and then press T to display the Opacity property for the layer.

● **Note:** Instead of changing the opacity for the entire layer, you could change the opacity for the original shape. The value would apply to all the duplicates as well.

4   Change the Opacity value to **25%**.

5   Press T to hide the Opacity property.

6   Select Shape Layer 1, press Enter or Return, and type **Suns** for the layer name. Press Enter or Return again to accept the new name.

7   Lock the layer to prevent accidental changes to it.

Creating stars

The Star tool is similar to the Polygon tool. A polygon is simply a star without an Inner Radius or Inner Roundness property; both tools create shapes called poly-stars. You'll use the Star tool to draw a star for the background, and then use the Pucker & Bloat operation to change the star's shape. Then you'll duplicate the star and rotate the stars around the layer's anchor point.

Drawing a star

The Star tool is grouped with the other shape tools. To draw a star, drag the Star tool in the Composition panel.

1 Select the Star tool (☆), which is hidden beneath the Polygon tool (⬡).

2 Change the fill and stroke settings for the shape before you draw the star:

- Click the Fill Color box, and select a medium blue. (We used R=75, G=120, B=200.) Then click OK.

- Click the word *Stroke*, and click None (▱) in the Stroke Options dialog box. Click OK.

3 Draw a star near the center of the composition. After Effects adds a shape layer named Shape Layer 1 to the Timeline panel.

4 In the Timeline panel, expand Shape Layer 1 > Contents > Polystar 1 > Polystar Path 1.

5 Change the Points to **6** and the Rotation to **150** degrees.

6 Change the Inner Radius to **50** and the Outer Radius to **90**. The radius values change the shape of the star.

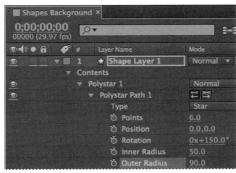

● **Note:** If you have trouble seeing the star in front of the background, you can temporarily hide the Suns and Background layers by clicking the Video switches (eye icons) for the layers in the Timeline panel.

7 Expand the Transform: Polystar 1 properties.

8 Change the Position to **−180, −70**.

9 Collapse the Polystar 1 properties to hide them.

Applying Pucker & Bloat

After Effects includes a powerful path operation called Pucker & Bloat. You can pucker a shape by pulling the path's vertices outward while curving segments inward, or bloat a shape by pulling the vertices inward while curving segments outward. Negative values pucker a shape; positive values bloat it. You'll pucker the star to give it a distinctive look.

1 Select Shape Layer 1.

2 Choose Pucker & Bloat from the Add pop-up menu.

3　Expand Pucker & Bloat 1.

4　Change the Amount to **–125** to pucker the star.

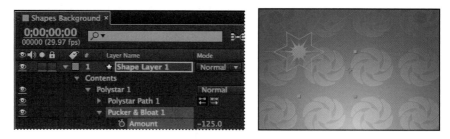

This star shape will go well in the background. Now you can duplicate and animate it.

Duplicating shapes

You want to have multiple stars in slightly different sizes rotating around the screen. You'll use the Repeater path operation again, but this time you'll modify the Transform properties for the Repeater to get different results.

1　Select Shape Layer 1, and choose Repeater from the Add pop-up menu.

2　Expand Repeater 1, and change the number of copies to **6**.

Now there are six stars on the screen.

3　Expand Transform: Repeater 1.

4　Change the Position to **0, 0** and the Rotation to **230** degrees.

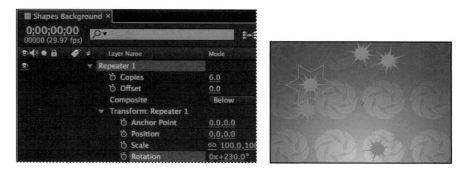

Because you applied the rotation to the Repeater, rather than the shape, each star rotates around the layer's anchor point to a different degree. When you change the Transform properties for the Repeater, the change is multiplied by the number of copies created. For example, if there are 10 copies of a shape and you change the Rotation value to 10 degrees, the first shape retains the original value of 0, the second shape rotates 10 degrees, the third shape rotates 20 degrees, and so on. The same concept applies to each of the Transform properties.

In this project, the anchor point for the layer differs from the position of the shapes, so the chain of stars begins to wrap in on itself.

5   Change the End Opacity to **65%**. Each star is more transparent than the one before it.

6   Hide the Repeater 1 properties.

7   Select the Shape Layer 1 layer, and choose Repeater from the Add pop-up menu again to add another Repeater.

8   Expand Repeater 2 > Transform: Repeater 2.

9   Change the Position to **–140, 0** and the Rotation to **40** degrees.

10 Change the Scale to **80%**.

Each duplicate star will be smaller than the one before it. Because there are three duplicates of the first group of stars, some will be 64% the size of the original.

11 Change the End Opacity to **0%**.

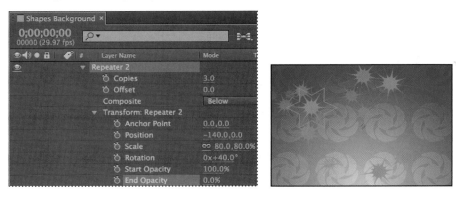

12 Collapse the Repeater 2 properties to hide them.

13 Choose File > Save.

Rotating shapes

You've rotated the stars around the anchor point for the layer. Now you want to animate each star to rotate around its own axis. To achieve this, you'll animate the Rotation property for the polystar shape itself, not the layer or the Repeater.

1   Expand Polystar 1 > Transform: Polystar 1.

2   Press the Home key or drag the current-time indicator to the beginning of the timeline.

3   Click the stopwatch icon (⏱) for the Rotation property to create an initial keyframe.

4   Press the End key, or drag the current-time indicator to the end of the timeline.

5   Change the Rotation to **180** degrees.

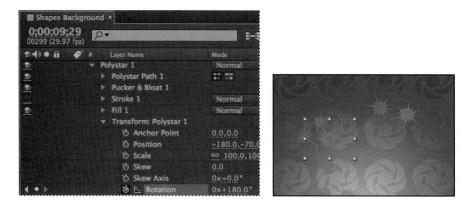

6   Manually preview the composition by dragging the current-time indicator along the timeline. After you confirm that everything is rotating, collapse the layer.

7   Rename the Shape Layer 1 layer **Stars**, and press Enter or Return to accept the layer name.

8   Lock the Stars layer.

Positioning layers with snapping

The rotating suns and stars are a good start. Now you'll add a checkerboard pattern to the mix using solid-color layers. Positioning the layers will be easy with the snapping feature in After Effects. You'll create a new composition and nest it within the main composition.

Creating a new composition

This checkerboard background includes multiple layers, so you'll create a new composition for it.

1   Press Ctrl+N (Windows) or Command+N (Mac OS) to create a new composition.

2 In the Composition Setting dialog box, name the composition **Checkerboard**, choose NTSC DV from the Preset menu, and type **10:00** for Duration. Then click OK.

After Effects open the new Checkerboard composition in the Timeline and Composition panels. You'll start by adding two solid layers, the building blocks of the checkerboard background.

3 Choose Layer > New > Solid to create a solid layer.

4 In the Solid Settings dialog box, do the following, and then click OK:

- Name the layer Dark Blue.

- Change both the Width and Height to **100** px.

- Choose Square Pixels from the Pixel Aspect Ratio menu.

- Select a dark blue color. (We used R=25, G=50, B=150.)

5   With the Dark Blue layer selected in the Timeline panel, press R to display
    the Rotation property for the layer. Then change the Rotation to **45** degrees.

6   Select the Selection tool. Then, in the Composition panel, drag the layer
    up so that only the bottom half of the diamond appears in the composition.

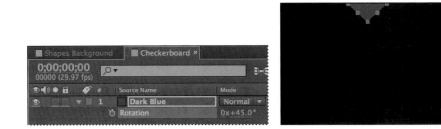

7   Press Ctrl+Y (Windows) or Command+Y (Mac OS) to create another solid layer.

8   In the Solid Settings dialog
    box, name the layer **Light
    Blue**, and change the color
    to a light blue (we used
    R=70, G=100, B=230).
    Then click OK.

The default width and height
for a new solid layer match the
settings you used previously,
so the Light Blue layer has the
same dimensions as the Dark
Blue layer.

9   With the Light Blue layer selected in the Timeline panel, press R to display
    the Rotation property. Then change the Rotation to **45** degrees.

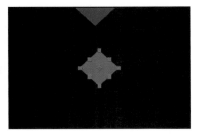

Snapping layers into position

You've created two layers, but they have no relationship to each other in the composition. You'll use the Snapping option in After Effects to quickly align the layers. When the Snapping option is enabled, the layer feature that is closest to your pointer when you click becomes the snapping feature. As you drag the layer near other layers, features on other layers are highlighted, showing you where the snapping feature would snap if you released the mouse button.

Note: You're snapping solid-color layers in this exercise, which works well, but you cannot snap shape layers. Also, a layer must be visible to snap to it. 2D layers can snap to 2D layers, and 3D layers can snap to 3D layers.

1 Select Snapping in the options section of the Tools panel, if it's not already selected.

2 Using the Selection tool (▶), select the Light Blue layer in the Composition panel.

When you select a layer in the Composition panel, After Effects displays the layer handles and anchor point. You can use any of these points as the snapping feature for a layer.

Tip: If the Snapping option isn't selected, you can temporarily enable it by holding down the Control key (Windows) or Command key (Mac OS) as you click and drag a layer.

3 Click near the corner handle on the left side of the Light Blue layer, and drag it near the lower right edge of the Dark Blue layer until it snaps into place, with the sides abutted. Be careful not to drag the corner itself, or you'll resize the layer.

As you drag the layer, a box appears around the left corner handle you selected, indicating that it is the snapping feature.

4 In the Timeline panel, select both of the layers, and press R to hide the Rotation property for both layers.

5 With both layers still selected, choose Edit > Duplicate to copy them.

Tip: Instead of choosing Edit > Duplicate, you can press Ctrl+D (Windows) or Command+D (Mac OS) to duplicate layers.

6 In the Composition panel, drag the two new layers down to the left, and then down to the right, so that the new Dark Blue layer abuts the original Light Blue layer. Remember that the snapping feature is determined by where you initially click when you begin to drag.

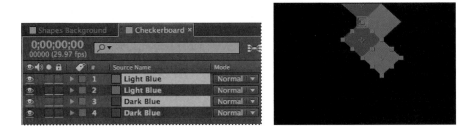

7 Repeat steps 5–6 twice, so that you have a column of diamonds filling the screen.

8 Choose Edit > Select All to select the layers in the Timeline panel.

9 Press Ctrl+D (Windows) or Command+D (Mac OS) to duplicate the layers. Then move them to the left in the Composition panel until they snap into place.

● **Tip:** If you need to generate a checkerboard more quickly, use the Checkerboard effect. For more information, see After Effects Help.

10 Repeat step 9 until the the Composition panel is full. Pull the duplicate layers to the left or right as necessary. Remember to click near an appropriate snapping feature as you begin dragging each time.

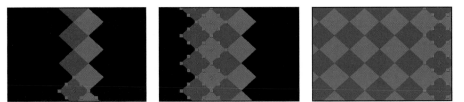

Nesting the composition

Now that the Checkerboard composition is complete, you'll nest it inside the main composition. To blend the checkerboard with the rest of the background, you'll change its blending mode, too.

1 Select the Shapes Background tab in the Timeline panel.

2 Drag the Checkerboard composition from the Project panel to the Timeline panel, placing it just above the Background layer.

3 Choose Soft Light from the Mode menu for the Checkerboard layer in the Timeline panel.

4 Lock the Checkerboard layer to ensure you don't accidentally change it.

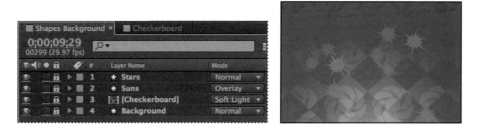

5 Save your work so far.

Incorporating video and audio layers

The background is in place. Now you can add the video of the DJ and the audio track that accompanies it.

Adding audio and video files

You imported files at the beginning of the lesson. Now you'll add them to the composition. The DJ.mov clip has no background and was rendered with a premultiplied alpha channel, so the underlying layers are visible.

1 Press the Home key or drag the current-time indicator to the beginning of the composition.

2 Open the Assets folder in the Project panel, if it isn't already open.

3 Drag the DJ.mov footage item to the Timeline panel, placing it above the other layers.

4 Drag the gc_adobe_dj.mp3 item from the Project panel to the Timeline panel, placing it beneath the other layers.

5 Lock the audio layer that you just added to the Timeline panel so that you can't accidentally change it later. Then choose File > Save.

● **Note:** You can place an audio layer anywhere in the layer stack, but moving it to the bottom keeps it out of the way while you work.

Trimming the work area

The DJ.mov clip is only 5 seconds long, but the composition is 10 seconds. If you rendered this movie now, the DJ would disappear halfway through the movie. To fix the problem, you'll move the work area end point to the 5-second mark. Then only the first 5 seconds will render.

1   Move the current-time indicator to the 5-second mark. You can drag the current-time indicator in the Timeline panel, or click the Current Time box and then type **500**.

Note: Alternatively, if you do not want to keep the last five seconds of the composition, you can change the duration of the composition to 5 seconds. To do so, choose Composition > Composition Settings, and then type **5.00** in the Duration box.

2   Press N to move the work area end point to the current time.

Applying a Cartoon effect

After Effects includes a Cartoon effect, which makes it easy to create a stylized look for your video. Since this intro for the *DJ Quad Master* reality series is very different from other reality series, the Cartoon effect will work perfectly here.

1   Select the DJ.mov layer in the Timeline panel.

2   Choose Effect > Stylize > Cartoon.

The Cartoon effect performs three operations on a layer. First, it smooths the layer, removing a great deal of detail. Therefore, it works best on video footage rather than a graphic layer, such as the background in this project. Next, the Cartoon effect emphasizes the edges of shapes, based on their brightness values. Finally, it simplifies the color in the layer.

The default settings do a pretty good job, but you'll fine-tune them in the Effect Controls panel.

▶ **Tip:** For interesting results, try changing the Cartoon Render options from Fill & Edges to Fill (for a color-only effect) or Edges (for black-and-white line art).

3   In the Effect Controls panel, choose Fill from the Render pop-up menu.

For this project, you're selecting Fill only temporarily so that you can more easily see the results of the Fill settings as you make adjustments.

4 Change the Detail Radius amount to **20** and the Detail Threshold amount to **50**.

These settings control how much detail is removed and how it is smoothed. Higher values remove more detail.

5 In the Fill area, change the Shading Steps value to **10,** and make sure the Shading Smoothness value is 70.

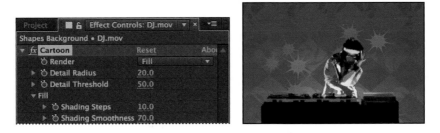

These settings determine how color is reduced and how gradients are preserved. In this project, changing these values reduces the number of colors in the DJ's shirt, creating a simpler design.

6 Choose Edges from the Render pop-up menu so you can focus on the edge controls. The layer becomes black and white temporarily.

7 In the Edge area, change the Threshold to **1.25** and the Width to **1**.

These settings reduce the number of black lines on the subject.

8 Leave the Softness value at its current setting (60), but lower the Opacity to **60%** to make the lines more subtle.

9 Choose Fill & Edges from the Render pop-up menu to restore the color.

10 Expand Advanced to see the advanced controls, which give you precise control over the edges.

11 Change the Edge Enhancement value to **50** to sharpen the edges of the layer.

12 Change the Edge Black Level to **2** to fill in more areas of the image with solid black. This makes the image even more cartoonish.

13 Lock the DJ.mov layer to ensure you don't accidentally make changes to it as you continue the project.

Adding a title bar

You've created an exciting background and added the video of the DJ and the audio track. The only thing missing is the title to identify the program. You'll use the Rectangle tool and path operations to create a dynamic shape, and then you'll add the text.

Creating a self-animating shape

Wiggle Paths turns a standard rectangle into a series of jagged peaks and valleys. You'll use it to create a shape that looks like a soundwave. Because the operation is self-animating, you need to change only a few properties for the entire shape to move on its own.

1 Select the Rectangle tool (▢), which is hidden beneath the Star tool (☆).

2 Click the Fill Color box, and select a light yellow. (We used R=255, G=255, B=130.) Click OK.

3 Click the word *Stroke*. In the Stroke Options dialog box, select Solid Color, and click OK.

4 Click the Stroke Color box, and select a light gray. (We used R=200, G=200, B=200.) Click OK.

5   Change the Stroke Width to **10** pixels.

6   Draw a rectangle across the composition—near the bottom and approximately 50 pixels high.

▶ **Tip:** If you need to reposition the rectangle, use the Selection tool to drag it into place in the Composition panel.

7   In the Timeline panel, expand Rectangle 1 > Rectangle Path 1.

8   Unlink the Size values, and then change them to **680, 50**.

9   Expand Stroke 1, and then change the Stroke Opacity to **30%**.

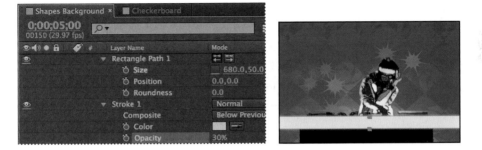

10 Hide the Rectangle 1 properties.

11 Select Shape Layer 1, and choose Wiggle Paths from the Add pop-up menu.

12 Expand Wiggle Paths 1. Then change the Size to **150** and the Detail to **80**.

13 Choose Smooth from the Points menu to make the path less jagged.

14 Change Wiggles/Second to **5** to speed up the movement.

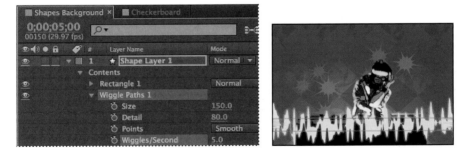

15 Move the current-time indicator across the timeline to see the shape move.

It's not exactly an audio waveform, but it's a stylistic version of one.

16 Hide all the properties for the layer.

17 Rename the layer **Lower Third**, and then lock the layer.

Adding text

All you need to do now is add the title of the program. You'll use an animation preset to make the text stand out.

1   Press the Home key or move the current-time indicator to the beginning of the composition.

2   Select the Horizontal Type tool (T). In the Character panel, select a sans serif font, such as Arial Bold or Helvetica Bold, and specify a size of **60** pixels.

3   Click the Fill Color box in the Character panel, and select black (R=**0**, G=**0**, B=**0**). Then click the Stroke Color box, and select white (R=**255**, G=**255**, B=**255**).

4   Change the Stroke Width to **2** pixels.

5   Click an insertion point in the Composition panel, and type **DJ Quad Master**.

6   Select the Selection tool (➤), and then reposition the text over the wave-form shape.

7   Select the text in the Composition panel. In the Effects & Presets panel, type **3D Rotate In By Character** in the Search box. Then drag the 3D Rotate In By Character animation preset onto the text.

After Effects applies the preset to the selected text.

8 Make a RAM preview to see the movie so far. Press the spacebar to stop the preview.

● **Note:** With the Cartoon effect in place, the RAM preview may take longer than usual to render and begin playing.

Using Brainstorm to experiment

The Brainstorm feature makes it easy to try different settings for effects, and to quickly apply the one you like. To use the Brainstorm feature, select the layer or properties you want to include, and then click the Brainstorm icon. The Brainstorm dialog box displays multiple variations of your image, based on randomized settings. You can save one or more of the variants, apply one to a composition, or redo the Brainstorm operation.

The Brainstorm feature works especially well with animation presets. You'll use it to explore possibilities for the Suns layer you created for this project.

1 Save the project, and then choose File > Save As > Save A Copy. Name the copy of the project **Brainstorm**, and save it in the Lesson04/Finished_Project folder.

2 Unlock the Suns layer in the Timeline panel.

3 Click the Solo switches (●) for the Suns and Background layers, so that you see only these two layers in the Composition panel.

You can isolate one or more layers for animating, previewing, or rendering by *soloing*. Soloing excludes all other layers of the same type from the Composition panel.

4 Expand the Suns layer, and then select Contents.

5 Click the Brainstorm icon (🔎) at the top of the Timeline panel to open the Brainstorm dialog box.

6 Select the level of randomness Brainstorm should apply to the layer properties. The default value is 25%; for drastic changes, try a higher number.

7 Click the Brainstorm button. The feature randomizes the properties and displays variants. You can click the Brainstorm button multiple times; each time, it randomizes the settings by the percentage you've selected.

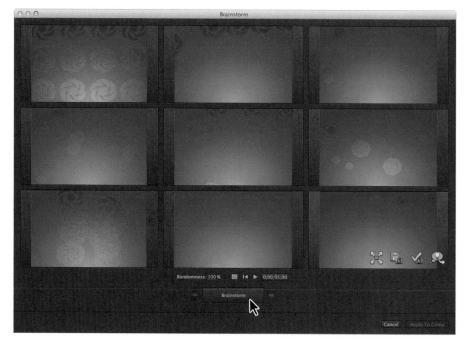

8 When you find a variation you like, move the pointer over the variant, and then click the check mark icon to apply it to the composition.

9 If you don't want to apply any of the variants, click Cancel to close the Brainstorm dialog box. Then unsolo the Suns and Background layers.

Extra credit

Animating layers to match audio

Currently, the suns and stars move at their own pace. The movie will be more compelling if the checkerboard background is animated with the music. You can scale the diamonds that make up the background in time with the amplitude of the audio file. First, you need to create keyframes from the audio information.

1   Unlock the gc_adobe_dj.mp3 layer in the Timeline panel. Then right-click or Control-click the layer, and choose Keyframe Assistant > Convert Audio To Keyframes.

After Effects adds the Audio Amplitude layer. The new layer is a null object layer, meaning it has no size or shape and won't appear in a final render. Null objects let you parent layers or drive effects.

2   Select the Audio Amplitude layer, and choose Edit > Cut.

3   Select the Checkerboard tab in the Timeline panel. Then choose Edit > Paste to paste the Audio Amplitude layer into that composition.

4   With the Audio Amplitude layer selected, press E to display the effects properties for the layer.

Three categories of effects properties are available for the layer: Left Channel, Right Channel, and Both Channels. You need only the Both Channels properties, so you'll delete the others.

5   Delete the Left Channel and Right Channel categories. Then expand the Both Channels category. Move the current time indicator across the timeline, and notice how the Slider value changes as you move across the keyframes.

When you converted the audio to keyframes, After Effects created keyframes that specify the amplitude of the audio file in each frame of the layer. You'll sync the scale of the background to those values.

6   Select a light blue diamond in the Composition panel. Then press S to display its Scale property in the Timeline panel.

7   In the Timeline panel, Alt-click (Windows) or Option-click (Mac OS) the Scale stopwatch to add an expression. The words *transform.scale* appear in the time ruler for the layer.

continues on next page

Extra credit (continued)

8 With the transform.scale expression selected in the time ruler, click the pick whip icon (◎) on the Expression:Scale line, and drag it to the Slider property name in the Audio Amplitude layer. You may need to expand the Timeline panel to see both the selected Light Blue layer and the Audio Amplitude layer, depending on which light blue layer you selected. If necessary, you can move the Audio Amplitude layer to a different position in the layer stack.

When you release the mouse, the pick whip snaps, and the expression in the solid layer time ruler now reads "temp = thisComp.layer("Audio Amplitude").effect("Both Channels")("Slider"); (temp,temp)" This means that the Scale values for the solid layer will depend on the Slider values of the Audio Amplitude layer.

Note: *You'll learn more about expressions in Lesson 6.*

9 Choose Edit > Deselect All to deselect the layers. Then move the current time indicator through the time ruler to see the diamond resize with the audio's amplitude.

The scale definitely changes, but because the amplitude of the sound file isn't very loud, the size of the layer remains small. You'll modify the expression to increase the size of the diamond.

10 Select the expression for the Light Blue layer in the time ruler. Click an insertion point just before the semicolon, and type ***2.5** to multiply the scale by 2.5. Then click outside the time ruler to accept the change. Now scrub through the time ruler to watch the diamond scale.

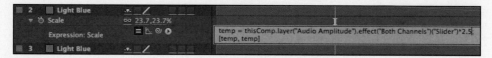

11 Select the Scale property name for the Light Blue layer, and choose Edit > Copy to copy the property and expression.

12 Select all the other solid layers in the Timeline, and choose Edit > Paste so that all the diamonds will change scale with the music. Then scrub through the time ruler to see the results.

13 Click the Shapes Background tab in the Timeline panel to return to the main composition. Hide the Suns layer so the background isn't quite so busy, and then make a RAM preview to watch the diamonds shrink and grow in time with the music.

Review questions

1 What is a shape layer, and how do you create one?

2 How can you quickly create multiple copies of a shape?

3 How can you snap one layer to another?

4 What does the Pucker & Bloat path operation do?

5 How does the Cartoon effect work?

Review answers

1 A shape layer is simply a layer that contains a vector graphic called a shape. To create a shape layer, draw a shape directly in the Composition panel using any of the drawing tools or the Pen tool.

2 To quickly duplicate a shape multiple times, apply a Repeater operation to the shape layer. The Repeater path operation creates copies of all paths, strokes, and fills included in the layer.

3 To snap one layer to another in the Composition panel, select Snapping in the options section of the Tools panel. Then click next to the handle or point you want to use as a snapping feature, and drag the layer close to the point to which you want to align it. After Effects highlights the points to which it will align when you release the mouse button. Note that you cannot snap shape layers.

4 The Pucker & Bloat operation pulls the path's vertices outward while curving segments inward (puckering), or pulls the vertices inward while curving segments outward (bloating). Negative values pucker a shape; positive values bloat it.

5 The Cartoon effect stylizes a layer by removing some details and emphasizing others, and by simplifying color. You can change settings in the Effect Controls panel to fine-tune the effect's behavior.

5 ANIMATING A MULTIMEDIA PRESENTATION

Lesson overview

In this lesson, you'll learn how to do the following:

- Create a complex animation with multiple layers.

- Adjust the duration of a layer.

- Clip live motion video using a shape layer.

- Animate with Position, Scale, and Rotation keyframes.

- Animate a precomposed layer.

- Apply the Radio Waves effect to a solid layer.

- Add audio to a project.

- Loop an audio track using time remapping.

 This lesson will take about an hour to complete. Download the Lesson05 project files from the Lesson & Update Files tab on your Account page at www.peachpit.com, if you haven't already done so. As you work on this lesson, you'll preserve the start files. If you need to restore the start files, download them from your Account page.

PROJECT: ANIMATED PORTFOLIO

Adobe After Effects projects typically use a variety of imported footage, arranged in a composition, which is edited and animated using the Timeline panel. In this lesson, you'll become more familiar with animation fundamentals as you build a multimedia presentation.

Getting started

For this project, professional illustrator Gordon Studer has created a Photoshop file of a city scene with several objects on separate layers that you will animate in After Effects. In fact, he has prepared an After Effects project that already contains this layered Photoshop file, as well as the video and audio clips that you will need later in the lesson.

You will animate an illustration of the artist driving a car on a city street. The animation ends with an easel that displays a slide show of samples of the artist's work. This is a complex animation. First, you'll animate the background and some objects so that the virtual camera appears to move from left to right across the scene. Then you'll animate the car driving down the road, and mask a photograph of the illustrator's face into the driver's seat. Next, you'll animate some passing traffic and buildings to add interest to the background. Finally, you'll animate the slide show of the artwork on the easel.

1 Make sure the following files are in the AECC_CIB/Lessons/Lesson05 folder on your hard disk, or download them from your Account page at www.peachpit.com now:

   • In the Start_Project_File folder: Lesson05_Start.aep

   • In the Assets folder: CarRide.psd, GordonsHead.mov, piano.wav, and several JPEG images whose filenames begin with "studer_"

   • In the Animation_preset folder: HeadShape.ffx

   • In the Sample_Movie folder: Lesson05.mov

2 Open and play the Lesson05.mov sample movie to see what you will create in this lesson. When you're done, quit QuickTime Player. You may delete the sample movie from your hard disk if you have limited storage space.

As you start After Effects, restore the default application settings. See "Restoring default preferences" on page 2.

3 Start After Effects, and then immediately hold down Ctrl+Alt+Shift (Windows) or Command+Option+Shift (Mac OS) to restore default preferences settings. When prompted, click OK to delete your preferences.

4 Click Close to close the Welcome screen.

5   Choose File > Open Project.

6   Navigate to the AECC_CIB/Lessons/Lesson05/Start_Project_File folder, select Lesson05_Start.aep, and click Open.

The CarRide composition is already open in the Composition and Timeline panels.

7   Choose File > Save As > Save As.

8   In the Save As dialog box, navigate to the AECC_CIB/Lessons/Lesson05/ Finished_Project folder. Name the project **Lesson05_Finished.aep**, and then click Save.

Animating the scenery using parenting

To animate the various elements of the scenery efficiently with the background, you're going to use parenting. As you learned in Lesson 3, "Animating Text," creating a parenting relationship between layers synchronizes the changes in the parent layer with the corresponding transformation values of the child layers. In Lesson 3, you used parenting to quickly apply one layer's scale transformation to another layer. Now, you will use it to synchronize the movement of the objects in three layers— the leaves, full skyline, and the FG (foreground) layers—with the BG (background) layer of the animation.

Setting up parenting

First, you'll set up the parent-child relationship between the relevant layers in the Timeline panel.

1   In the Timeline panel, Ctrl-click (Windows) or Command-click (Mac OS) to select the leaves, FG, and full skyline layers.

▶ **Tip:** If you don't see the Parent column, choose Columns > Parent from the Timeline panel menu.

2 In the Parent column for any one of the selected layers, choose 8.BG from the pop-up menu. This establishes the three selected layers as child layers to the parent layer, which is layer 8, named BG (the background).

Animating the parent layer

Now you'll animate the position of the background layer—the parent layer—so that it moves horizontally. This, in turn, will animate the child layers in the same way.

1 Press the Home key or move the current-time indicator to the beginning of the time ruler.

2 Select the BG layer in the Timeline panel, and press P to reveal its Position property.

3 Set the BG layer's Position values to **1029, 120,** and click the stopwatch icon (⏱) to create a Position keyframe.

The background layer moves off to the left side of the scene, as if the camera had been moved.

▶ **Tip:** A quick way to go to a frame is to press Alt+Shift+J (Windows) or Option+Shift+J (Mac OS) to open the Go To Time dialog box. Then type the desired time without punctuation (as in **1015** for 10:15), and press Enter or Return.

4 Go to 10:15.

5   Set the BG layer's Position values to **−626, 120**.

After Effects automatically creates a second keyframe and shows you the motion path of the animation in the Composition panel. The background now moves across the composition, and because the leaves, full skyline, and FG layers are child layers to the BG (parent) layer, they also move horizontally from the same starting position.

6   Select the BG layer, and press **P** to hide its Position property and keep the Timeline panel neat.

Animating the bee's position

Another element of the composition that moves across the scene at the beginning of the animation is the bee. You will animate it next.

1   Press the Home key or go to 0:00.

2   Select the Bee layer in the Timeline panel, and press P to reveal its Position property. (The bee is not visible at 0:00 in the Composition panel.)

3   Set the Position values of the Bee layer to **825, 120**, so that the bee is offscreen to the left at the beginning of the animation. Then click the stopwatch icon (⏱) to create a Position keyframe.

4   Go to 1:00, and set the Bee layer's Position values to **1411, 120**, putting the bee offscreen to the right. After Effects adds a keyframe.

5   Select the Bee layer, and press P to hide its Position property in the Timeline panel.

Tip: You can also change the Bee layer's Position values by dragging the layer in the Composition panel (using the Selection tool) until the layer is in the correct position.

Trimming a layer

Because you don't want the bee to appear in the composition after 1:00, you need to *trim* the layer. Trimming (hiding) footage at the beginning or end of a layer lets you change which frames are first or last in the composition. The first frame to appear is called the *In point*, and the last frame is called the *Out point*. You can trim footage by changing the In and Out points in the Layer panel or the Timeline panel, depending on what you want to change. Here, you'll change the Out point of the Bee layer in the Timeline panel.

▶ **Tip:** You can also drag the right side of the layer duration bar to change the Out point.

1 Make sure the current-time indicator is at 1:00 and the Bee layer is selected in the Timeline panel.

2 Press Alt+] (Windows) or Option+] (Mac OS) to set the Out point at 1:00.

Applying motion blur

To finish the bee's animation, you'll apply motion blur for more realistic movement.

1 Click the Motion Blur switch (⊘) for the Bee layer to apply motion blur.

2 Click the Enable Motion Blur button (⊘) at the top of the Timeline panel to view the motion blur in the Composition panel.

Previewing the animation

A quick manual preview will show you how the elements in the scenery move.

1 Drag the current-time indicator from 0:00 to 10:15. The animation of the background, leaves, bee, foreground objects, and objects in the skyline makes it appear as if a camera is panning across the scene.

2 After you preview, return the current-time indicator to 0:00, and then choose File > Save to save your work.

Adjusting an anchor point

The background is moving; now it's time to animate the artist in his red car so that he appears to drive across the composition. To begin that process, you must first move the anchor point of the layer that contains the red car, without moving the layer's relative position in the composition. The red car is on the Artist layer. To edit the anchor point of the Artist layer, you need to work on the Artist layer in the Layer panel.

1   Double-click the Artist layer in the Timeline panel to open it in the Layer panel.

2   At the bottom right of the Layer panel, choose Anchor Point Path from the View menu.

This view displays the layer's anchor point, which by default is set at the center of the layer.

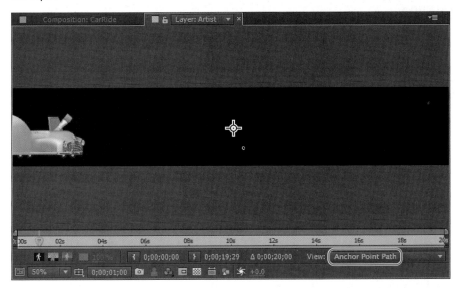

3   Select the Pan Behind tool (⌖) in the Tools panel (or press Y to activate it).

4   Choose Fit Up To 100% from the Magnification Ratio pop-up menu to see the entire layer, and then drag the anchor point to the lower left corner of the car.

5   Click the Composition: CarRide tab to view the CarRide composition.

6   Select the Artist layer in the Timeline panel, and press P to reveal its Position property.

7   Set the Position values for the Artist layer to **50, 207** so that the car is in the center of the frame, and then click the stopwatch icon (⏱) to set a Position keyframe.

This is a temporary position that lets you see the car onscreen while you mask the driver into place, which is your next task. Then you'll animate the car so that it drives across the composition.

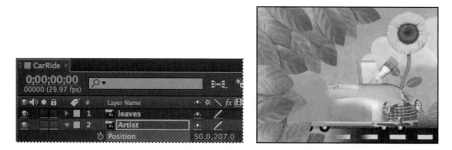

8   Select the Artist layer, press P to hide its Position property, and then choose File > Save to save your work.

Masking video using vector shapes

● **Note:** You'll learn much more about masking in Lesson 7.

With the car positioned onscreen, you can add the driver. You will use a custom animation preset to create a mask from a shape layer. This shape turns a frontal head shot into a side-view profile shape, which is a "Picasso-esque" signature style of the artist's work.

Creating a new composition

To help you manage the movement of this layer later, you will create a new composition, which you'll add to the main composition.

1   Drag the GordonsHead.mov clip from the Source folder in the Project panel onto the Create A New Composition button (▣) at the bottom of the panel.

After Effects creates a new composition named GordonsHead based on the settings applied to the movie. It opens the new composition in both the Timeline and Composition panels.

Unfortunately, the GordonsHead movie has a different resolution than the CarRide composition. You need to fix that now.

2   Select the GordonsHead composition in the Project panel, and then choose Composition > Composition Settings.

3   In the Composition Settings dialog box, change the Width to **360** pixels. If the Lock Aspect Ratio option is selected, After Effects automatically changes the Height to 240 pixels. Click OK.

Now you'll scale the layer to fit the composition.

4   Select the GordonsHead layer in the Timeline panel, and choose Layer > Transform > Fit To Comp.

Using animation presets with shape layers

If you're the creative type, like Gordon Studer, you can create shape layers and save them as animation presets to apply to future projects. You'll apply an animation preset to a shape layer to change the appearance of Gordon's head.

1 Choose Layer > New > Shape Layer. After Effects adds a new shape layer to the composition.

2 Select Shape Layer 1 in the Timeline panel, and then choose Animation > Apply Animation Preset.

3 In the Open dialog box, navigate to the AECC_CIB/Lessons/Lesson05/ Animation_preset folder on your hard disk.

4 Select the HeadShape.ffx file, and click Open to apply it.

Constraining a layer with an alpha matte

There are many ways to mask layers in After Effects. For example, you can use shape tools or the Pen tool to draw a mask. In this lesson, you'll use an alpha matte, which uses the alpha channel of a layer to mask another layer.

1 Click Toggle Switches/Modes at the bottom of the Timeline panel to view the Mode column.

2 In the TrkMat menu for the GordonsHead layer, choose Alpha Matte "Shape Layer 1."

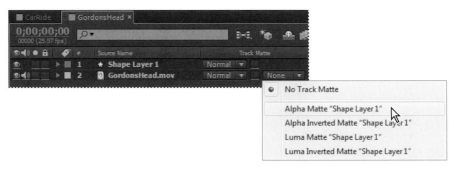

The layer is now constrained by the shape layer.

Swapping a composition into a layer

Now that Gordon Studer's mug is constrained to the vector shape, you need to attach it to the car. You'll return to the main CarRide composition and swap the GordonsHead composition into the Head layer, which is currently a solid layer that serves as a placeholder.

1   Click the CarRide tab in the Timeline panel.

2   Select the head layer in the Timeline panel, and then do one of the following:

  •   Select the GordonsHead composition in the Project panel, and press Ctrl+Alt+/ (Windows) or Command+Option+/ (Mac OS).

  •   Alt-drag (Windows) or Option-drag (Mac) the GordonsHead composition from the Project panel to the head layer in the Timeline panel.

3   Using the Selection tool (▶), drag the head layer in the Composition panel so that Gordon is sitting properly in the car.

Now, you'll use parenting again so that Gordon's head will move with the car.

4 In the head layer in the Timeline panel, choose 2. Artist from the Parent menu.

5 Choose File > Save to save your work.

Keyframing a motion path

Finally, you're ready to animate the car so that it drives onscreen at the beginning of the composition, scales larger during the middle of the composition—as if it's approaching the camera—and then pops a wheelie and drives offscreen. You'll start by keyframing the car's position to get it on the screen.

1 Press the Home key or move the current-time indicator to the beginning of the time ruler.

2 Click the Video switch (◉) for the leaves layer in the Timeline panel to hide the layer, so that you can clearly see the Artist layer below it.

3 Select the Artist layer in the Timeline panel, and expand its Transform properties.

● **Note:** There's already a keyframe at this time from the anchor-point exercise.

4 Change the layer's Position values to **–162, 207** to move it offscreen to the left (behind the leaves).

5   Go to 2:20, and change the Position values for the Artist layer to **54.5, 207**. After Effects adds a keyframe.

6   Go to 6:00, and click the Add Or Remove Keyframe At Current Time button (in the Switches column) for the Artist layer to add a Position keyframe for the Artist layer at the same values (54.5, 207).

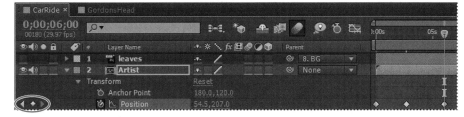

Note: You can't add a keyframe here by clicking the stopwatch—it's already active. And After Effects won't automatically add a new keyframe if you haven't entered new values. Thus, you must click the Add Or Remove Keyframe At Current Time button to add a keyframe with the same values.

When you animate the Position property, After Effects displays the movement as a motion path. You can create a motion path for the position of the layer or for the anchor point of a layer. A position motion path appears in the Composition panel; an anchor-point motion path appears in the Layer panel. The motion path appears as a sequence of dots in which each dot marks the position of the layer at each frame. A box in the path marks the position of a keyframe. The density of dots between the boxes in a motion path indicates the layer's relative speed. Dots close together indicate a slower speed; dots farther apart indicate a faster speed.

Keyframing scale and rotation transformations

The car is zooming onscreen; now, you'll make it appear as if the car is getting closer to the camera by scaling it larger. Then you'll make it pop a wheelie by keyframing the Rotation property.

1   Go to 7:15, and set the Scale values for the Artist layer to **80, 80%**. Then click the stopwatch (⏱) to set a Scale keyframe.

2   Go to 10:10, and set the Position values for the Artist layer to **28, 303**.
    After Effects adds a keyframe.

3   Still at 10:10, change the Scale values to **120, 120%**. After Effects adds a keyframe.

4   Still at 10:10, click the stopwatch icon (⏱) for the Rotation property to set
    a Rotation keyframe at the default value, 0.0 degrees.

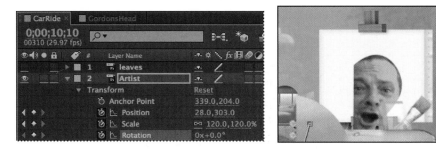

5   Go to 10:13, and change the Rotation value to **0x −14.0 degrees**. After Effects adds
    a keyframe, and now the car pops a wheelie.

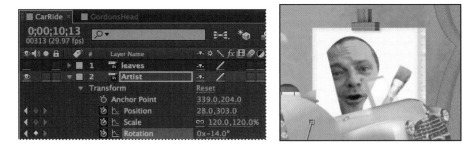

Now, you'll animate the car driving offscreen.

6   Go to 10:24, and set the Position values for the Artist layer to **369, 258**. After Effects
    adds a keyframe.

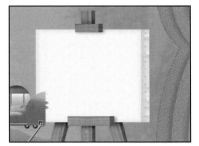

Adding motion blur

Finally, apply a motion blur to smooth out the driving sequence.

1 Hide the Artist layer properties in the Timeline panel.

2 Turn on the Motion Blur switch (⊘) for the Artist and head layers.

The blur will be visible as the car drives offscreen, and it will be visible for the flying bee as well, because you applied motion blur to that layer earlier in the lesson. You'll see all of this when you preview the composition.

Previewing your work

Now that the keyframes are set for the moving car, preview the entire clip, and make sure the driver is framed to create a pleasant composition.

1 Click the Video switch (👁) for the leaves layer to make it visible.

2 Click the RAM Preview button in the Preview panel to preview the animation.

3 Choose File > Save to save your work so far.

Animating additional elements

You'll get more practice creating keyframe animations as you animate the passing traffic and the buildings in the background.

Animating the passing traffic

Perhaps you noticed in the preview you just watched that the blue car is tailgating the artist in his red speedster. The blue car is actually on a precomposed layer that also contains a yellow car. Next, you'll make the scene more dynamic by animating the blue and yellow cars so that they drive past the artist's car in the background.

● **Note:** Remember, a precomposition is simply a layer with nested layers in it. In this example, the vehicles layer contains one nested layer with a blue car and one nested layer with a yellow car.

1 Select the vehicles layer in the Timeline panel, and click the Solo switch (●) to isolate it as you work.

2 Press the P key to reveal the layer's Position property.

3 Go to 3:00.

4 Using the Selection tool (▶), drag the vehicles layer in the Composition panel so that both cars are offscreen to the right. Press Shift after you start to drag to constrain the movement vertically. Or, simply set the vehicles layer's Position values to **684, 120**.

5   Click the stopwatch icon (⏱) to create a Position keyframe for the vehicles layer.

6   Go to 4:00, and drag the vehicles layer in the Composition panel so that both cars are offscreen to the left. Or, simply set the layer's Position values to **93, 120**. After Effects adds a keyframe.

7   Turn on motion blur for the vehicles layer.

8   Select the vehicles layer in the Timeline panel, and then press P to hide its Position property.

9   Unsolo the vehicles layer, and then manually preview the passing traffic by dragging the current-time indicator from about 2:25 to 4:06.

Animating the buildings

Animated buildings? You bet. You'll animate a couple of buildings rising and "jumping" in the background as the artist cruises through downtown San Francisco. Once again, you'll be working with a precomposition (full skyline), but you'll open it to animate its nested layers individually.

1   Double-click the full skyline composition in the Project panel to open it in its own Timeline and Composition panels.

Notice that this composition has three layers: skyline, building, and buildings. You'll start with the buildings layer.

2   Go to 5:10, select the buildings layer in the Timeline panel, and press P to reveal its Position property.

3 Click the stopwatch icon (⏱) to set a Position keyframe for the buildings layer at the default values (127, 120).

4 Go to 4:20. Then, in the Composition panel, use the Selection tool (▶) to drag the buildings layer down, off the bottom of the composition, until its y Position value is 350. Press Shift after you start to drag to constrain the horizontal axis. After Effects adds a keyframe.

▶ **Tip:** Dragging the layer into position is good practice, but you can also directly enter the y coordinates in steps 4 and 5 if you don't want to drag the layer in the Composition panel.

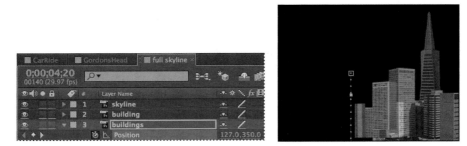

5 Go to 5:02, and drag the buildings layer up in the Composition panel until its y Position value is 90. After Effects adds a keyframe.

Great. You've got your first animated building. Next, you'll finesse the movement at the high point of the jump to make it more natural. (Naturally jumping buildings? Aw, come on. This is fun.)

Adding Easy Ease

Finesse the movement at the high point of the jump by adding Easy Ease.

1   Right-click (Windows) or Control-click (Mac OS) the keyframe at 5:02, and choose Keyframe Assistant > Easy Ease.

This adjusts the speed of change as the motion approaches and retreats from the keyframe.

2   Drag the current-time indicator from 4:20 to 5:10 to preview the jumping building.

Copying the building animation

To animate the other layers in the full skyline composition, you'll copy and paste the buildings layer's keyframes to those other layers—but at different times—so that the elements jump in sequence.

1   Click the Position property name for the buildings layer to select all of the property's keyframes, and then choose Edit > Copy or press Ctrl+C (Windows) or Command+C (Mac OS).

2   Go to 5:00, and select the building layer in the Timeline panel. Choose Edit > Paste or press Ctrl+V (Windows) or Command+V (Mac OS) to paste the keyframes to this layer. (You won't see the pasted keyframes if the Position property isn't visible.)

3   Go to 5:10, and select the skyline layer. Choose Edit > Paste or press Ctrl+V (Windows) or Command+V (Mac OS) again to paste the keyframes to this layer, too.

4   If the Position properties are not already visible, select the building layer name, and press the P key to see the copied keyframes. Then do the same for the skyline layer.

5   Apply motion blur to all three layers. Then switch to the CarRide Timeline panel, and turn on motion blur for the full skyline precomposed layer. This applies motion blur to all of the nested layers.

You've done a lot of work. Take a look at the animation from the beginning.

6   Watch a RAM preview, and then choose File > Save to save your work.

Applying an effect

You've created several keyframed animations in this project. You'll switch gears now and apply an effect in this next exercise. The effect will animate some radio waves emitting from the Transamerica Pyramid building.

Adding a solid-color layer

You need to apply the radio wave effect on its own layer, which will be a solid-color layer.

About solid-color layers

You can create solid images of any color or size (up to 30,000 x 30,000 pixels) in After Effects. After Effects treats solids as it does any other footage item: You can modify the mask, transform properties, and apply effects to a solid layer. If you change settings for a solid that is used by more than one layer, you can apply the changes to all layers that use the solid or to only the single occurrence of the solid. Use solid layers to color a background or to create simple graphic images.

1 Make sure the CarRide Timeline panel is open.

2 Choose Layer > New > Solid. In the Solid Settings dialog box, name the layer **radio waves**, and then click the Make Comp Size button. Then click OK to create the layer.

3 Drag the radio waves layer in the Timeline panel so that it sits directly above the BG layer.

By default, the radio waves layer lasts the duration of the composition. However, it needs to be only a few seconds long, to last the length of the effect. So you'll change the layer's duration.

4   Click the Expand Or Collapse The In/Out/Duration/Stretch Panes button (⚹) in the lower left corner of the Timeline panel to view those four columns.

5   Click the orange Duration value for the radio waves layer.

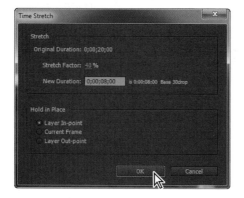

6   In the Time Stretch dialog box, set the New Duration to **8:00**. Then click OK.

7   In the time ruler, drag the radio waves layer duration bar (from the center) so that it starts at 6:00. Watch the In value for the layer to see when it's at 6:00, or you can enter the In value manually.

8   Go to 6:00—the first frame of the radio waves effect.

Applying the effect

Now you're ready to apply the radio waves effect to the solid layer.

1   With the radio waves layer selected in the Timeline panel, choose Effect > Generate > Radio Waves.

Nothing changes in the Composition panel, because the first wave hasn't emitted yet.

2   In the Effect Controls panel, expand the Wave Motion and Stroke properties, if they aren't already visible. Then do the following:

- Choose Each Frame from the Parameters Are Set At menu.
- Set the Expansion to **0.40**.
- Set the Velocity to **1.00**.
- Set the Color to white (R=**255**, G=**255**, B=**255**).
- Set the Opacity to **0.50**.
- Set both the Start Width and End Width to **3.00**.

3   Still in the Effect Controls panel, click the cross-hair button for the Producer Point setting near the top of the panel. Then, in the Composition panel, click to set the producer point at the top of the pyramid.

Radio waves with the settings you specified will now emit from the top of the pyramid building. You just need to parent the radio waves layer to the full skyline layer so that the waves travel with the pyramid building across the composition.

4   In the Parent column of the radio waves layer, choose 7. full skyline from the pop-up menu.

5   Go to 5:28, just before the Radio Waves effect begins, and select From Current Time in the Preview panel. (You may need to expand the Preview panel to see all the options.)

6   Click the RAM Preview button (▋▶) to view a RAM preview from the point that the Radio Waves effect begins.

After watching the preview, tidy up the Timeline panel.

7   Click the Expand Or Collapse The In/Out/Duration/Stretch Panes button (↿↾) to hide those columns. Then press the Home key or move the current-time indicator to the beginning of the time ruler.

8   Choose File > Save to save your work.

Creating an animated slide show

Now that you've completed this complex animation of the artist driving through a stylized cityscape, it's time to add samples of his work to the easel. The point, after all, is to show off the artist's work to potential new clients. However, this slide-show technique could easily be adapted to other uses, such as exhibiting family photos or making a business presentation.

Importing the slides

The artist has provided a folder of sample artwork, but you'll include only some of the images. To help you choose, use Adobe Bridge to preview them.

Note: If Bridge isn't installed, you'll be prompted to install it when you choose Browse In Bridge. For more information, see page 2.

1 Choose File > Browse In Bridge to jump to Adobe Bridge.

2 In the Folders panel, navigate to the AECC_CIB/Lessons/Lesson05/Assets folder on your hard disk.

3 Click the various "studer_" images, and study them in the Preview panel.

4 Ctrl-click (Windows) or Command-click (Mac OS) to select your five favorite images, and then double-click to add all of them to the After Effects Project panel. We chose studer_Comcast.jpg, studer_Map.jpg, studer_music.jpg, studer_Puzzle.jpg, and studer_Real_Guys.jpg.

5 Leave Adobe Bridge open in the background.

Making a new composition

You'll put these images into their own composition, which will make it easier to turn them into a slide show, complete with transition effects between slides.

1 In After Effects, click the Project tab to view the Project panel.

2 Deselect all items in the Project panel. Then Shift-click to select the five Studer images, and drag them onto the Create A New Composition button (⊞) at the bottom of the panel.

3   In the New Composition From Selection dialog box, do the following:

   - In the Create area, select Single Composition.

   - In the Options area, set the Still Duration to **2:00**.

   - Select the Sequence Layers and Overlap options.

   - Set the Duration to **0:10**.

   - Choose Cross Dissolve Front And Back Layers from the Transition menu.

   - Click OK.

The transition option creates a sequence of still images that dissolve from one to the next. When you click OK, After Effects opens the new composition, named for the Studer image at the top of the list in the Project panel, in the Composition and Timeline panels. Before continuing, you'll give the composition a more intuitive name.

4   Choose Composition > Composition Settings, and rename the composition **Artwork**. Then click OK.

Positioning the slide show

Wasn't it easy to make the slide show? Now, you'll position the slide show on the canvas of the easel. The slides are actually larger than the canvas, but because they're in a composition, you can size them as a unit.

1   Switch to the CarRide Timeline panel, and go to 11:00, which is when the canvas is centered in the composition.

2   Drag the Artwork composition from the Project panel into the CarRide Timeline panel, placing it at the top of the layer stack.

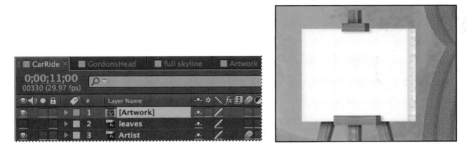

Currently, the Artwork layer is set to start at 0:00. You need to adjust the timing of the layer so that it appears at 11:00.

3   Drag the layer duration bar (from the center) for the Artwork layer in the time ruler so that its In point is at 11:00. You can click the Expand Or Collapse The In/Out/Duration/Stretch Panes button (↔) to see the In point precisely.

Now, you'll scale the slides to fit the canvas.

4   With the Artwork layer selected in the Timeline panel, press S to reveal its Scale property, and set the Scale values to **45, 45%**.

5   Press P to reveal the Position property, and then drag the x Position value down (to the left) until the slide is centered (about 144.0).

6 Select the Artwork layer in the Timeline panel, and choose Layer > Blending Mode > Darken. This drops out the pure white in each image and replaces it with the softer white of the canvas.

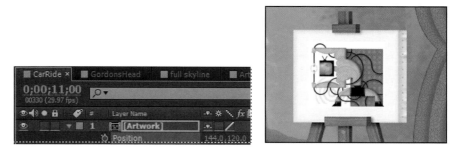

7 Click the RAM Preview button (▮▶) in the Preview panel to watch a RAM preview of the slide show. (Make sure From Current Time is selected to start the RAM preview at 11:00.)

Fading in the first slide

As it stands, the first slide instantly appears in the easel at 11:00. You'll animate the Artwork layer's opacity so that the first slide fades in.

1 Select the Artwork layer in the Timeline panel, and press T to reveal its Opacity property.

2 Go to 11:00.

3 Set the Artwork layer's Opacity to **0%**, and click the stopwatch icon (⏱) to set an Opacity keyframe.

4 Go to 11:03, and set the Artwork layer's Opacity to **100%**. After Effects adds a keyframe. Now the artwork appears gradually.

5 Manually preview the animation from 11:00 to 11:03 to see the first slide fade in.

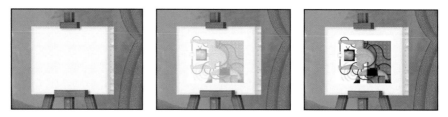

6 Select the Artwork layer in the Timeline panel, and press T to hide its Opacity property. Then choose File > Save to save your work.

Adding an audio track

Give yourself a hand—you've done a lot of animating in this project. But you're not quite done. Gordon Studer speaks to the viewer while he drives his car across the composition, but you'll add some polish by dropping in a background audio track.

1   Choose File > Browse In Bridge to jump to Adobe Bridge.

2   In the Content panel, select the piano.wav thumbnail preview.

Adobe Bridge lets you preview audio.

3   If the file doesn't automatically play when you select it, click the Play button (▶) in the Preview panel to hear the track. Click the Pause button (❙❙) or press the spacebar to stop.

4   Double-click the piano.wav file to import it into the After Effects Project panel.

5   Deselect everything in the Project panel, and then drag the piano.wav item from the Project panel into the CarRide Timeline panel, placing it at the bottom of the layer stack.

Supported audio file formats

You can import any of the following types of audio files into After Effects:

*   Adobe Sound Document (ASND; multitrack files import as merged single track)
*   Advanced Audio Coding (AAC, M4A)
*   Audio Interchange File Format (AIF, AIFF)
*   MP3 (MP3, MPEG, MPG, MPA, MPE)
*   Video for Windows (AVI, WAV; requires QuickTime on Mac OS)
*   Waveform (WAV)

Looping the audio track

The duration of the piano layer isn't as long as the composition, so you'll need to loop it. Luckily, this music track has been composed to loop cleanly. You're going to loop the audio clip using the time-remapping feature. You'll learn to use time remapping in more depth in Lesson 6, "Animating Layers."

1 Select the piano.wav layer in the Timeline panel.

2 Choose Layer > Time > Enable Time Remapping. A Time Remap property appears for the layer in the Timeline panel, and two Time Remap keyframes appear for the layer in the time ruler.

3 Alt-click (Windows) or Option-click (Mac OS) the stopwatch icon (⏱) for the layer's Time Remap property. This sets the default expression for time remapping; it has no immediate effect in the Composition panel.

4 In the Expression: Time Remap property for the piano layer, click the Expression Language pop-up menu, and choose Property > loopOut(type = "cycle", numKeyframes = 0).

The audio is now set to loop in a cycle, repeating the clip endlessly. All you need to do is extend the Out point of the layer to the end of the composition.

5 Select the piano layer in the Timeline panel, and go to the end of the time ruler. Then press Alt+] (Windows) or Option+] (Mac OS) to extend the layer to the end of the composition.

You'll preview the entire composition soon.

6 Hide the piano layer's properties, and then choose File > Save to save your work.

Zooming in for a final close-up

Everything is looking good, but zooming in for a final close-up of the slide show will really focus the viewer's attention on the artwork.

1   In the Project panel, drag the CarRide composition onto the Create A New Composition button (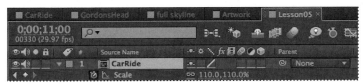) at the bottom of the panel.

After Effects creates a new composition, named CarRide 2, and opens it in the Timeline and Composition panels. You'll rename the composition to avoid confusion.

2   Select the CarRide 2 composition in the Project panel, press Enter or Return, and type **Lesson05**. Then press Enter or Return again to accept the new name.

3   In the Lesson05 Timeline panel, go to 10:24, the first frame where the car clears the right side of the composition.

4   Select the CarRide layer in the Lesson05 Timeline panel, and press S to reveal its Scale property.

5   Click the stopwatch icon (⏱) to set a Scale keyframe at the default values, 100, 100%.

6   Go to 11:00, and change the Scale values to **110, 110%**. After Effects adds a keyframe, and for the rest of the composition, the slide show will be prominent and eye-catching.

7   Select the CarRide layer, and press S to hide its Scale property.

Previewing the entire composition

It's time to see how the whole thing comes together.

1   In the Preview panel, deselect From Current Time, and then click the RAM Preview button (⏵) to watch a RAM preview of the entire composition.

2   Press the spacebar to stop playback when you're done.

3   Choose File > Save.

Congratulations. You've just created a complex animation, practicing all kinds of After Effects techniques and capabilities along the way, from parenting to audio looping.

Extra credit

Editing audio files in Adobe Audition

You can make some very simple changes to audio in After Effects. For more substantial edits, use Adobe Audition. Audition is available with a full Adobe Creative Cloud membership.

You'll use Audition to alter the pitch of the background music in the movie you just created. Changes you save to the audio file will be reflected the next time you play a RAM preview or otherwise render the composition in After Effects.

1 Open the Lesson05_Finished.aep file if you closed it previously.

2 Select the piano.wav file in the Project panel, and choose Edit > Edit In Adobe Audition.

3 In Audition, press the Play button to sample a few seconds of the audio file.

4 Choose Effects > Time And Pitch > Stretch And Pitch.

5 In the Effects - Stretch And Pitch dialog box, move the Stretch slider to **100%** and the Pitch Shift value to **20**. Then click OK.

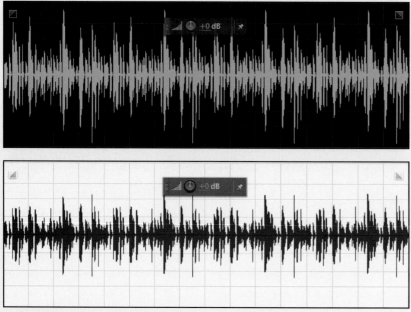

Changes you make are reflected in the Editor panel in Audition.

6 Click the Play button to preview the higher-pitched sound.

7 Choose File > Save.

8 In After Effects, play a RAM preview to hear how your edited audio track sounds in context.

Review questions

1 How does After Effects display an animation of the Position property?

2 What is a solid-color layer, and what can you do with it?

3 What types of audio can you import into an After Effects project?

Review answers

1 When you animate the Position property, After Effects displays the movement as a motion path. You can create a motion path for the position of the layer or for the anchor point of a layer. A position motion path appears in the Composition panel; an anchor-point motion path appears in the Layer panel. The motion path appears as a sequence of dots, where each dot marks the position of the layer at each frame. A box in the path marks the position of a keyframe.

2 You can create solid images of any color or size (up to 30,000 x 30,000 pixels) in After Effects. After Effects treats solids as it does any other footage item: You can modify the mask, transform properties, and apply effects to the solid layer. If you change settings for a solid that is used by more than one layer, you can apply the changes to all layers that use the solid or to only the single occurrence of the solid. Use solid layers to color a background or create simple graphic images.

3 You can import any of the following types of audio files into After Effects: Adobe Sound Document (ASND; multitrack files import as merged single track), Advanced Audio Coding (AAC, M4A), Audio Interchange File Format (AIF, AIFF), MP3 (MP3, MPEG, MPG, MPA, MPE), Video for Windows (AVI, WAV; requires QuickTime on Mac OS), and Waveform (WAV).

6 ANIMATING LAYERS

Lesson overview

In this lesson, you'll learn how to do the following:

- Animate a layered Adobe Photoshop file.

- Duplicate an animation using the pick whip.

- Work with imported Photoshop layer styles.

- Apply a track matte to control the visibility of layers.

- Animate a layer using the Corner Pin effect.

- Apply the Lens Flare effect to a solid layer.

- Use time remapping and the Layer panel to dynamically retime footage.

- Edit Time Remap keyframes in the Graph Editor.

 This lesson will take approximately an hour to complete. Download the Lesson06 project files from the Lesson & Update Files tab on your Account page at www.peachpit.com, if you haven't already done so. As you work on this lesson, you'll preserve the start files. If you need to restore the start files, download them from your Account page.

PROJECT: SUNRISE EFFECT IN A FILM SHORT

Animation is all about making changes over time—
changes to an object or image's position, opacity, scale,
and other properties. This lesson provides more practice
animating the layers of a Photoshop file, including
dynamically remapping time.

Getting started

Adobe After Effects provides several tools and effects that let you simulate motion video using a layered Photoshop file. In this lesson, you will import a layered Photoshop file of the sun appearing through a window, and then animate it to simulate the motion of the sun rising behind the panes of glass. This is a stylized animation in which the motion is first accelerated, and then slows down as clouds and birds move through the window frame at the end.

First, you'll preview the final movie and set up the project.

1   Make sure the following files are in the AECC_CIB/Lessons/Lesson06 folder on your hard disk, or download them from your Account page at www.peachpit.com now:

   •   In the Assets folder: clock.mov, sunrise.psd

   •   In the Sample_Movies folder: Lesson06_regular.mov, Lesson06_retimed.mov

2   Open and play the Lesson06_regular.mov file to see the straightforward time-lapse animation you will create in this lesson.

3   Open and play the Lesson06_retimed.mov file to see the same animation after time has been remapped, which you will also do in this lesson.

4   When you're done, quit QuickTime Player. You may delete the sample movies from your hard disk if you have limited storage space.

When you begin the lesson, restore the default application settings for After Effects. See "Restoring default preferences" on page 2.

5   Start After Effects, and then immediately hold down Ctrl+Alt+Shift (Windows) or Command+Option+Shift (Mac OS) to restore default preferences settings. When prompted, click OK to delete your preferences file. Click Close to close the Welcome screen.

After Effects opens to display an empty, untitled project.

6   Choose File > Save As > Save As.

7   In the Save As dialog box, navigate to the AECC_CIB/Lessons/Lesson06/ Finished_Project folder.

8   Name the project **Lesson06_Finished.aep**, and then click Save.

Importing the footage

You need to import one source item for this lesson.

1   Double-click an empty area of the Project panel to open the Import File dialog box.

2   Navigate to the AECC_CIB/Lessons/Lesson06/Assets folder on your hard disk, and select the sunrise.psd file.

3   Choose Composition – Retain Layer Sizes from the Import As menu, so the dimensions of each layer will match the layer's content.

4   Click Import or Open.

5   In the Sunrise.psd dialog box, make sure Composition – Retain Layer Sizes is selected in the Import Kind menu, and click OK.

Before continuing, take a moment to study the layers of the file you just imported.

6   In the Project panel, expand the sunrise Layers folder to see the Photoshop layers. Resize the Name column to make it wider and easier to read, if necessary.

Each of the elements you'll animate in After Effects—the shadows, birds, clouds, and sun—is on a separate layer. In addition, there is one layer representing the initial, predawn lighting conditions in the room (Background), and a second layer that represents the final, bright daylight conditions in the room (Background Lit). Similarly, there are two layers for the two lighting conditions outside the window: Window and Window Lit. The Window Pane layer includes a Photoshop layer style that simulates a pane of glass.

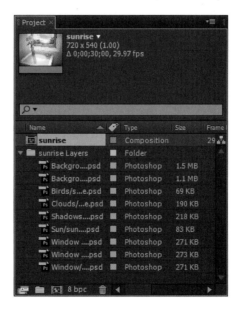

After Effects preserves the layer order, transparency data, and layer styles from the source Photoshop document. It also preserves other features, such as adjustment layers and type, which you don't happen to be using in this project.

Preparing layered Photoshop files

Before you import a layered Photoshop file, name its layers carefully to reduce preview and rendering time, and to avoid problems importing and updating the layers:

- Organize and name layers. If you change a layer name in a Photoshop file after you have imported it into After Effects, After Effects retains the link to the original layer. However, if you delete an imported layer, After Effects will be unable to find the original layer and will list it as missing in the Project panel.

- Make sure that each layer has a unique name to avoid confusion.

Creating the composition

For this lesson, you'll use the imported Photoshop file as the basis of the composition.

1   Double-click the sunrise composition in the Project panel to open it in the Composition panel and in the Timeline panel.

2   Choose Composition > Composition Settings.

3 In the Composition Settings dialog box, change the Duration to **10:00** to make the composition 10 seconds long, and then click OK.

About Photoshop layer styles

Adobe Photoshop provides a variety of layer styles—such as shadows, glows, and bevels—that change the appearance of a layer. After Effects can preserve these layer styles when you import Photoshop layers. You can also apply layer styles in After Effects.

Though layer styles are referred to as *effects* in Photoshop, they behave more like blending modes in After Effects. Layer styles follow transformations in the standard render order, whereas effects precede transformations. Another difference is that each layer style blends directly with the underlying layers in the composition, whereas an effect is rendered on the layer to which it's applied, the result of which then interacts with the underlying layers as a whole.

The layer style properties are available for the layer in the Timeline panel.

To learn more about working with layer styles in After Effects, see After Effects Help.

Simulating lighting changes

The first part of the animation involves lightening the dark room. You'll use Opacity keyframes to animate the light.

1 In the Timeline panel, click the Solo switch (●) for both the Background Lit and Background layers.

Soloing the layers isolates them to speed animating, previewing, and rendering.

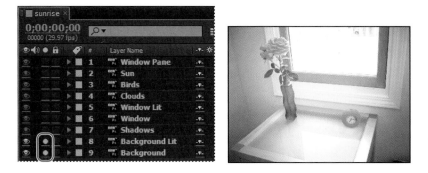

Currently, the lit background is on top of the regular (darker) background, obscuring it and making the initial frame of the animation light. However, you want the animation to start dark, and then lighten. To accomplish this, you will make the Background Lit layer initially transparent, and have it "fade in" and appear to lighten the background over time.

2 Go to 5:00.

3 Select the Background Lit layer in the Timeline panel, and press T to reveal its Opacity property.

4 Click the stopwatch icon (⏱) to set an Opacity keyframe. Note that the Opacity value is 100%.

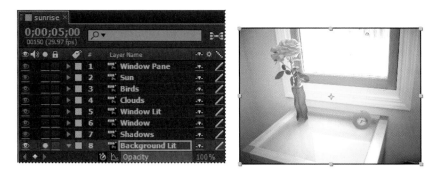

5 Press the Home key or drag the current-time indicator to 0:00. Then set the Opacity for the Background Lit layer to **0%**. After Effects adds a keyframe.

Now, when the animation begins, the Background Lit layer is transparent, which allows the dark Background layer to show through.

6 Click the Solo switches (●) for the Background Lit and Background layers to restore the view of the other layers, including Window and Window Lit. Make sure to leave the Opacity property for the Background Lit layer visible.

7 Expand the Window Pane layer's Transform properties. The Window Pane layer has a Photoshop layer style that creates a bevel on the window.

8 Go to 2:00, and click the stopwatch next to the Opacity property for the Window Pane layer to create a keyframe at the current value, 30%.

9 Press the Home key or drag the current-time indicator to the beginning of the time ruler, and change the Opacity property to **0%**.

10 Hide the Window Pane properties.

11 Click the Play/Pause button (▶) in the Preview panel, or press the spacebar to preview the animation.

The interior of the room transitions gently from dimly to brightly lit.

12 Press the spacebar to stop playback at any time after 5:00.

13 Choose File > Save.

About expressions

When you want to create and link complex animations, such as multiple car wheels spinning, but want to avoid creating tens or hundreds of keyframes by hand, you can use *expressions* instead. With expressions, you can create relationships between layer properties and use one property's keyframes to dynamically animate another layer. For example, if you set rotation keyframes for a layer and then apply the Drop Shadow effect, you can use an expression to link the Rotation property's values with the Drop Shadow effect's Direction values; that way, the drop shadow changes with the layer as it rotates.

Expressions are based on the JavaScript language, but you don't need to know JavaScript to use them. You can create expressions by using simple examples and modifying them to suit your needs, or by chaining objects and methods together.

You work with expressions in the Timeline panel or the Effect Controls panel. You can use the pick whip to create expressions, or you can enter and edit expressions manually in the expression field—a text field in the time graph under the property.

For more about expressions, see After Effects Help.

Duplicating an animation using the pick whip

Now you need to lighten the view through the window. To do this, you'll use the pick whip to duplicate the animation you just created. You can use the pick whip to create expressions that link the values of one property or effect to another.

1 Press the Home key or move the current-time indicator to the beginning of the time ruler.

2 Select the Window Lit layer, and press T to reveal its Opacity property.

3   Alt-click (Windows) or Option-click (Mac OS) the Opacity stopwatch for the
    Window Lit layer to add an expression for the default Opacity value, 100%.
    The words *transform.opacity* appear in the time ruler for the Window Lit layer.

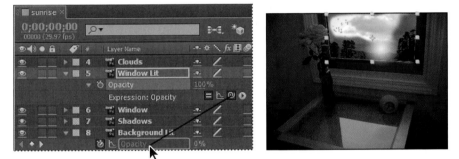

4   With the transform.opacity expression selected in the time ruler, click the
    pick whip icon (◉) on the Window Lit Expression: Opacity line, and drag it to
    the Opacity property name in the Background Lit layer. When you release the
    mouse, the pick whip snaps, and the expression in the Window Lit layer time
    ruler now reads "thisComp.layer("Background Lit").transform.opacity." This
    means that the Opacity value for the Background Lit layer (0%) replaces the
    previous Opacity value (100%) for the Window Lit layer.

5   Drag the current-time indicator from 0:00 to 5:00. Notice that the Opacity
    values for the two layers match.

6   Go to the beginning of the time ruler, and then press the spacebar to preview
    the animation again. Notice that the sky outside the window lightens as the
    room inside the window does.

7   Press the spacebar to stop playback.

8   Hide the Window Lit and Background Lit layers' properties to keep the Timeline
    panel tidy for your next task.

9   Choose File > Save to save your project.

Animating movement in the scenery

The scenery outside the window is unrealistically static. For one thing, the sun should actually rise. In addition, shifting clouds and flying birds would bring this scene to life.

Animating the sun

To make the sun rise in the sky, you'll set keyframes for its Position, Scale, and Opacity properties.

1 In the Timeline panel, select the Sun layer, and expand its Transform properties.

2 Go to 4:07, and click the stopwatch icons (⏱) to set keyframes for the Position, Scale, and Opacity properties at their default values.

3 Go to 3:13.

4 Still working with the Sun layer, set its Scale to **33, 33%** and its Opacity to **10%**. After Effects adds a keyframe for each property.

5 Press the End key, or move the current-time indicator to the end of the composition.

6   For the Position property of the Sun layer, set the y value to **18**, and then set the Scale values to **150, 150%**. After Effects adds two keyframes.

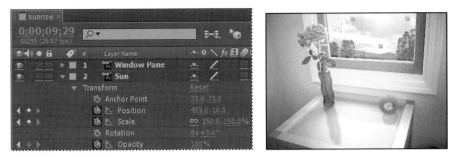

You've just set keyframes that instruct the sun to move up and across the sky, and to become slightly larger and brighter as it rises.

7   Hide the Sun layer's properties.

Animating the birds

Next, you'll animate the motion of the birds flying by. To create the animation faster, you'll take advantage of the Auto-Keyframe button in the Timeline panel. When the Auto-Keyframe button is selected, After Effects automatically creates a keyframe whenever you change a value.

1   Select the Birds layer in the Timeline panel, and press P to reveal its Position property.

2   Click the Auto-Keyframe button (◉) at the top of the Timeline panel.

The stopwatch icon becomes red when it's selected.

3   Go to 4:20, and set the Position values for the Birds layer to **200, 49**. After Effects automatically adds a keyframe.

● **Note:** While the Auto-Keyframe button can make your life easier, it can also create more keyframes than you intended. Enable the Auto-Keyframe button only when you need it for a specific task, and remember to turn it off when you're done with that task!

4   Go to 4:25, and set the Position values of the Birds layer to **670, 49**. After Effects adds a keyframe.

5   Select the Birds layer, and press P to hide its Position property.

Animating the clouds

Next, you'll animate the clouds drifting across the sky.

1   Select the Clouds layer in the Timeline panel, and expand its Transform properties.

2   Go to 5:22, and click the stopwatch icon (⏱) for the Position property to set a Position keyframe at the current value (406.5, 58.5).

3   Still at 5:22, set the Opacity for the Clouds layer to **33%**.

After Effects automatically adds a keyframe, because the Auto-Keyframe button is still selected.

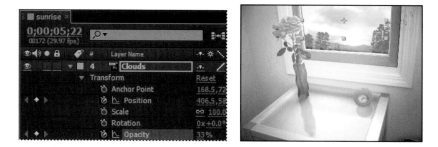

4   Click the Auto-Keyframe button to deselect it.

5   Go to 5:02, and set the Clouds layer Opacity value to **0%**.

After Effects adds a keyframe, even though the Auto-Keyframe button is deselected. After Effects adds a keyframe when you change the value for a property that already has a keyframe in the timeline.

6   Go to 9:07, and set the Clouds layer Opacity value to **50%**. After Effects adds a keyframe.

7   Press the End key, or move the current-time indicator to the last frame of the composition.

8   Set the Position of the Clouds layer to **456.5, 48.5**. After Effects adds a keyframe.

Previewing the animation

Now, see how it all comes together.

1   Press the Home key or go to 0:00.

2   Press F2 or click an empty area in the Timeline panel to deselect everything, and then press the spacebar to preview the animation.

The sun rises in the sky, the birds fly by (very quickly), and the clouds drift. So far, so good! However, there's a fundamental problem: These elements all overlap the window frame—the birds even appear to be flying inside the room. You'll solve this next.

3   Press the spacebar to stop playback.

4   Hide the Clouds layer's properties, and then choose File > Save.

Adjusting the layers and creating a track matte

To solve the problem of the sun, birds, and clouds overlapping the window frame, you must first adjust the hierarchy of the layers within the composition. Then you'll use an alpha track matte to allow the outside scenery to show through the window, but not appear to be inside the room.

Precomposing layers

You'll start by precomposing the Sun, Birds, and Clouds layers into one composition.

1 Shift-click to select the Sun, Birds, and Clouds layers in the Timeline panel.

2 Choose Layer > Pre-compose.

3 In the Pre-compose dialog box, name the new composition **Window Contents**. Make sure the Move All Attributes Into The New Composition option is selected, and select Open New Composition. Then click OK.

A new Timeline panel named Window Contents appears. It contains the Sun, Birds, and Clouds layers you selected in step 1 above. The Window Contents composition also appears in the Composition window.

4 Click the sunrise Timeline panel to see the contents of the main composition. Notice that the Sun, Birds, and Clouds layers have been replaced by the Window Contents layer, which refers to the Window Contents composition.

Creating the track matte

Now, you will create the track matte to hide the outside scenery behind all areas of the image except the windowpane. To do that, you'll duplicate the Window Lit layer and use its alpha channel.

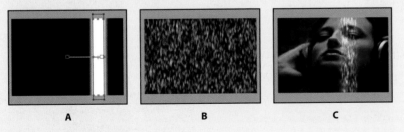

1 In the sunrise Timeline panel, select the Window Lit layer.

2 Choose Edit > Duplicate.

3 Drag the duplicate layer, Window Lit 2, up in the layer stack so that it's above the Window Contents layer.

4 Click Toggle Switches/Modes in the Timeline panel to display the TrkMat column, so you can apply the track matte.

5 Select the Window Contents layer, and choose Alpha Matte "Window Lit 2" from the TrkMat pop-up menu.

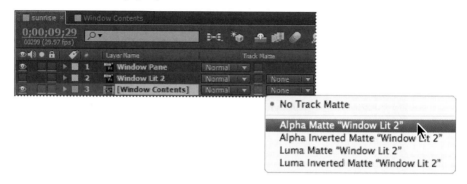

The alpha channel of the layer above (Window Lit 2) is used to set transparency for the Window Contents layer, so the scenery outside the window shows through the transparent areas of the windowpane.

6 Press the Home key or move the current-time indicator to the beginning of the time ruler, and then press the spacebar to preview the animation. Press the spacebar again when you're done.

7 Choose File > Save to save your project.

Adding motion blur

The birds will look more authentic if they include motion blur. You'll add the motion blur and then set the shutter angle and phase, which control the intensity of the blur.

1 Switch to the Window Contents Timeline panel.

2   Go to 4:22—the middle of the birds animation. Then select the Birds layer, and choose Layer > Switches > Motion Blur to turn on motion blur for the layer.

3   Click the Enable Motion Blur button (⊘) at the top of the Timeline panel to display the motion blur for the Birds layer in the Composition panel.

4   Choose Composition > Composition Settings.

5   In the Composition Settings dialog box, click the Advanced tab, and reduce the Shutter Angle to **30** degrees.

The Shutter Angle setting imitates the effect of adjusting a shutter angle on a real camera, which controls how long the camera aperture is open, gathering light. Larger values create more motion blur.

6   Change the Shutter Phase to **0** degrees, and then click OK.

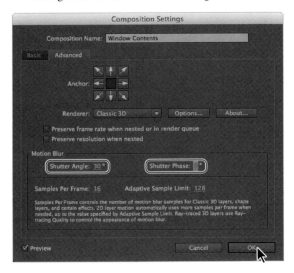

Animating the shadows

It's time to turn your attention to the shadows cast on the table by the clock and the vase. In a realistic time-lapse image, those shadows would shorten as the sun rises.

There are a few ways to create and animate shadows in After Effects. For example, you could use 3D layers and lights. In this project, however, you'll use the Corner Pin effect to distort the Shadows layer of the imported Photoshop image. Using the Corner Pin effect is like animating with the Photoshop Free Transform tool—the effect distorts an image by repositioning each of its four corners. You can use it to stretch, shrink, skew, or twist an image, or to simulate perspective or movement that pivots from the edge of a layer, such as a door opening.

1 Switch to the sunrise Timeline panel, and make sure you're at the beginning of the time ruler.

2 Select the Shadows layer in the Timeline panel, and then choose Effect > Distort > Corner Pin. Small circles appear around the corner points of the Shadows layer in the Composition panel.

Note: If you don't see the controls, choose View Options from the Composition panel menu. In the View Options dialog box, select the Handles and Effect Controls options, and then click OK.

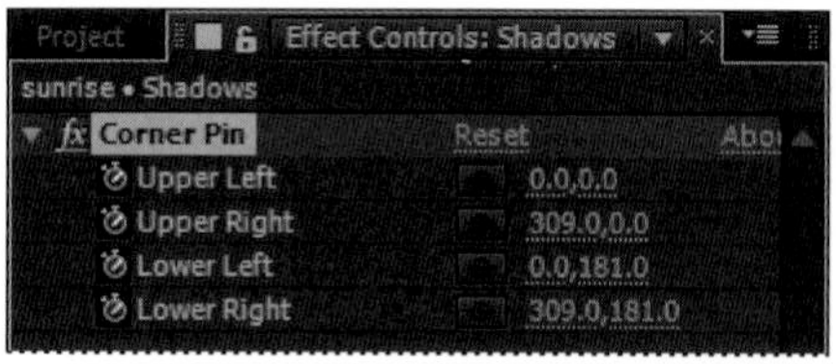

You'll start by setting the four corners of the Shadows layer to correspond to the four corners of the glass tabletop. Begin about midway into the animation, when the sun is high enough to start affecting the shadow.

3 Go to 6:00, and then drag each of the four corner-pin handles to the respective corners of the glass tabletop. Notice that the x and y coordinates update in the Effect Controls panel.

Tip: The lower right corner of the Shadows layer is offscreen. To adjust that corner, switch to the Hand tool (), and drag up in the Composition panel so that you can see some of the pasteboard below the image. Then switch back to the Selection tool (), and drag the lower right corner-pin handle to the approximate location of the lower right corner of the glass tabletop.

If you have trouble getting the shadows to look right, you can manually enter the values shown in the figure that follows step 4.

4   Set a keyframe for each corner at 6:00 by clicking the stopwatch icon (⏱) for each position in the Effect Controls panel.

5   Press the End key, or move the current-time indicator to the last frame of the composition.

6   Using the Selection tool (▶), shorten the shadows: Drag the two lower corner-pin about 25% closer to the back edge of the tabletop. You may also need to move the two upper corners in slightly so that the bases of the shadows still align properly with the vase and the clock. Your corner-pin values should be similar to those in the figure below; you can enter the values directly if you prefer not to drag the corners. After Effects adds keyframes.

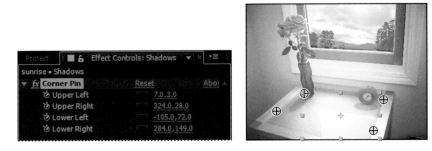

7   If necessary, select the Hand tool (✋), and drag the composition down to center it vertically in the Composition panel. Then switch back to the Selection tool, and deselect the layer.

8 Go to 0:00, and then press the spacebar to preview the entire animation, including the corner-pin effect. When you're done, press the spacebar again.

9 Choose File > Save to save your project.

Adding a lens flare effect

In photography, when bright light (such as sunlight) reflects off the lens of a camera, it causes a flare effect. Lens flares can be bright, colorful circles and halos, depending on the type of lens in the camera. After Effects offers a few lens flare effects. You'll add one now to enhance the realism of this time-lapse photography composition.

1 Go to 5:10, where the sun is shining brightly into the lens of the camera.

2 Choose Layer > New > Solid.

3 In the Solid Settings dialog box, name the layer **Lens Flare,** and click the Make Comp Size button. Then set the Color to black by clicking the swatch and setting all the RGB values to 0 in the Solid Color dialog box. Click OK to return to the Solid Settings dialog box.

4 Click OK to create the Lens Flare layer.

5 With the Lens Flare layer selected in the sunrise Timeline panel, choose Effect > Generate > Lens Flare.

The Composition panel and the Effect Controls panel display the visual and numeric default Lens Flare settings, respectively; you'll customize the effect for this composition.

6 Drag the Flare Center cross-hair icon (⊕) in the Composition panel to the center of the sun. You cannot see the sun in the Composition panel; the x, y coordinates, which you can read in the Effect Controls or Info panel, are approximately 455, 135.

▶ **Tip:** You can also enter the Flare Center values directly in the Effect Controls panel.

7 In the Effect Controls panel, change the Lens Type to 35mm Prime, a more diffuse flare effect.

8 Make sure you're still at 5:10. In the Effect Controls panel, click the stopwatch icon (ö) for the Flare Brightness property to set a keyframe at the default value of 100%.

9 Adjust the brightness of the lens flare to peak when the sun is highest:

- Go to 3:27, and set the Flare Brightness value to **0%**.
- Go to 6:27, and set the Flare Brightness value to **0%**, also.
- Go to 6:00, and set the Flare Brightness to **100%**.

10 With the Lens Flare layer selected in the Timeline panel, choose Layer > Blending Mode > Screen to change the blending mode.

▶ **Tip:** You can also choose Screen from the Mode pop-up menu in the Timeline panel.

11 Press the Home key or move the current-time indicator to the beginning of the time ruler, and then press the spacebar to preview the Lens Flare effect. When you're done, press the spacebar again.

12 Choose File > Save to save your project.

Animating the clock

● **Note:** You'll learn more about 3D layers in Lessons 11 and 12.

The animation now looks very much like a time-lapse photo—except the clock isn't working yet! The hands of the clock should be spinning quickly to show the progress of time. To show this, you will add an animation that was created specifically for this scene. The animation was created in After Effects as a set of 3D layers that are lit, textured, and masked to blend into the scene.

1 Bring the Project panel forward. Close the sunrise Layers folder, and then double-click an empty area in the panel to open the Import File dialog box.

2 In the AECC_CIB/Lessons/ Lesson06/Assets folder, select the clock.mov file, and click Import or Open.

The QuickTime movie clock.mov now appears at the top of the Project panel.

3 Click in the sunrise Timeline panel to make it active, and then go to the beginning of the time ruler. Drag the clock.mov footage item from the Project panel to the top of the layer stack in the Timeline panel.

4 Preview the animation by pressing the spacebar. Press the spacebar again to stop playback when you're done.

5 Choose File > Save to save the project.

Rendering the animation

To prepare for the next task—retiming the composition—you need to render the sunrise composition and export it as a movie.

1 Select the sunrise composition in the Project panel, and then choose Composition >
   Add To Render Queue.

The Render Queue panel opens.

2 Choose Maximize Frame from the Render
   Queue panel menu to make the panel larger.

3 Accept the default Render Settings in the Render Queue panel. Then click the
   orange, underlined words *Not Yet Specified* next to the Output To pop-up menu.

4 Navigate to the AECC_CIB/Lessons/Lesson06/Assets folder, and name the
   file **Lesson06_retime.avi** (Windows) or **Lesson06_retime.mov** (Mac OS).
   Then click Save.

5 Expand the Output Module group, and then choose Import from the Post-Render
   Action menu. After Effects will import the movie file after it's rendered.

6 Hide the Output Module section.

7 Click the Render button in the Render Queue panel.

After Effects displays a progress bar as it renders and exports the composition, and plays an audio alert when it is finished. It also imports the resulting movie file into the project.

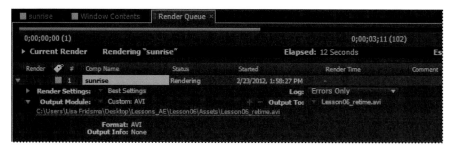

8 When After Effects has finished rendering and exporting the composition, choose Restore Frame Size from the Render Queue panel menu, and then close the Render Queue panel.

Retiming the composition

Tip: You can get even finer control with the Timewarp effect, which you'll use in Lesson 13.

So far, you have created a straightforward time-lapse simulation. That's fine, but After Effects offers more ways to play with time using the time-remapping feature. Time remapping lets you dynamically speed up, slow down, stop, or reverse footage. You can also use it to do things like create a freeze-frame result. The Graph Editor and the Layer panel are a big help when remapping time, as you'll see in the following exercise, when you retime the project so that the time-lapse speed changes over the course of the movie.

For this exercise, you'll use the movie that you just imported as the basis of a new composition, which will be easier to remap than the original.

1 Drag the Lesson06_retime movie onto the Create A New Composition button (■) at the bottom of the Project panel.

After Effects creates a new composition named Lesson06_retime, and displays it in the Timeline and Composition panels. Now you can remap all of the elements of the project at once.

2 With the Lesson06_retime layer selected in the Timeline panel, choose Layer > Time > Enable Time Remapping.

After Effects adds two keyframes, at the first and last frames of the layer, visible in the time ruler. A Time Remap property also appears under the layer name in the Timeline panel; this property lets you control which frame is displayed at a given point in time.

3   Double-click the Lesson06_retime layer name in the Timeline panel to open it in the Layer panel.

The Layer panel provides a visual reference of the frames you change when you remap time. It displays two time rulers: The time ruler at the bottom of the panel displays the current time. The Source Time ruler, just above the time ruler, has a remap-time marker that indicates which frame is playing at the current time.

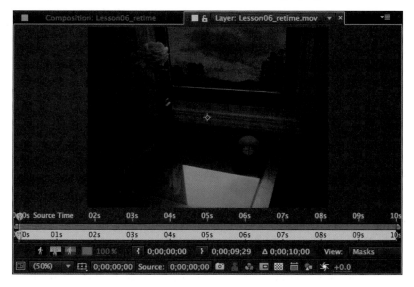

4   Drag the current-time indicator across the time ruler in the Timeline panel, and notice that the source-time and current-time markers in the two Layer panel rulers are synchronized. That will change as you remap time.

5   Go to 4:00, and change the Time Remap value to **2:00**.

This remaps time so that frame 2:00 plays at 4:00. In other words, the composition now plays back at half-speed for the first 4 seconds of the composition.

6   Press the spacebar to preview the animation. The composition now runs at half-speed until 4:00, and at a regular speed thereafter. Press the spacebar again when you have finished previewing the animation.

Viewing time remapping in the Graph Editor

Using the Graph Editor, you can view and manipulate all aspects of effects and animations, including effect property values, keyframes, and interpolation. The Graph Editor displays changes in effects and animations as a two-dimensional graph, with playback time represented horizontally (from left to right). In layer bar mode, in contrast, the time ruler represents only the horizontal time element, without a graphical display of changing values.

1   Make sure the Time Remap property is selected for the Lesson06_retime layer in the Timeline panel.

2   Click the Graph Editor button (⛊) to display the Graph Editor.

The Graph Editor displays a time-remap graph that shows a white line connecting the keyframes at 0:00, 4:00, and 10:00. The angle of the line is shallow up to 4:00, and then becomes steeper. The steeper the line, the faster the playback time.

Using the Graph Editor to remap time

When remapping time, you can use the values in the time-remap graph to determine and control which frame of the movie plays at which point in time. Each Time Remap keyframe has a time value associated with it that corresponds to a specific frame in the layer; this value is represented vertically on the time-remap graph. When you enable time remapping for a layer, After Effects adds a Time Remap keyframe at the start and end points of the layer. These initial Time Remap keyframes have vertical time values equal to their horizontal position.

By setting additional Time Remap keyframes, you can create complex motion effects. Every time you add a Time Remap keyframe, you create another point at which you can change the playback speed or direction. As you move the keyframe up or down in the time-remap graph, you adjust which frame of the video is set to play at the current time.

Have some fun with the timing of this project.

1   In the time-remap graph, drag the middle keyframe vertically from 2 up to 10 seconds.

2   Drag the last keyframe down to 0 seconds.

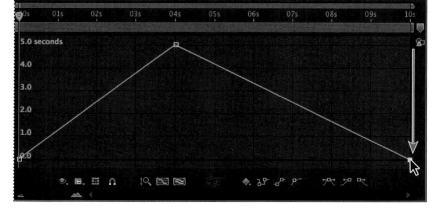

▶ **Tip:** Watch the Info panel as you drag to see more information as you adjust the keyframe.

3   Go to 0:00, and then press the spacebar to preview the results. Watch the time ruler and Source Time ruler in the Layer panel to see which frames are playing at any given point in time.

The animation progresses rapidly over the first 4 seconds of the composition, and then plays in reverse for the rest of the composition.

4   Press the spacebar to stop the preview.

Having fun yet? Keep going.

5   Ctrl-click (Windows) or Command-click (Mac OS) the last keyframe to delete it. The composition is still in fast-forward mode for the first 4 seconds, but now it holds on a single frame (the last frame) for the rest of the composition.

6   Press the Home key or move the current-time indicator to the beginning of the time ruler, and then press the spacebar to preview the animation. Press the spacebar again when you're done.

● **Note:** Pressing Ctrl or Command temporarily activates the Add Vertex tool.

7   Ctrl-click (Windows) or Command-click (Mac OS) the dotted line at 6:00 to add a keyframe at 6:00 with the same value as the keyframe at 4:00.

8   Ctrl-click (Windows) or Command-click (Mac OS) at 10:00 to add another keyframe, and then drag it down to 0 seconds.

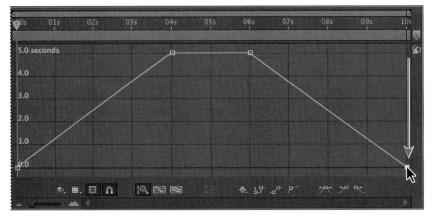

The animation progresses rapidly, holds for two seconds on the last frame, and then runs in reverse.

9   Go to the beginning of the composition, and then press the spacebar to preview the change. Press the spacebar again when you're done.

Adding an Easy Ease Out

Soften the shift in time that occurs at 6 seconds with an Easy Ease Out.

1   Click to select the keyframe at 6:00, and then click the Easy Ease Out button (⟑) at the bottom of the Graph Editor. This slows the shift into reverse—the footage runs slowly in reverse at first, and then gradually speeds up.

► **Tip:** You can refine the amount of ease on this transition further by dragging the Bezier handle that appears out of the right side of the keyframe at 6:00. If you drag it to the right, the transition is softer; if you drag it down or to the left, the transition is more pronounced.

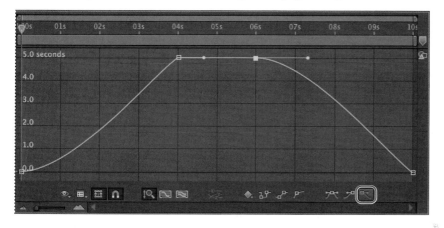

2   Choose File > Save to save your work so far.

Scaling the animation in time

Finally, use the Graph Editor to scale the entire animation in time.

1   Click the Time Remap property name in the Timeline panel to select all of the Time Remap keyframes.

2   Make sure the Show Transform Box button (⊞) at the bottom of the Graph Editor is selected; a free-transform selection box should be visible around all of the keyframes.

3   Drag one of the upper transform handles from 10 seconds to 5 seconds.

► **Tip:** If you press Ctrl (Windows) or Command (Mac OS) while you drag, the entire free-transform box scales around the center point, which you can also drag to offset. If you press Alt (Windows) or Option (Mac OS) and drag one corner of the free-transform box, the animation is skewed in that corner as you drag. You can also drag one of the right transform handles to the left to scale the entire animation so that it happens more quickly.

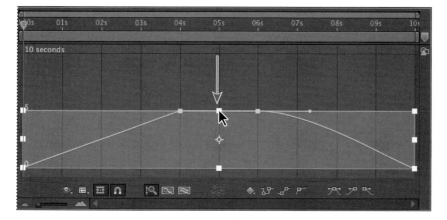

The entire graph shifts, reducing the top keyframe values and slowing playback.

4   Press the Home key or move the current-time indicator to the beginning of the time ruler, and then press the spacebar to preview the change. Press the spacebar again when you're done.

5   Choose File > Save.

Congratulations. You've completed a complex animation, including shifts in time. You can render and export the time-remap project if you'd like. Follow the instructions in "Rendering the animation" in this lesson, or see Lesson 14, "Rendering and Outputting," for detailed instructions on rendering and exporting a composition.

Review questions

1 How does After Effects import Photoshop files?

2 What is the pick whip, and how do you use it?

3 What is a track matte, and how do you use it?

4 How do you remap time in After Effects?

Review answers

1 When you import a layered Photoshop file into After Effects as a composition, After Effects preserves the layer order, transparency data, and layer styles from the source Photoshop document. It also preserves other features, such as adjustment layers and type. When you import a layered Photoshop file as a single footage item, however, After Effects flattens and merges the Photoshop layers into one image.

2 The pick whip creates expressions that link the values of one property or effect to another layer. The pick whip is also a way to create parenting relationships. To use the pick whip, simply drag the pick whip icon from one property to another.

3 When you want one layer to show through a hole in another layer, you can use a track matte. To create a track matte, you need two layers: one to act as a matte, and another to fill the hole in the matte. You can animate either the track matte layer or the fill layer. When you animate the track matte layer, you create a traveling matte.

4 There are several ways to remap time in After Effects. Time remapping lets you dynamically speed up, slow down, stop, or reverse footage. When remapping time, you can use the values in the time-remap graph in the Graph Editor to determine and control which frame of the movie plays at which point in time. When you enable time remapping for a layer, After Effects adds a Time Remap keyframe at the start and end points of the layer. By setting additional Time Remap keyframes, you can create complex motion effects. Every time you add a Time Remap keyframe, you create another point at which you can change the playback speed or direction.

7 WORKING WITH MASKS

Lesson overview

In this lesson, you'll learn how to do the following:

- Create a mask using the Pen tool.

- Change a mask's mode.

- Edit a mask shape by controlling vertices and direction handles.

- Feather a mask edge.

- Replace the contents of a mask shape.

- Adjust the position of a layer in 3D space to blend it with the rest of a shot.

- Create a reflection effect.

- Modify a mask using the Mask Feather tool.

- Create a vignette.

- Use Auto Levels to correct the color of the shot.

 This lesson will take approximately an hour to complete. Download the Lesson07 project files from the Lesson & Update Files tab on your Account page at www.peachpit.com, if you haven't already done so. As you work on this lesson, you'll preserve the start files. If you need to restore the start files, download them from your Account page.

PROJECT: NETWORK NEWS OPENER

There will be times when you won't need (or want) everything in a shot to be included in the final composite. Use masks to control what appears.

About masks

A mask in Adobe After Effects is a path, or outline, that is used to modify layer effects and properties. The most common use of masks is to modify a layer's alpha channel. A mask consists of segments and vertices: Segments are the lines or curves that connect vertices. Vertices define where each segment of a path starts and ends.

A mask can be either an open or a closed path. An open path has a beginning point that is not the same as its end point; for example, a straight line is an open path. A closed path is continuous and has no beginning or end, such as a circle. Closed-path masks can create transparent areas for a layer. Open paths cannot create transparent areas for a layer, but are useful as parameters for an effect. For example, you can use an effect to generate a running light around a mask.

A mask belongs to a specific layer. Each layer can contain multiple masks.

You can draw masks in common geometric shapes—including polygons, ellipses, and stars—with the shape tools, or you can use the Pen tool to draw an arbitrary path.

Getting started

In this lesson, you will create a mask for the screen of a desktop computer and replace the screen's original content with a TV news promo. Then you'll adjust the positioning of the new footage so that it fits the perspective of the shot. Finally, you'll polish the scene by adding a reflection, creating a vignette effect, and adjusting the color.

Begin by previewing the movie and setting up the project.

1 Make sure the following files are in the AECC_CIB/Lessons/Lesson07 folder on your hard disk, or download them from your Account page at www.peachpit.com now:

   • In the Assets folder: news_promo.mov, office_mask.mov

   • In the Sample_Movie folder: Lesson07.mov

2 Open and play the Lesson07.mov sample movie to see what you will create in this lesson. When you are done, quit QuickTime Player. You may delete the sample movie from your hard disk if you have limited storage space.

When you begin the lesson, restore the default application settings for After Effects. See "Restoring default preferences" on page 2.

3   Start After Effects, and then immediately hold down Ctrl+Alt+Shift (Windows) or Command+Option+Shift (Mac OS) to restore default preferences settings. When prompted, click OK to delete your preferences. Click Close to close the Welcome screen.

After Effects opens to display a new, untitled project.

4   Choose File > Save As > Save As, and navigate to the AECC_CIB/Lessons/Lesson07/Finished_Project folder.

5   Name the project **Lesson07_Finished.aep**, and then click Save.

Importing the footage

You'll import two footage items for this exercise.

1   Double-click an empty area of the Project panel to open the Import File dialog box.

2   Navigate to the AECC_CIB/Lessons/Lesson07/Assets folder, Shift-click to select the news_promo.mov and office_mask.mov files, and then click Import or Open.

3   In the Interpret Footage dialog box that appears, select Ignore, and then click OK.

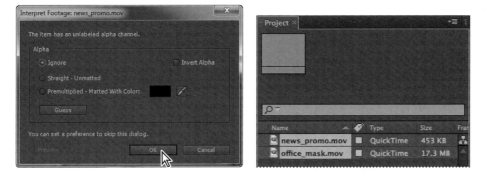

There's an alpha channel in the news_promo movie, but it isn't needed for this project.

You'll start by organizing the files in the Project panel.

4   Choose File > New > New Folder to create a new folder in the Project panel, or click the Create A New Folder button (■) at the bottom of the Project panel.

5   Type **mov_files** to name the folder, press Enter or Return to accept the name, and then drag the two movies into the mov_files folder.

6   Click the triangle to expand the folder so that you can see the footage items inside.

Creating the composition

Now, you'll create the composition based on the aspect ratio and duration of one of the footage items.

1   Select the office_mask.mov footage item in the Project panel, and drag it to the Create A New Composition button (■) at the bottom of the panel.

After Effects creates a composition named office_mask, and opens it in the Composition and Timeline panels.

2   Choose File > Save to save your work so far.

Creating a mask with the Pen tool

The computer screen currently contains a word-processing document. To replace it with the news promo, you need to mask the screen.

1   Press the Home key or move the current-time indicator to the beginning of the time ruler.

2   Zoom in to the Composition panel until the monitor screen nearly fills the view. You may need to use the Hand tool (✋) to reposition the view in the panel.

3   Select the Pen tool (✒) in the Tools panel.

The Pen tool creates straight lines or curved segments. The monitor appears to be rectangular, so you'll try using straight lines first.

4   Click the upper left corner of the monitor screen to place the first vertex.

5   Click the upper right corner of the monitor to place the second vertex. After Effects connects the two points with a segment.

6   Click to place a third vertex in the lower right corner of the monitor, and then click to place a fourth vertex in the lower left corner of the monitor.

7   Move the Pen tool over the first vertex (in the upper left corner). When a circle appears next to the pointer (as in the middle image below), click to close the mask path.

▶ **Tip:** You can also create a mask using the Mocha Shapes plug-in, which comes with After Effects, and then import it into After Effects. To learn more about using the plug-in, see After Effects Help.

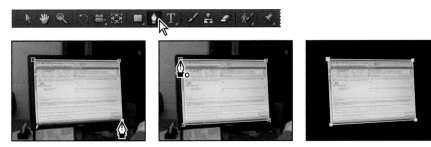

Editing a mask

The mask looks pretty good, but instead of masking the information *inside* the monitor, the mask has removed everything *outside* the monitor. You need to invert the mask. (Alternatively, you could change the mask mode, which is set to Add by default.)

About mask modes

Blending modes for masks (mask modes) control how masks within a layer interact with one another. By default, all masks are set to Add, which combines the transparency values of any masks that overlap on the same layer. You can apply one mode to each mask, but you cannot change a mask's mode over time.

The first mask you create interacts with the layer's alpha channel. If that channel doesn't define the entire image as opaque, then the mask interacts with the layer frame. Each additional mask that you create interacts with masks located above it in the Timeline panel. The results of mask modes vary depending on the modes set for the masks higher up in the Timeline panel. You can use mask modes only between masks in the same layer. Using mask modes, you can create complex mask shapes with multiple transparent areas. For example, you can set a mask mode that combines two masks and sets the opaque area to the regions where the two masks intersect.

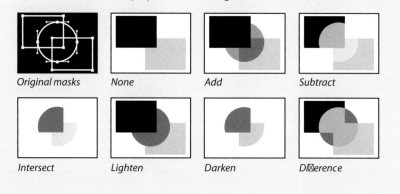

Original masks   None   Add   Subtract

Intersect   Lighten   Darken   Difference

Inverting the mask

For this project, you need everything inside the mask to be transparent and everything outside the mask to be opaque. You'll invert the mask now.

▶ **Tip:** Pressing the M key twice in quick succession displays all mask properties for the selected layer.

1 Select the office_mask layer in the Timeline panel, and press the M key to see the Mask Path property for the mask.

There are two ways to invert this mask: by choosing Subtract from the Mask Mode pop-up menu, or by selecting the Inverted option.

2 Select the Inverted option for Mask 1.

The mask inverts.

3 Press F2, or click an empty area of the Timeline panel, to deselect the office_mask layer.

If you look closely at the monitor, you will probably see portions of the screen still appearing around the edges of the mask.

These errors will certainly call attention to changes being made to the layer, and they need to be fixed. To fix them, you'll change the straight lines to curves.

Creating curved masks

Curved or freeform masks use Bezier curves to define the shape of the mask. Bezier curves give you the greatest control over the shape of the mask. With them, you can create straight lines with sharp angles, perfectly smooth curves, or a combination of the two.

1 In the Timeline panel, select Mask 1, the mask for the office_mask layer. Selecting Mask 1 makes the mask active and also selects all the vertices.

2 In the Tools panel, select the Convert Vertex tool (⌐), which is hidden behind the Pen tool.

3   In the Composition panel, click any of the vertices. The Convert Vertex tool changes the corner vertices to smooth points.

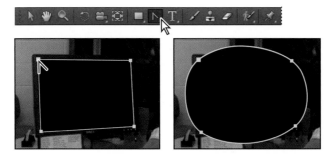

4   Switch to the Selection tool (▶), click anywhere in the Composition panel to deselect the mask, and then click the first vertex that you created.

Two direction handles extend off the smooth point. The angle and length of these handles control the shape of the mask.

5   Drag the right handle of the first vertex around the screen. Notice how this changes the shape of the mask. Notice also that the closer you drag the handle to another vertex, the less the shape of the path is influenced by the direction handle of the first vertex, and the more it is influenced by the direction handle of the second vertex.

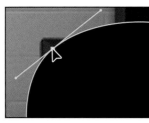

Click the vertex.   Drag the handle.

6   Once you are comfortable moving the handles, position the handle of the upper left vertex as in the preceding figure. As you have seen, you can create very fluid shapes.

Breaking direction handles

By default, the direction handles of any smooth point are connected to one another. As you drag one handle, the opposite handle moves as well. However, you can break this connection to get greater control over the shape of the mask, and you can create sharp points or long, smooth curves.

1   Select the Convert Vertex tool (ⴷ) in the Tools panel.

2   Drag the right direction handle of the upper left vertex. The left direction handle remains stationary.

▶ **Tip:** If you make a mistake, press Ctrl+Z (Windows) or Command+Z (Mac OS) to undo your last action. You can also change the zoom level and use the Hand tool to reposition the image in the Composition panel as you work.

3   Adjust the right direction handle until the top segment of the mask shape more closely follows the curve of the monitor in that corner. It doesn't have to be perfect.

4   Drag the left direction handle of the same vertex until the left segment of the shape more closely follows the curve of the monitor in that corner.

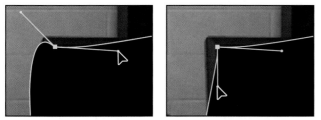

Drag the right direction handle of the upper left vertex, and then the left direction handle, to follow the curve of the monitor.

5   For each of the remaining corner points, click with the Convert Vertex tool, and then repeat steps 2–4 until the mask's shape more closely matches the curvature of the monitor. If you need to shift a corner point, use the Selection tool.

6   When you're done, deselect the office_mask layer in the Timeline panel to check the edge of your mask. You should not see any of the monitor screen.

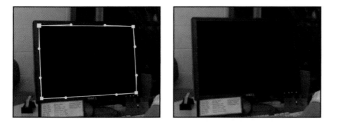

▶ **Tip:** Again, you may need to adjust your view in the Composition panel as you work. You can drag the image with the Hand tool. To temporarily switch to the Hand tool, press and hold the spacebar.

7   Choose File > Save to save your work.

Creating a Bezier mask

You used the Convert Vertex tool to change a corner vertex to a smooth point with Bezier handles, but you could have created a Bezier mask in the first place. To do so, click in the Composition panel with the Pen tool where you want to place the first vertex. Then click where you want to place the next vertex, and drag in the direction you want to create a curve. When you are satisfied with the curve, release the mouse button. Continue to add points until you've created the shape you want. Close the mask by either clicking on the first vertex or double-clicking the last vertex. Then switch to the Selection tool to refine the mask.

Feathering the edges of a mask

The mask looks good, but you need to soften the edges a bit.

1 Choose Composition > Composition Settings.

2 Click the Background Color box, and choose white for the background color (R=**255**, G=**255**, B=**255**). Then click OK to close the Color Picker, and OK again to close the Composition Settings dialog box.

The white background allows you to see that the edge of the monitor screen looks a little too sharp and unrealistic. To address this, you'll feather, or soften, the edges.

3 Select the office_mask layer in the Timeline panel, and press the F key to display the Mask Feather property for the mask.

4 Increase the Mask Feather amount to **1.5, 1.5** pixels.

5 Hide the properties for the office_mask layer, and then choose File > Save to save your work.

Replacing the content of the mask

You are now ready to replace the background with the TV news promo movie and blend it with the overall shot.

1   In the Project panel, select the news_promo.mov file, and drag it to the Timeline panel, placing it below the office_mask layer.

2   Choose Fit Up To 100% from the Magnification Ratio pop-up menu at the bottom of the Composition panel so that you can see the whole composition.

3   Using the Selection tool (**⬉**), drag the news_promo layer in the Composition panel until the anchor point is centered in the monitor screen.

Repositioning and resizing the news clip

The news promo clip is too big for the monitor screen, so you'll resize it as a 3D layer, which will give you more control over its shape and size.

1   With the news_promo layer selected in the Timeline panel, click the 3D switch for the layer.

2   Press the P key to show the Position property for the news_promo layer.

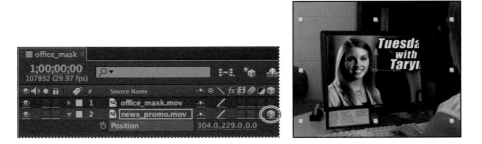

The Position property for a 3D layer has three values: From left to right, they represent the x, y, and z axes of the image. The z axis controls the depth of the layer. You can see these axes represented in the Composition panel.

● **Note:** You'll learn more about 3D layers in Lessons 11 and 12.

3 Position the pointer in the Composition panel over the red arrow so that a small x appears. The red arrow controls the x (horizontal) axis of the layer.

4 Drag left or right as necessary to center the clip horizontally in the monitor screen.

5 Position the pointer in the Composition panel over the green arrow so that a small y appears. Then drag up or down as necessary to position the clip vertically in the monitor screen.

6 Position the pointer in the Composition panel over the blue cube where the red and green arrows meet so that a small z appears. Then drag down and to the right to increase the depth of field.

▶ **Tip:** You can also enter the Position values directly in the Timeline panel instead of dragging in the Composition panel.

7 Continue to drag the x, y, and z axes until the entire clip fits into the monitor screen, as shown in the following image. The final x, y, and z values should be approximately 114, 219, 365.

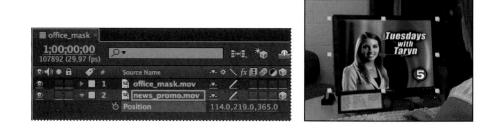

Rotating the clip

The news clip fits better, but you need to rotate it slightly to improve the perspective.

1 Select the news_promo layer in the Timeline panel, and press the R key to reveal its Rotation properties. Again, since this is a 3D layer, you can control rotation on the x, y, and z axes.

2 Change the Y Rotation value to **−10** degrees. This swivels the layer to match the perspective of the monitor.

3 Change the Z Rotation value to **−2** degrees to align the layer with the monitor.

Your composition should now resemble the preceding image.

4 Hide the properties for the news_promo layer, and then choose File > Save to save your work.

Adding a reflection

The masked image looks convincing, but you can make it look even more realistic by adding a reflection to the monitor.

1 Choose Layer > New > Solid.

2 In the Solid Settings dialog box, name the layer **Reflection**, click the Make Comp Size button, change the Color to white, and then click OK.

Instead of trying to exactly re-create the shape of the office_mask layer's mask, it is easier to copy it to the Reflection layer.

3 Select the office_mask layer in the Timeline panel, and press the M key to display the Mask Path property for the mask.

4 Select Mask 1, and then choose Edit > Copy or press Ctrl+C (Windows) or Command+C (Mac OS).

5 Select the Reflection layer in the Timeline panel, and then choose Edit > Paste or press Ctrl+V (Windows) or Command+V (Mac OS).

This time, you want to keep the area inside the mask opaque and make the area outside the mask transparent.

6 Select the office_mask layer, and then press U to hide the mask properties.

7   Select the Reflection layer in the Timeline panel, and press the F key to reveal the Mask 1 Mask Feather property for the layer.

8   Change the Mask Feather value to **0** (zero).

9   Deselect the Inverted option. The Reflection layer now obscures the news_promo layer.

10 Zoom in to see the screen, and then select the Mask Feather tool (✐), hidden beneath the Convert Vertex tool (⌐), in the Tools panel.

When you feather a mask, the width of the feather is the same all the way around the mask. The Mask Feather Tool lets you vary the feathering width at points you define on the closed mask.

11 Click the Reflection layer in the Timeline panel to select it. Then click the lower left vertex to create a feather point, and without releasing the mouse button, drag that feather point inward so that only the center of the screen is reflected, and so that the feather point is centered, as in the image at right.

Currently the feather extends evenly across the mask. You'll add more feather points for greater flexibility.

12 Click in the center of the top of the mask to create another feather point. Then drag the feather point down slightly, into the mask.

13 Right-click or Control-click the feather point you just created, and choose Edit Radius. Change the Feather Radius to **0**, and click OK.

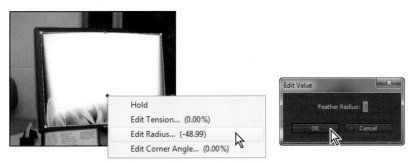

This is a good start, but the sides slope in too sharply. You'll add more feather points to change the angle.

14 Add another feather point by clicking the left edge of the matte, about one-third of the way from the top.

15 Add a similar feather point on the right side.

The shape of the reflection is good, but it's obscuring the image. You'll change the opacity to reduce its effect.

16 Select the Reflection layer in the Timeline panel, and then press the T key to reveal the Opacity property. Change its value to **25%**.

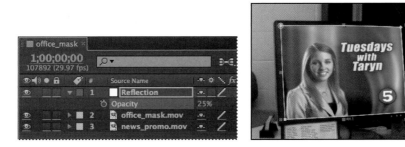

17 Press T to hide the Opacity property, and then press F2 or click an empty area in the Timeline panel to deselect all layers.

Applying a blending mode

To create unique interactions between layers, you may want to experiment with blending modes. Blending modes control how each layer blends with, or reacts to, layers beneath it. Blending modes for layers in After Effects are identical to blending modes in Adobe Photoshop.

1   In the Timeline panel menu, choose Columns > Modes to display the Mode pop-up menu.

2   Choose Add from the Reflection layer's Mode pop-up menu.

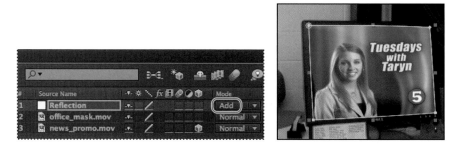

This creates a hard glare on the monitor screen image and boosts the colors underneath.

3   Choose File > Save to save your work.

Adding a 3D light layer

Instead of creating the reflection using a solid layer and a feathered mask, you could also use a 3D light layer to create realistic surface reflection. You'll learn more about 3D layers, including using 3D light layers, in Lessons 11 and 12. If you're ambitious, however, you can follow these steps to create a 3D light layer now with this project. This exercise is optional.

1   Hide the Reflection layer by clicking its Video switch.

2   Choose Layer > New > Light.

3   Click OK to accept the default values in the Light Settings dialog box.

4   With the Light 1 layer selected in the Timeline panel, press P to display its Position property.

The Position property affects the placement of the light in the scene.

5   Set the Position values for the Light 1 layer to **260**, **–10**, **–350**, which moves the light above the monitor and off the image.

6   Select the Light 1 layer in the Timeline panel, and press A to reveal its Point Of Interest property.

The point of interest determines where the light is "looking."

7   Set the Point Of Interest values to **135**, **200**, **0**.

8   Select the news_promo.mov layer in the Timeline panel, and press AA to reveal the layer's Material Options properties.

Material Options properties determine how a 3D layer interacts with light and shadow, both of which are important components of realism and perspective in 3D animation.

9   Increase the Specular Intensity value to **75%** and the Specular Shininess value to **50%**.

10 Lower the Metal value to **50%**.

The Metal value determines how much of the layer's color reflects the light. Because there are dark blues in the layer, little light is being reflected. Because you are simulating glass in front of the layer, lowering this value causes the reflection to take on the same color as the light.

11 Hide the properties for the news_promo.mov layer.

That's it. You've created the same effect using a 3D light layer.

Creating a vignette

A popular effect in motion graphic design is to apply a vignette to the composition. This is often done to simulate light variations of a glass lens. It creates an interesting look that focuses the attention on the subject and sets the shot apart.

1 Zoom out to see the whole image.

2 Choose Layer > New > Solid.

3 In the Solid Settings dialog box, name this layer **Vignette**, click the Make Comp Size button, change the Color to black (R=**0**, G=**0**, B=**0**), and then click OK.

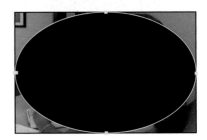

In addition to the Pen tool, After Effects provides tools that let you easily create square and elliptical masks.

4 In the Tools panel, select the Ellipse tool (◯), hidden behind the Rectangle tool (▢).

5 In the Composition panel, position the cross-hair pointer in the upper left corner of the image. Drag to the opposite corner to create an elliptical shape that fills the image. Adjust the shape and position using the Selection tool, if necessary.

6 Expand the Mask 1 property in the Vignette layer to display all of the mask properties for the layer.

7 Choose Subtract from the Mask 1 Mode pop-up menu.

8 Increase the Mask Feather amount to **200, 200** pixels.

Using the Rectangle and Ellipse tools

The Rectangle tool, as the name suggests, creates a rectangle or square. The Ellipse tool creates an ellipse or circle. You create mask shapes with these tools by dragging them in the Composition or Layer panel.

If you want to draw a perfect square or circle, press the Shift key as you drag with the Rectangle tool or the Ellipse tool. To create your mask from the center, press Ctrl (Windows) or Command (Mac OS) after you start to drag. Press Ctrl+Shift or Command+Shift after you start to drag to create a perfect square or circle mask from a center anchor point.

Be careful! If you use these tools without a layer selected, you'll draw a shape, not a mask.

Your composition should now resemble the following figure.

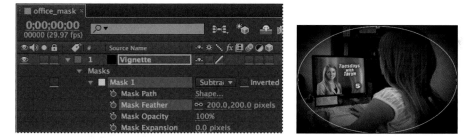

Even with this large feather amount, the vignette is a bit intense and constricting. You can give the composition more breathing room by adjusting the Mask Expansion property. The Mask Expansion property represents, in pixels, how far from the original mask edge you are expanding or contracting the adjusted edge.

9 Increase Mask Expansion to **90** pixels.

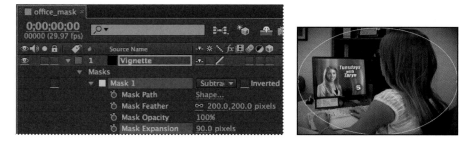

10 Hide the properties for the Vignette layer, and then choose File > Save.

Tips for creating masks

If you have worked with Adobe Illustrator, Photoshop, or similar applications, you're probably familiar with masks and Bezier curves. If not, here are a few additional tips to help you create them effectively:

- Use as few vertices as possible.

- As you saw in this lesson, you can close a mask by clicking the starting vertex. You can also open a closed mask: Click a mask segment, choose Layer > Mask And Shape Path, and deselect Closed.

- To add points to an open path, press Ctrl (Windows) or Command (Mac OS), and click the last point on the path with the Pen tool. When the point is selected, you can continue adding points.

Adjusting the color

The shot is looking quite polished, but the color of the office_mask.mov layer is rather dull. Warming it up will make the image really pop.

1 Select the office_mask.mov layer in the Timeline panel.

2 Choose Effect > Color Correction > Auto Levels.

The Auto Levels effect sets highlights and shadows by defining the lightest and darkest pixels in each color channel as white and black, and then redistributing intermediate pixel values proportionately. Because Auto Levels adjusts each color channel individually, it may remove or introduce color casts.

Why apply this effect? Sometimes video cameras favor a certain color channel that makes the image cooler (bluer) or warmer (redder). The Auto Levels effect sets the black and white pixels for each channel, so the end result looks much more natural.

The color of the office_mask.mov layer should look much better now.

3 Choose File > Save to save the finished project.

In this lesson you have worked with the mask tools to hide, reveal, and adjust portions of a composition to create a stylized inset shot. Next to keyframes, masks are probably the most-used feature of After Effects.

You can preview the clip now, if you'd like, or render and export it following the steps in Lesson 14, "Rendering and Outputting."

Review questions

1 What is a mask?

2 Name two ways to adjust the shape of a mask.

3 What is a direction handle used for?

4 What is the difference between an open mask and a closed mask?

5 How is the Mask Feather tool useful?

Review answers

1 A mask in After Effects is a path, or outline, that is used to modify layer effects and properties. The most common use of masks is to modify a layer's alpha channel. A mask consists of segments and vertices.

2 You can adjust the shape of a mask by dragging individual vertices or by dragging a segment.

3 A direction handle is used to control the shape and angle of a Bezier curve.

4 An open mask can be used to control effects or the placement of text; it does not define a region of transparency. A closed mask defines a region that will affect the alpha channel of a layer.

5 The Mask Feather tool lets you vary the width of feathering at different points on a mask. With the Mask Feather tool, click to add a Feather point, and then drag it.

8 DISTORTING OBJECTS WITH THE PUPPET TOOLS

Lesson overview

In this lesson, you'll learn how to do the following:

- Place Deform pins using the Puppet Pin tool.

- Define areas of overlap using the Puppet Overlap tool.

- Stiffen part of an image using the Puppet Starch tool.

- Animate the position of Deform pins.

- Smooth motion in an animation.

- Record animation using the Puppet Sketch tool.

This lesson will take approximately an hour to complete. Download the Lesson08 project files from the Lesson & Update Files tab on your Account page at www.peachpit.com, if you haven't already done so. As you work on this lesson, you'll preserve the start files. If you need to restore the start files, download them from your Account page.

PROJECT: ANIMATED ILLUSTRATION

Pull, squash, stretch, and otherwise deform objects on the screen using the Puppet tools. Whether you're creating realistic animations, fantastic scenarios, or modern art, the Puppet tools will expand your creative freedom.

Getting started

The Puppet tools in Adobe After Effects let you add natural motion to raster images and vector graphics. Three tools create pins to define the point of deformation, areas of overlap, and areas that should remain more rigid. An additional tool, the Puppet Sketch tool, lets you record animation in real time. In this lesson, you'll use the Puppet tools to animate a character slipping on a banana peel.

Start by previewing the final movie and then setting up the project.

1   Make sure the following files are in the AECC_CIB/Lessons/Lesson08 folder on your hard disk, or download them from your Account page at www.peachpit.com now:

   •   In the Assets folder: backdrop.psd, banana.psd, man.psd

   •   In the Sample_Movie folder: Lesson08.mov

2   Open and play the Lesson08.mov file to see what you will create in this lesson. When you are done, quit QuickTime Player. You may delete this sample movie from your hard disk if you have limited storage space.

When you begin this lesson, restore the default application settings for After Effects. See "Restoring default preferences" on page 2.

3   Start After Effects, and then immediately hold down Ctrl+Alt+Shift (Windows) or Command+Option+Shift (Mac OS). When prompted, click OK to delete your preferences. Click Close to close the Welcome screen.

After Effects opens to display a blank, untitled project.

4   Choose File > Save As > Save As.

5   In the Save As dialog box, navigate to the AECC_CIB/Lessons/Lesson08/ Finished_Project folder.

6   Name the project **Lesson08_Finished.aep**, and then click Save.

Importing footage

You'll import three Adobe Photoshop files, which you'll use to create the scene.

1   Choose File > Import > File.

2   Navigate to the AECC_CIB/Lessons/Lesson08/Assets folder. Shift-click to select the backdrop.psd, banana.psd, and man.psd files, and then click Import or Open. The footage items appear in the Project panel.

3 Click the Create A New Folder
   button at the bottom of the
   Project panel.

4 Name the new folder **Assets**, and
   then drag the footage items into
   the folder.

5 Expand the Assets folder to see
   its contents.

Creating the composition

As with any project, you need to create a new composition.

1 Choose Composition > New Composition.

2 Name the composition **Walking Man**.

3 Choose NTSC DV from the Preset pop-up menu. The preset automatically
   sets the width, height, pixel aspect ratio, and frame rate for the composition.

4 In the Duration field, type **500** to specify 5 seconds, and then click OK.

After Effects opens the new composition in the Timeline and Composition panels.

Adding the background

It's easier to animate a character in context, so first you'll add the background to the composition.

1 Press the Home key or move the current-time indicator to the beginning of the composition.

2 Drag the backdrop.psd file to the Timeline panel.

3 Lock the layer to prevent accidental changes to it.

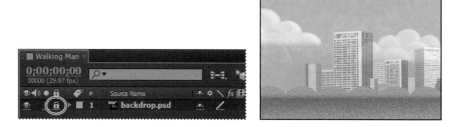

Scaling an object

Next, you'll add the banana peel. At its default size, it's large enough to do real damage to anyone who slips on it. You'll scale it to a more proportional size for the scene.

1 Drag the banana.psd file from the Project panel to the top layer in the Timeline panel.

2 Select the banana.psd layer in the Timeline panel, and press S to display its Scale property.

3 Change the Scale value to **15%**.

4 Press P to display the layer's Position property.

5 Change the Position to **160, 420**. The banana peel moves to the left side of the composition.

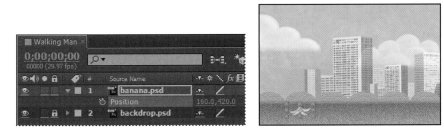

6 Hide the properties for the banana.psd layer.

Adding the character

The last element in the scene is the character himself. You'll add him to the composition and then scale and position him appropriately.

1 Drag the man.psd footage item from the Project panel to the Timeline panel at the top of the layer stack.

2 Select the man.psd layer, and press S to display its Scale property.

3 Change the Scale value to **15%**.

4 Press P to display the Position property, and change the Position to **575, 300**.

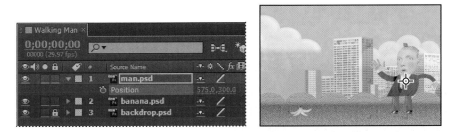

● **Note:** In the original drawing, the character has already slipped on the banana peel and was falling. To make it easier to animate, the character has been modified to be more upright. Sometimes you can make your work easier by making some adjustments before animation.

5 Press P again to hide the Position property for the layer.

6 Choose File > Save to save your work so far.

About the Puppet tools

The Puppet tools turn raster and vector images into virtual marionettes. When you move the string of a marionette, the body part attached to that string moves; pull the string attached to the hand, and the hand goes up. The Puppet tools use pins to indicate where strings would be attached.

The Puppet effect deforms parts of an image based on the positions of pins that you place and animate. These pins determine which parts of the image should move, which parts should remain rigid, and which parts should be in front when areas overlap.

There are three kinds of pins, each placed by a different tool:

- The Puppet Pin tool (✦) places and moves Deform pins, which deform a layer.
- The Puppet Overlap tool (✿) places Overlap pins, which indicate the parts of an image that should be in the front when areas overlap.
- The Puppet Starch tool (🗍) places Starch pins, which stiffen parts of the image so that they are distorted less.

● **Note:** The mesh is calculated at the frame where the Deform pins are applied. If you add more pins anywhere in the timeline, they are placed based on the original position of the mesh.

As soon as you place a pin, the area within an outline is automatically divided into a mesh of triangles. Each part of the mesh is associated with the pixels of the image, so as the mesh moves, so do the pixels. When you animate a Deform pin, the mesh deforms more in the area closest to the pin, while keeping the overall shape as rigid as possible. For example, if you animate a pin in a character's hand, the hand and arm will be deformed, but most of the character will remain in place.

Adding Deform pins

Deform pins are the main component of the Puppet effect. Where you place these pins and how you position them determine how the objects move on the screen. You'll place Deform pins and display the mesh that After Effects creates to determine the area of influence for each pin.

When you select the Puppet Pin tool, the Tools panel displays the Puppet tool options. Each pin has its own properties in the Timeline panel, and After Effects automatically creates an initial keyframe for each pin.

1. Select the Puppet Pin tool (✱) in the Tools panel.

2. In the Composition panel, place a Deform pin in the character's right arm, near the wrist. You may find it helpful to zoom in to see the character more clearly.

● **Note:** Be careful! The character's right arm is on the left side of the image, and vice versa. Pin the character according to *his* left and right, not yours!

A yellow dot representing the Deform pin appears in the Composition panel. If at this point you were to use the Selection tool (▶) to move the Deform pin, the entire character would move with it. You need more pins to keep the other parts of the mesh in place.

3. Using the Puppet Pin tool, place another Deform pin in the left arm near the wrist.

Now you can move the right hand with the Selection tool. The more pins you place, the smaller the area of influence for each pin, and the less each area will stretch. If you experimented, undo any stretching by pressing Ctrl+Z (Windows) or Command+Z (Mac OS).

4. Place additional Deform pins in the man's right and left legs (near the ankles), torso (near the bottom of the tie), and forehead.

5. In the Timeline panel, expand the Mesh 1 > Deform properties. Each Deform pin is listed. To keep track of each pin, you'll rename them.

6. Select Puppet Pin 1, press Enter or Return, and rename the pin **Right Arm**. Press Enter or Return again to accept the new name.

7. Rename the remaining pins (Puppet Pin 2 through Puppet Pin 6) **Left Arm**, **Right Leg**, **Left Leg**, **Torso**, and **Head**, respectively.

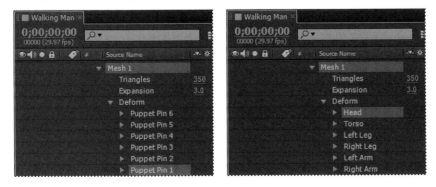

Tip: You can extend the mesh beyond the outline of the layer in order to ensure a stroke is included in the deformation. To expand the mesh, increase the Expansion property in the options section of the Tools panel.

8   Select Show in the options section of the Tools panel to display the distortion mesh.

9   Change the Triangles value in the options section of the Tools panel to **300**.

The Triangles setting determines how many triangles are included in the mesh. Increasing the number of triangles results in a smoother animation, but also increases rendering time.

Defining areas of overlap

Note: You must select the Show option separately for each Puppet tool. You can also place pins without viewing the mesh.

Normal human movement requires the arms to swing, so as the character walks across the screen, portions of his right arm and leg will be behind other areas of his body. You'll use the Puppet Overlap tool to define the areas that should appear in front when areas overlap.

1   Select the Puppet Overlap tool (), which is hidden behind the Puppet Pin tool in the Tools panel.

2   Select Show in the options area of the Tools panel to view the distortion mesh.

Tip: If the mesh doesn't appear when you select Show, click outside the path shape in the Composition panel.

3   Zoom in, and use the Hand tool ( ) to position the man in the Composition window so that you can see his torso and legs clearly. Then select the Puppet Overlap tool again.

4   In the options area of the Tools panel, change In Front to **100%**.

The In Front value determines the apparent proximity to the viewer; setting the value to 100% prevents those parts of the body that are overlapped from showing through.

5   Click intersections in the mesh to place Overlap pins on the right side of the
    character's torso and left leg, which are the areas that should remain in the front.
    As you add a pin, you may want to adjust its Extent value in the options area
    of the Tools panel. The Extent value determines how far the overlap influence
    extends for the pin; the affected area appears lighter in the Composition panel.
    Use this image as a guide.

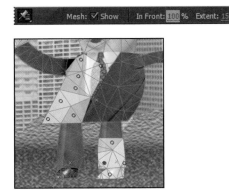

Stiffening an area

The character's arms and legs should move as he walks, but his torso should stay
fairly firm. You'll use the Puppet Starch tool to add Starch pins where you want the
character to be stiffer.

1   Select the Puppet Starch tool (icon), which
    is hidden behind the Puppet Overlap tool,
    in the Tools panel.

2   Select Show in the options area of the Tools
    panel to display the distortion mesh.

3   Place Starch pins on intersections to stiffen the
    lower half of the torso, as in the image at right.

4   Hide the properties for the man.psd layer in the
    Timeline panel.

5   Choose File > Save to save your work so far.

● Note: The Amount
value determines how
rigid the area will be.
Typically, a low value is
fine; higher values make
the area more rigid. You
can also use negative
numbers to reduce the
rigidity of another pin.

Animating pin positions

The Deform, Overlap, and Starch pins are in place. Now you can change the Deform pin positions to animate the character. The Overlap pins keep the front areas in the front, and the Starch pins keep specific areas (in this case, the torso) from moving too much.

Creating a walking cycle

Initially, the character should be walking across the screen. To create a realistic walking cycle, keep in mind that as humans walk, wave patterns develop in the motion path. You'll create a wave pattern in the pin positions. However, the values will vary slightly to add a bit of randomness, and to keep the character from looking too much like a robot.

1 Select the man.psd layer in the Timeline panel, and then press U to display all the keyframes for the layer.

2 Press Home, or move the current-time indicator to the beginning of the timeline.

Squash and stretch

As the character moves, his body squashes and stretches. Squash and stretch is a traditional animation technique that adds realism and weight to objects. It's an exaggeration of the effect that occurs in real life when a moving object comes into contact with a stationary object, such as the ground. When squashing and stretching are applied correctly, the volume of the character doesn't change.

The easiest way to understand the principle of squash and stretch is to view an animation of a bouncing ball. As the ball lands, it partially flattens, or squashes. As it bounces up, it stretches.

To see squash and stretch in action, open the Squash_and_stretch.aep project file in the Lesson08/End_Project_Files folder.

3 In the Timeline panel, change the position of the Deform pins as follows:

- Head: **845, 295**
- Torso: **821.5, 1210**
- Left Leg: **1000.5, 1734**
- Right Leg: **580.5, 1734**
- Left Arm: **1384.5, 1214.7**
- Right Arm: **478.5, 1108**

Note: After Effects automatically creates keyframes when you place Deform pins, so you don't need to click the stopwatch for each pin before setting its initial position.

4 To complete the walking cycle, move the pins to the positions at the times indicated in the chart below. Where the chart says "Add keyframe," click the Add Or Remove Keyframe At Current Time button (◇) in the Timeline panel to create a keyframe at the pin's current position.

Note: To add a keyframe, click the diamond (between two arrows) on the left side of the Timeline panel.

TIME	HEAD	TORSO	LEFT LEG	RIGHT LEG	LEFT ARM	RIGHT ARM
0:07	593, 214	570.5, 1095	604, 1614.5			
0:15	314, 295	312.5, 1210	118.5, 1748.3	Add keyframe (◇)	886.5, 1208	−325.5, 1214.7
0:18	−6, 217	37.5, 1098.3		352.5, 1618.6		
1:00	−286, 295	−253.5, 1210	Add keyframe (◇)	−561.5, 1734	−121.5, 1234.7	Add keyframe (◇)
1:07	−614, 218.3	−530, 1094	−70.3, 1628.8			
1:15	−883, 300.7	−803.5, 1213.3	−1003.5, 1728.7	Add keyframe (◇)	Add keyframe (◇)	−1309.5, 1101.3
1:23	−1153, 212.7	−1055.5, 1099.7	−789.3, 1609.4			
2:00	−1412, 319.3	−1283.5, 1213	−1003.4, 1728.7	−1545.5, 1740.7	−1147.5, 1241.3	Add keyframe (◇)
2:08	−1622, 246	−1505.5, 1099.7	−996, 1617	−1926.5, 1677.1		

▶ **Tip:** The Timeline panel measures time in seconds and frames, depending on the frames-per-second (fps) rate. So 1:15 equals 1 second and 15 frames. At 29.97 fps, 1:15 is frame 45.

Animating a slip

The character steps on a banana peel, loses his balance, and falls. The falling movements occur more quickly than the walking cycle. To surprise the viewer, you'll animate the character to fall off the screen.

1   Choose File > Save to save the work you've just done.

2   Move the current-time indicator to 2:11, and then change the position of the Left Leg pin to **−2281, 1495.3**.

3   At 2:15, move the Deform pins to the following positions:

   - Head: **−1298, 532.7**
   - Torso: **−1667.5, 1246.3**
   - Left Leg: **−2398.8, 1282.7**
   - Right Leg: **−2277.5, 874**
   - Left Arm: **−1219.5, 1768**
   - Right Arm: **−1753.5, 454.7**

4   At 2:20, make the character fall off the screen by moving the Deform pins to the following positions:

   - Head: **−1094, 2452.7**
   - Torso: **−1643.5, 3219.7**
   - Left Leg: **−2329.5, 2682**
   - Right Leg: **−2169.5, 2234**
   - Left Arm: **−1189.5, 3088**
   - Right Arm: **−1597.5, 2654.7**

5   Hide the properties for the man.psd layer, and save your work so far.

Moving an object

Of course, when the man slips on the banana peel, the banana peel moves, too. It should slide out from beneath the man's feet and fly off the screen. You didn't add any pins to the banana, and you don't need them. Instead, you'll move the entire layer, using its Position and Rotation properties.

1   Move the current-time indicator to 2:00.

2   Select the banana.psd layer in the Timeline panel, and press P to display its Position property.

3   Press Shift+R to also display the layer's Rotation property.

▶ **Tip:** To view multiple layer properties at the same time, press the Shift key while you press the keyboard shortcut for the additional layer property.

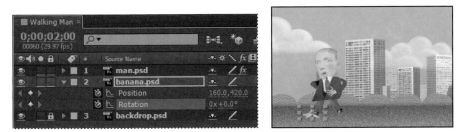

4   Click the stopwatches (◉) next to Position and Rotation to create initial keyframes for each property.

5   Move to 2:06, and change the Position to **80**, **246** and the Rotation to **19** degrees.

6   Move to 2:15, and change the Position to **−59**, **361**, so that the banana peel moves completely off the screen.

7   At 2:15, change the Rotation to **42** degrees, so that the peel continues to rotate slightly as it moves off the screen.

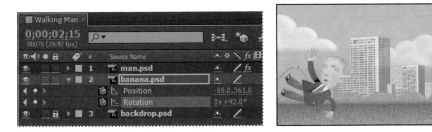

8   Choose Fit Up To 100% in the Magnification pop-up menu at the bottom of the Composition panel so you can see the entire composition. Then make a RAM preview and view your animation. If necessary, adjust the Position property for the Deform pins in the Timeline panel. Then choose File > Save.

Extra credit

The character in this animation walks, but his movement is a little bit stiff. You can use the Easy Ease and roving keyframe features to help him move more naturally.

You've used Easy Ease in other lessons. The Easy Ease In, Easy Ease Out, and Easy Ease options adjust the speed of an object.

Roving keyframes create smooth movement across several keyframes at once. They are not linked to a specific time; their speed and timing are determined by the keyframes near them. To create a roving keyframe, right-click (Windows) or Control-click (Mac OS) the keyframe, and then choose Rove Across Time from the keyframe menu.

Note: *The first and last keyframes cannot be roving keyframes.*

Go ahead and experiment with the Easy Ease and roving keyframe features, but start by trying to make your keyframes match those shown below.

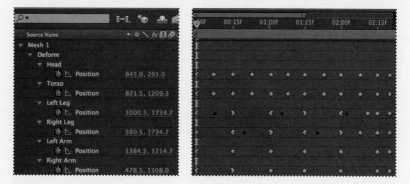

Recording animation

Changing the Position property for each pin at each keyframe worked, but you probably found the process to be slow and tedious. If you were creating a much longer animation, you'd quickly tire of entering precise numbers for each keyframe. Instead of manually animating keyframes, you can use the Puppet Sketch tool to drag the objects into position in real time. After Effects starts recording the motion as soon as you begin dragging a pin, and it stops recording when you release the mouse button. The composition moves forward through time as you move the pin. When you stop recording, the current-time indicator returns to the point at which you began recording, so that you can record the path for another pin during the same time period.

Experiment with this method of animation as you re-create the slipping motion using the Puppet Sketch tool.

1   Choose File > Save As > Save As, and name the project **Motionsketch.aep**. Save it in the Lesson08/Finished_Project folder.

2   Move the current-time indicator 2:08.

3   In the man.psd layer, delete all keyframes after 2:08.

The walking cycle remains, but you've removed the keyframes that animate the character slipping and falling.

4   Select the Puppet Pin tool (✦) in the Tools panel.

5   In the Timeline panel, expand the man.psd layer, and then expand Effects. Select Puppet to see the pins in the Composition panel.

6   Select a pin in the Composition panel, and press Ctrl (Windows) or Command (Mac OS) to activate the Puppet Sketch tool (a clock icon appears next to the pointer).

7   Continue to press Ctrl or Command as you drag the pin into a new position. Release the mouse button when you've finished. The current-time indicator returns to 2:08.

8   Press Ctrl or Command and drag another pin into position. Use the outline of the character to guide you.

9   Continue using the Puppet Sketch tool to move all the pins through the animation until you're satisfied with the movement.

10 Create a RAM preview to view the final animation.

Now you've used all the Puppet tools to create a realistic, engaging animation. Remember that you can use the Puppet tools to deform and manipulate many kinds of objects, not just drawn art. And watch out for banana peels!

▶ **Tip:** By default, the motion is played back at the speed at which it was recorded. To change the ratio of recording speed to playback speed, click Record Options in the Tools panel, and change the Speed value before recording.

Review questions

1 What's the difference between the Puppet Pin tool and the Puppet Overlap tool?

2 When would you use the Puppet Starch tool?

3 How can you make your animation more fluid?

4 Describe two methods of animating pin positions.

Review answers

1   The Puppet Pin tool creates Deform pins, which define the position of a portion of the image as the image is deformed. The Puppet Overlap tool creates Overlap pins, which determine which areas of an object remain in front when two areas overlap.

2   Use the Puppet Starch tool to add Starch pins to an area that you want to remain more rigid while other areas of the object are distorted.

3   To make your animation more fluid, you can use the Easy Ease feature or roving keyframes. Additionally, you can create smoother movement by increasing the number of triangles in the distortion mesh, but increasing the number of triangles also increases the time it takes to render the animation.

4   You can manually animate pin positions by changing the value of the Position property for each pin in the Timeline panel. To animate pin positions more quickly, use the Puppet Sketch tool: With the Puppet Pin tool selected, press Ctrl or Command, and drag a pin to record its movement.

9 USING THE ROTO BRUSH TOOL

Lesson overview

In this lesson, you'll learn how to do the following:

- Extract a foreground object from the background using the Roto Brush tool.

- Correct the segmentation boundary across a span of frames.

- Touch up a matte with the Refine Edge Tool.

- Freeze a matte across a clip.

- Animate properties for creative effects.

 This lesson will take approximately an hour to complete. Download the Lesson09 project files from the Lesson & Update Files tab on your Account page at www.peachpit.com, if you haven't already done so. As you work on this lesson, you'll preserve the start files. If you need to restore the start files, download them from your Account page.

PROJECT: TV COMMERCIAL

With the Roto Brush tool, you can quickly separate a foreground object from a background across many frames. You can achieve professional results in a fraction of the time you'd spend with traditional rotoscoping.

About rotoscoping

When you draw or paint on the frames of a movie, you're *rotoscoping*. For example, a common use of rotoscoping is to trace an object, using the path as a mask to separate it from the backgroud so you can work with it separately. Traditionally in After Effects, you drew masks, animated the mask paths, and then used the masks to define a matte. (A *matte* is a mask used to hide part of an image so that another image can be superimposed.) While effective, this is a time-intensive, tedious process, especially if the object moves a great deal or the background is complex.

If a background or foreground object is a consistent, distinct color, you could use color keying to separate the object from the background. If the subject was shot against a green or blue background (green screen or blue screen), keying is usually much easier than rotoscoping.

The Roto Brush tool in After Effects is much faster than conventional rotoscoping, and for movies with complex backgrounds, it's much easier than keying. You use the Roto Brush tool to define the foreground and background elements; then, After Effects creates a matte and tracks the movement of the matte over time. The Roto Brush tool does much of the work for you, leaving only a little cleanup work to be done.

Getting started

In this lesson, you'll use the Roto Brush tool to isolate a young boy from a wet winter background so you can color-treat the background without affecting the boy. To finish up the project, you'll add an animated title.

First, you'll preview the final movie and set up your project.

1 Make sure the following files are in the AECC_CIB/Lessons/Lesson09 folder on your hard disk, or download them from your Account page at www.peachpit.com now:

- In the Assets folder: boy.mov
- In the Sample_Movie folder: Lesson09.mov

2   Open and play the Lesson09.mov file to see what you will create in this lesson. When you're done, quit QuickTime Player. You may delete the sample movie from your hard disk if you have limited storage space.

When you begin this lesson, restore the default application settings for After Effects. See "Restoring default preferences" on page 2.

3   Start After Effects, and then immediately hold down Ctrl+Alt+Shift (Windows) or Command+Option+Shift (Mac OS). When prompted, click OK to delete your preferences. Click Close to close the Welcome screen.

After Effects opens to display an empty, untitled project.

4   Choose File > Save As > Save As.

5   In the Save As dialog box, navigate to the AECC_CIB/Lessons/Lesson09/ Finished_Project folder.

6   Name the project **Lesson09_Finished.aep**, and then click Save.

Creating the composition

You need to import one footage item for this lesson.

1   Choose File > Import > File.

2   Navigate to the AECC_CIB/ Lessons/Lesson09/Assets folder, select the boy.mov file, and then click Import or Open.

3   Drag the boy.mov clip onto the Create A New Composition button (■) at the bottom of the Project panel.

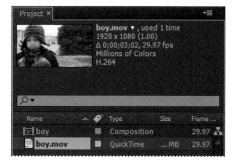

After Effects creates a composition named boy, based on the settings in the boy.mov file. The composition is three seconds long, and it uses the HD (1920x1080) preset. The movie file was shot at a rate of 29.97 frames per second.

4   Choose File > Save to save the project so far.

Using Adobe Premiere Pro with After Effects

You can work with a clip in both Adobe Premiere Pro and After Effects, moving easily between the two applications as you edit your project.

To edit an Adobe Premiere Pro clip in After Effects, do the following:

1   Right-click the clip in Adobe Premiere Pro, and choose Replace With After Effects Composition.

After Effects starts and opens the Adobe Premiere Pro clip.

2   Save the project when you're prompted by After Effects. Then work in the composition just as you'd work in any other After Effects project.

3   When you're finished, save the project, and return to Adobe Premiere Pro.

Your changes are automatically reflected in the timeline.

Note that the codec you use must be available to anyone viewing the project. For instance, if you use a hardware codec on a capture card, viewers must have the same capture card installed, or a software codec that emulates it.

For more about compression and codecs, see After Effects Help.

Creating a segmentation boundary

You use the Roto Brush tool to specify which parts of the clip are in the foreground and which are in the background. You add strokes to distinguish the two, and then After Effects creates a segmentation boundary between the foreground and background.

Creating a base frame

To use the Roto Brush tool to isolate a foreground object, you start by adding strokes to a base frame to identify foreground and background areas. You can start on any frame in the clip, but in this exercise, you'll use the first frame as the base frame. Then you'll add the strokes that identify the boy as the foreground object.

1 Move the current time indicator across the time ruler to preview the footage.

2 Press the Home key to move the current time indicator to the beginning of the time ruler.

3 Select the Roto Brush tool () in the Tools Panel.

You use the Roto Brush tool in the Layer panel, so you'll open it now.

4 Double-click the boy.mov layer in the Timeline panel to open the clip in the Layer panel.

By default, the Roto Brush tool creates green foreground strokes. You'll start by adding strokes to the foreground—the boy. Generally, it's most efficient to start with broad strokes and then use smaller brushes to refine the border.

5 Choose Window > Brushes to open the Brushes panel. Set up a hard round 100-pixel brush.

When you're drawing strokes to define the foreground object, follow the skeletal structure of the subject. Unlike traditional rotoscoping, you don't need to define a precise boundary around the object. Start with broad strokes, and work down to small regions as After Effects determines where the boundary is supposed to be.

6 Draw a green stroke from the boy's head down toward the bottom of the clip.

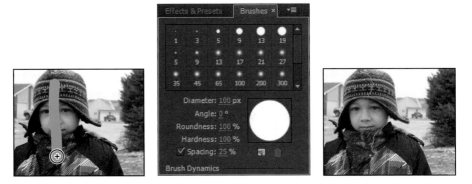

A magenta outline identifies the boundaries After Effects created for the foreground object. After Effects recognized only about half of the boy, because you initially sampled only a small area of the subject. You'll help After Effects find the boundary by adding some more foreground strokes.

7 Still using a large brush, draw a green stroke from left to right across the boy's coat, including the black strip on the right.

8 Use a smaller brush to add any neglected areas to the foreground.

It can be tricky to get some areas without accidentally adding background as well. It's okay if you haven't captured every detail in the foreground, or if you've included some of the background. You'll add background strokes to remove any extraneous areas of the matte.

9 Press Alt (Windows) or Option (Mac OS) to switch to the red background stroke brush.

10 Add red strokes to background areas you want to exclude from the matte. Switch back and forth between the foreground and background brushes to fine-tune the matte. Don't forget to deselect the area under the boy's hat where the background shows through. In fact, one click may be all it takes to exclude that area from the matte.

Don't worry about being exact about your brush strokes. Just make sure the matte is within 1 to 2 pixels of the edge of the foreground object. You'll have an opportunity to refine the matte later. However, After Effects uses the information on the base frame to adjust the matte for the rest of the span, so you want the matte to be accurate.

11 Click the Toggle Alpha button (▪) at the bottom of the Layer panel. The selected area is white against a black background, so you can see the matte clearly.

12 Click the Toggle Alpha Overlay button (▪) at the bottom of the Layer panel. The foreground area appears in color, and the background has a red overlay.

13 Click the Toggle Alpha Boundary button (▪) at the bottom of the Layer panel to see the outline around the boy again.

As you use the Roto Brush tool, the Alpha Boundary is the best way to see how accurate your boundary is, because you can see everything in the frame. However, the Alpha and Alpha Overlay options let you see your matte without the distraction of the background.

Refining the boundary across the initial span

You used the Roto Brush tool to create a base frame, which includes a segmentation boundary that divides the foreground from the background. After Effects applied the segmentation boundary across a span of frames. The Roto Brush span appears below the time ruler at the bottom of the Layer panel. As you move forward and backward through the footage, the segmentation boundary moves with the foreground object (in this case, the boy).

1 Extend the span range by dragging the end of the span to 1:00 in the Layer panel.

You'll step through the frames in the span and make adjustments to the segmentation boundary as necessary.

▶ **Tip:** To move forward one frame, press the 2 key on your keyboard; to move back one frame, press the 1 key.

2 Press the 2 key on the main keyboard (not the numeric keypad) to move forward one frame.

Working from the base frame, After Effects tracks the edge of the object and attempts to follow its movement. Depending on how complex your foreground and background elements are, the boundary may or may not conform exactly to the area you hoped it would. In this case, you may notice changes to the segmentation boundary along the boy's right sleeve (the left edge of the clip) as more of the coat is revealed in the frame. Likewise, the flaps of the cap and the edges of the hood need some adjustment, which means you need to refine the segmentation.

● **Note:** As it propagates the segmentation boundary for a frame, After Effects caches that frame. Cached frames have a green bar in the time ruler. If you jump ahead to a frame further along the span, After Effects may take longer to calculate the boundary.

3 Using the Roto Brush tool, paint foreground and background strokes to refine the matte for this frame. If the matte is accurate, you don't need to paint any strokes.

If you make a stroke you don't like, you can always undo the stroke and try again. As you move through the span, each change you make affects the frames after it. The more you refine your selection, the better the overall results will be. You may find it useful to move forward a few frames to see how changes affect the boundary.

4   Press the 2 key again to move forward to the next frame.

5   Use the Roto Brush tool to add to the foreground or subtract from the background as necessary to refine the boundary.

6   Repeat steps 4 and 5 until you reach 1:00.

Adding new base frames

After Effects creates an initial Roto Brush span of 20 frames (10 in each direction). As you move through the frames, the span range may increase automatically, or you can drag it to extend the span. However, the further you move from the base frame, the longer After Effects takes to propagate, or calculate, the segmentation for each frame, especially if the shot is complex. If the scene changes significantly, it may be better to create multiple base frames for your footage than to have one really long span. The scene in this project remains fairly consistent, so you could extend the span and make additional adjustments as needed. However, you'll create additional base frames to gain experience using the tools, learn to connect spans, and see how the segmentation shifts as you move further from a base frame.

You've reached 1:00 in the refining process. Now you'll add a new base frame to the project.

1   Go to 1:20 in the Layer panel. This frame isn't included in the initial span, so the segmentation boundary disappears.

2   Use the Roto Brush tool to add foreground and background strokes, defining
    the segmentation boundary.

A new base frame (represented by a gold rectangle) is added to the time ruler, and
the Roto Brush span extends ten frames behind and ahead of the new base frame.
There's a gap between the first span, which ends at 1:00, and the second span,
which begins at 1:10. You'll connect the two.

3   Drag the left edge of the new span to the edge of the previous span.

4   Press 1 to move backward one frame (from the new base frame), and refine
    the segmentation boundary.

5   Continue to move backwards through the span, refining the segmentation
    boundary until you reach the frame at 1:00.

6   Move back to the base frame at 1:20, and then press 2 to move forward,
    correcting the segmentation boundary for each frame if necessary.

7   When you reach the end of the span, drag the right edge to the end of the clip,
    and continue to refine each frame in the footage as needed. Pay special attention
    to the left earflap of the cap when it crosses in front of the tree. The dark areas
    overlap, making it more difficult to get a consistent edge. Remember that you are
    trying to get the segmentation boundary as close to the edge of the foreground
    object as possible.

8   When you have completed refining the segementation boundary for the entire
    clip, choose File > Save to save your work so far.

Fine-tuning the matte

Roto Brush does a pretty good job, but there may be stray bits of background in the
matte, or foreground areas that weren't included. You'll clean those up by refining
the edge.

Adjusting the Roto Brush & Refine Edge effect

When you use the Roto Brush tool, After Effects applies the Roto Brush & Refine
Edge effect to the layer. You can modify the effect using settings in the Effect
Controls panel. You'll use those settings to further refine the edge of the matte.

1   Press the spacebar to play the clip in the Layer panel.

As you preview the clip, you may notice that the segmentation boundary area jumps
around quite a bit. You'll use the Reduce Chatter setting to make it smoother.

2 In the Effect Controls panel, increase the Feather amount to **10**, and increase Reduce Chatter to **20%**.

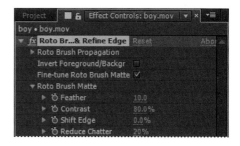

The Reduce Chatter value determines how much influence the current frame has when performing a weighted average across adjacent frames. Depending on how tight your matte was, you may need to increase Reduce Chatter to 50%.

3 Press the spacebar to play the clip again. Notice how much smoother the edge of the matte has become.

Using the Refine Edge tool

The boy's coat and face have hard edges, but his cap is fuzzy, and the Roto Brush tool didn't pick up the nuanced edge. The Refine Edge tool lets you include fine details such as wisps of hair in designated areas of the segmentation boundary.

Though it might be tempting to use the Refine Edge tool immediately after creating the base frame, it's best to wait until you've refined the segmentation boundary across the entire clip. Because of the way After Effects propagates the segmentation boundary, using the Refine Edge tool too early results in a matte that is difficult to use.

1 Select the Refine Edge tool ( ) (hidden beneath the Roto Brush tool) in the Tools panel, and then move to the beginning of the clip in the Layer panel.

2 Zoom in to at least 100% so that you can see the edges of the cap clearly.

The cap is relatively soft, so a small brush size will work well. For a fuzzier object, you might have better results with a much larger brush. The brush needs to overlap the stray edges that emerge from the object.

3 Change the brush size to **10** pixels.

When you use the Refine Edge tool, draw strokes across or along the edges of the matte.

4 In the Layer panel, move the Refine Edge tool over the edge of the cap, straddling the segmentation boundary, and including the fuzzy variations. You can use multiple strokes to move the tool around the entire cap.

When you release the mouse, After Effects switches to the Refine Edge X-ray view so that you can see how the Refine Edge tool changes the matte, capturing the detail in the edges.

5   Move to the second base frame in the Layer panel (1:20), and then repeat steps 1–4 to complete the rotoscoping process.

6   Zoom out to see the entire scene, and then choose File > Save to save your work.

Note: Use the Refine Edge tool only after you have cleaned up the matte across the entire clip.

Refine Soft Matte and Refine Hard Matte effects

After Effects includes two related effects for refining mattes: Refine Soft Matte and Refine Hard Matte. The Refine Soft Matte effect does the same thing as the Refine Edge Matte, except it applies the effect to the entire matte at a constant width. If you need to capture subtle variations across an entire matte, use this effect.

The Refine Hard Matte effect performs the same edge refinements as the Roto Brush when Fine-Tune Roto Brush Matte is turned on in the Roto Brush & Refine Edge Effect Controls panel.

Freezing your Roto Brush tool results

You've put a fair amount of time and effort into creating the segmentation boundary across the entire clip. After Effects has cached the segmentation boundary so it can recall it without having to make the calculations again. To keep that data easily accessible, you'll *freeze* it. This reduces the processing demands on your system so you can work faster in After Effects.

Once the segmentation is frozen, you cannot edit it unless you unfreeze it. Refreezing the segmentation is time-consuming, so it's best to refine the segmentation boundary as much as possible before freezing.

1 Click the Freeze button in the lower right area of the Layer panel.

The Freezing Roto Brush dialog box displays a progress bar as it freezes the Roto Brush and Refine Edge tool data. Freezing may take a few minutes, depending on your system. As After Effects freezes the information for each frame, the cache line turns from green to blue. When it has finished freezing, a blue warning bar appears above the time ruler in the Layer panel, reminding you that the segmentation is frozen.

2 Click the Toggle Alpha Boundary button (■) in the Layer panel to see the matte. Then click the Toggle Transparency Grid button (▩). Move the time marker across the time ruler to see the subject without the distractions of the background.

3 Click the Toggle Alpha Boundary button again to see the boundary.

4 Choose File > Save.

After Effects saves the frozen segmentation information with the project.

Changing the background

There are many reasons to isolate a foreground image from a background. Often, you want to replace the background entirely, moving the subject to a different setting. But rotoscoping is also useful if you want to change the foreground or background without modifying the other. In this lesson, you'll make the background blue to enhance the theme of winter and help the subject stand out.

1 Close the Layer panel to return to the Composition panel, and move the current time indicator to the beginning of the timeline.

The Composition panel displays the composition, which includes a single layer. The boy layer consists only of the foreground you isolated from the clip.

2 Click the Project tab to display the Project panel. Then drag another copy of the boy.mov clip from the Project panel to the Timeline panel, and place it below the original boy layer.

3 Click the new layer, press Enter or Return, and rename the layer **Background**. Then press Enter or Return again.

4 With the Background layer selected, choose Effect > Color Correction > Hue/Saturation.

5 In the Effect Controls panel, do the following:

- Select Colorize.
- Change Colorize Hue to **−122** degrees.
- Change Colorize Saturation to **29**.
- Change Colorize Lightness to **−13**.

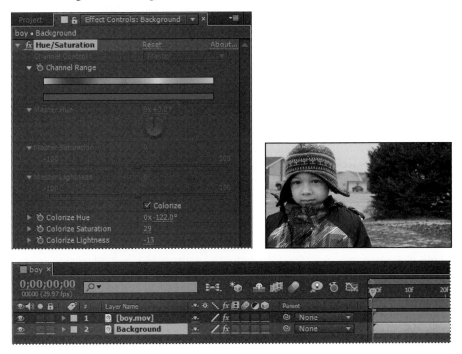

6 Choose File > Increment And Save.

If you save incrementally, you can return to earlier versions of your project to make adjustments later. This can be very useful if you're experimenting or want to try alternative effects. The Increment And Save feature preserves the previously saved version of the project and creates a new project with the same name with an increasing number in the filename.

Adding animated text

You're nearly done. All you need to do is to add the animated title between the boy and the background.

1   Move the current time indicator to the beginning of the time ruler.

2   Choose Layer > New > Text.

A new text layer appears in the Timeline panel at the top of the layer stack.

3   Double-click the Text 1 layer name to make the text editable, and then type **WINTER BLUES** in the Composition panel.

4   Select all the text in the Composition panel, and then do the following in the Character panel:

- • Choose Myriad Pro for the font.

- • Choose Black or Semibold for the font style.

- • Type **300** px for the font size.

- • Choose Optical from the Kerning menu.

- • Select white for the fill color.

- • Select black for the stroke color.

- • Make sure the stroke width is 1 px and Stroke Over Fill is selected.

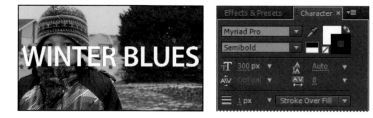

5 Select the text layer in the Timeline panel to deselect the text. Then press T to reveal the layer's Opacity property. Change the Opacity to **40%**.

6 Select the Effects & Presets tab to bring the panel to the front, and then type **Glow** in the search box. Double-click the Glow preset under Stylize.

The text gains some texture. The default settings are fine.

7 Drag the Winter Blues layer in the Timeline panel down to position it between the boy.mov and Background layers. Then move the current time indicator to the beginning of the time ruler, if it's not already there.

You'll animate the text so that it moves left behind the boy while he crosses to the right of the frame.

8 With the Winter Blues layer selected, press P to reveal its Position property. Change the Position to **1925, 540**. Click the stopwatch icon for the Position property to set a keyframe.

The text moves offscreen, so it's not visible when the movie begins.

9 Move the current time indicator to 3:01 (the end of the clip), and change the Position to **–1990, 540**.

The text moves to the left. After Effects creates a keyframe.

10 Deselect all layers in the Timeline panel, and move the current time indicator to the beginning of the time ruler. Press the spacebar to preview the clip.

11 Choose File > Save to save your work.

Outputting your project

Render your movie to complete the project.

1   Choose File > Export > Add To Render Queue.

2   In the Render Queue panel, click the orange, underlined words *Best Settings*.

3   In the Render Settings dialog box, choose Half from the Resolution pop-up menu, and select Use Comp's Frame Rate in the Frame Rate area. Then click OK.

4   Click the orange text next to Output Module. Then, at the bottom of the Output Module Settings dialog box, choose Audio Output Off, and click OK.

5   Click the orange text next to Output To. In the Output Movie To dialog box, navigate to the Lesson09/Finished_Project folder, and click Save.

6   Click Render in the top right corner of the Render Queue panel.

Congratulations! You've separated a foreground object from the background, including tricky details, and then modified the background and animated text to complete the movie. You're ready to use the Roto Brush tool on your own projects.

Review questions

1 When should you use the Roto Brush tool?

2 What is the segmentation boundary?

3 When should you use the Refine Edge tool?

Review answers

1 Use the Roto Brush tool any time you would have used traditional rotoscoping. It's particularly useful for removing a foreground element from the background.

2 The segmentation boundary is the boundary between the foreground and background. The Roto Brush tool adjusts the segmentation boundary as you progress through the frames in the Roto Brush span.

3 Use the Refine Edge tool when you need to rotoscope objects with fuzzy or wispy edges. The Refine Edge tool creates partial transparency for areas of fine detail, such as hair. Use the Refine Edge tool only after you've adjusted the segmentation boundary across the entire clip.

10 PERFORMING COLOR CORRECTION

Lesson overview

In this lesson, you'll learn how to do the following:

- Use the Levels effect to correct the color in a shot.

- Replace the sky with a different image.

- Use the Auto Levels effect to introduce a color shift.

- Correct a range of colors using Synthetic Aperture Color Finesse 3.

- Apply the Photo Filter effect to warm portions of an image.

- Remove unwanted elements with the Clone Stamp tool.

This lesson will take approximately an hour to complete. Download the Lesson10 project files from the Lesson & Update Files tab on your Account page at www.peachpit.com, if you haven't already done so. As you work on this lesson, you'll preserve the start files. If you need to restore the start files, download them from your Account page.

PROJECT: COLOR CORRECTED VIDEO CLIP

Most shots require some degree of color correction.
With Adobe After Effects, you can transform a dull,
lifeless shot into a bright, sharp clip in no time.

Getting started

As the name implies, color correction is a way of altering or adapting the color of the captured image. Color correction can help you achieve many different goals: optimizing source material, focusing attention on a key element in a shot, correcting errors in white balance and exposure, ensuring color consistency from one shot to another, and creating a color palette for a specific visual look desired by a director. In this lesson, you will improve the color of a video clip that was shot without the proper white-balance setting. You'll apply a variety of color-correction effects to clean up and enhance the image. Finally, you will remove an unwanted portion of the shot with the Clone Stamp tool.

First, you'll preview the final movie and set up your project.

1   Make sure the following files are in the AECC_CIB/Lessons/Lesson10 folder on your hard disk, or download them from your Account page at www.peachpit.com now:

   • In the Assets folder: Albertson_Hall.mov, storm_clouds.jpg

   • In the Sample_Movie folder: Lesson10.mov

● **Note:** This lesson includes the SA Color Finesse 3 effect, which requires registration. If you open the Lesson10_end file, you may be prompted to register the effect.

2   Open and play the Lesson10.mov file to see what you will create in this lesson. When you're done, quit QuickTime Player. You may delete the sample movie from your hard disk if you have limited storage space.

When you begin this lesson, restore the default application settings for After Effects. See "Restoring default preferences" on page 2.

3   Start After Effects, and then immediately hold down Ctrl+Alt+Shift (Windows) or Command+Option+Shift (Mac OS). When prompted, click OK to delete your preferences. Click Close to close the Welcome screen.

After Effects opens to display an empty, untitled project.

4   Choose File > Save As > Save As.

5   In the Save As dialog box, navigate to the AECC_CIB/Lessons/Lesson10/ Finished_Project folder.

6   Name the project **Lesson10_Finished.aep**, and then click Save.

Importing the footage

You need to import two footage items for this lesson.

1 Choose File > Import > File.

2 Navigate to the AECC_CIB/Lessons/Lesson10/Assets folder, Shift-click to select the Albertson_Hall.mov and storm_clouds.jpg files, and then click Import or Open.

3 Choose File > New > New Folder to create a new folder in the Project panel, or click the Create A New Folder button (■) at the bottom of the panel.

4 Type **Movies** to name the folder, press Enter or Return to accept the name, and then drag the Albertson_Hall.mov item into the Movies folder.

5 Create another new folder, and name it **Images**. Then drag the storm_clouds.jpg item into the Images folder.

6 Expand the folders so that you can see their contents.

Creating the composition

Now you will create a new composition based on the Albertson_Hall.mov file.

1 Drag the Albertson_Hall.mov footage item onto the Create A New Composition button (■) at the bottom of the Project panel.

After Effects creates a new composition named for the source file and displays it in the Composition and Timeline panels.

Previewing your project on a video monitor

If possible, perform color correction on a video monitor instead of a computer monitor. The gamma values between a computer monitor and a broadcast monitor vary greatly. What may look good on a computer screen may be too bright and washed out on a broadcast monitor.

You can view After Effects compositions on a broadcast monitor via the IEEE 1394 (FireWire) port on your computer. One way to accomplish this is to use a video tape recorder that accepts FireWire. You can loop the signal from your computer to the video tape recorder and then run a cable to your video monitor via the monitor/video output on the video tape recorder.

1   With a video monitor connected to your computer system, start After Effects CC.

2   Do one of the following, depending on your platform:

   • In Windows, choose Edit > Preferences > Video Preview. Then choose IEEE 1394 (OHCI Compliant) from the Output Device pop-up menu.

   • In Mac OS, choose After Effects > Preferences > Video Preview. Then choose FireWire from the Output Device pop-up menu.

3   For Output Mode (Windows and Mac OS), choose the appropriate format for your system. In North America, choose NTSC.

4   To view the composition you are working on, select the Previews, Mirror On Computer Monitor, Interactions, and Renders options. With all of these options selected, you will be able to see every update and change you make to the composition on the video monitor.

5   Click OK to close the Preferences dialog box.

Always be sure your video or computer monitor is properly calibrated before performing color correction. For instructions on calibrating a computer monitor, see After Effects Help.

2 (Optional) Choose Composition > Composition Settings to view the composition's aspect ratio and duration. This is an NTSC DV composition that is approximately 5 seconds long. Click Cancel to close the Composition Settings dialog box.

3 Drag the Albertson_Hall composition to an empty area of the Project panel to move it out of the Movies folder.

4 Drag the current-time indicator across the time ruler to preview the shot.

There is an unappealing blue cast to the entire image. You'll correct that first.

5 Choose File > Save to save your work.

Adjusting color balance

After Effects provides several tools for color correction. Some may do the job with a single click, but understanding how to adjust colors manually gives you the greatest freedom to achieve the look you want. You'll use the Levels effect to darken the shadows, remove the blue cast, and make the image pop a little more.

1 Press the Home key or move the current-time indicator to the beginning of the time ruler.

2 Select the Albertson_Hall.mov layer in the Timeline panel.

● **Note:** An additional color-correction tool, called Adobe SpeedGrade®, is available with Adobe Creative Cloud membership. To learn about SpeedGrade, see www.adobe.com/products/speedgrade.html.

3   Press Enter or Return, rename the layer **Building**, and then press Enter or Return to accept the new name.

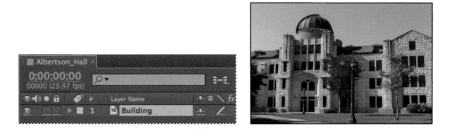

4   With the Building layer selected, choose Effect > Color Correction > Levels (Individual Controls).

The Levels (Individual Controls) effect may be a little intimidating at first, but it can give you great control over your shot. It remaps the range of input color or alpha channel levels onto a new range of output levels, functioning much the same as the Levels adjustment in Adobe Photoshop.

The Channel menu specifies the channel to be modified, and the histogram shows the number of pixels with each luminance value in the image. When the selected channel is RGB, you can adjust the overall brightness and contrast of the image. That's a good place to start.

5   In the Effect Controls panel, make sure RGB is selected in the Channel menu. Then click the triangle next to RGB to expand its properties.

6   Enter **2** for the Input Black value, slightly darkening the shadows.

The Input Black slider under the histogram moves accordingly.

7   Enter **0.85** for the Gamma value, increasing the contrast so that it pops a little more. The Gamma value represents the midtones.

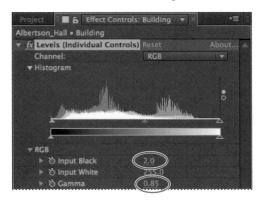

To correct the blue cast, you must first determine what areas are supposed to be gray (or white or black) in the image. In this shot, the building is supposed to be a neutral color.

8   Move the cursor over the concrete areas of the building, and note the RGB values in the Info panel. The values change as you move the cursor.

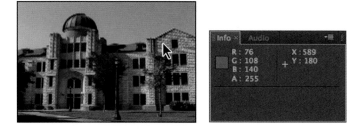

In a region near the door, the RGB value is R=70, G=95, B=125. To determine what the values should be, divide 255 (the highest possible RGB value) by the highest of the values in the sample. That gives you 255 divided by 125 (the blue value near the door), or 2.04. To equalize the colors so that blue is no longer prominent, you need to multiply 2.04 by the original red and green values (70 and 95, respectively). The new values are 142.8 for red and 193.8 for green.

9   In the Effect Controls panel, expand the Red and Green properties.

10 For the Red Input White value, enter **142.8**; for the Green Input White value, enter **193.8**.

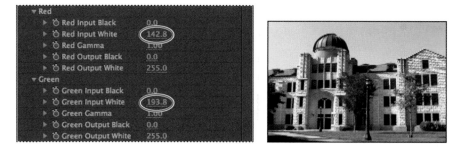

The blue cast is gone, revealing a much more realistic scene.

For each channel, the Input settings increase the value, while the Output settings decrease the value. For example, lowering the Red Input White value adds red to the highlights in the shot, and increasing the Red Output White value adds red to the shadows or dark areas in the shot.

Performing the math lets you zero in on the appropriate settings quickly. If you prefer, you could experiment with the settings to find the best values for the footage you're using.

11 Hide the Levels (Individual Controls) properties in the Effect Controls panel.

Replacing the background

This shot was taken on a clear day with a cloudless sky. To add a little drama, you'll key out the sky and replace it with storm clouds.

Keying out an area with the Color Range effect

The Color Range effect keys out a specified range of colors. This key effect is especially useful where the color to be keyed is unevenly lit. The current sky ranges in color from light blue to dark blue—a perfect candidate for the Color Range effect.

1 Press the Home key or move the current-time indicator to the beginning of the time ruler.

2 With the Building layer selected in the Timeline panel, choose Effect > Keying > Color Range.

Changing the background color of the composition can help you spot any keying errors.

3 Choose Composition > Composition Settings. Click the Background Color box, and select red (R=**255**, G=**0**, B=**0**). Click OK to close each dialog box.

● **Note:** Instead of changing the background color, you could click the Toggle Transparency Grid button (▨) to see transparent areas of the composition.

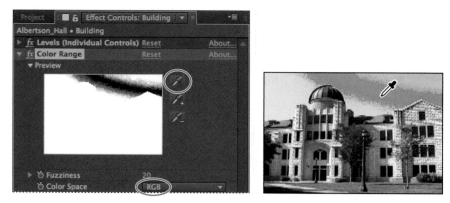

4 In the Effect Controls panel, choose RGB from the Color Space menu.

5 Select the Key Color eyedropper, next to the Preview window in the Effect Controls panel. Then, in the Composition panel, click a midtone blue color in the sky to sample it.

The keyed-out area appears red in the Composition panel, and black in the Preview window in the Effect Controls panel.

6 Select the Add To Key Color eyedropper in the Effect Controls panel, and then click another area of the sky in the Composition panel.

7 Repeat step 6 until the entire sky has been keyed out.

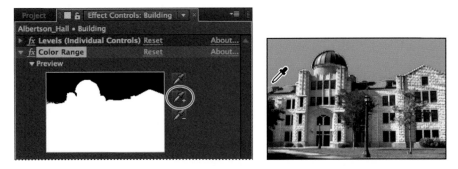

Even with the sky keyed out, a slight fringe of color remains around the building. You can remove that fringe by choking the matte.

8 Hide the Color Range properties in the Effect Controls panel.

9 Choose Effect > Matte > Matte Choker.

Use the Matte Choker effect to fill undesired holes in regions that should be opaque. The effect includes two stages: The first spreads the matte (using the first three settings), and the second chokes it (using the next three settings).

10 In the Effect Controls panel, lower the Geometric Softness 1 value to **2,** and increase the Geometric Softness 2 value to **2.5**.

Geometric Softness specifies the largest spread or choke, in pixels.

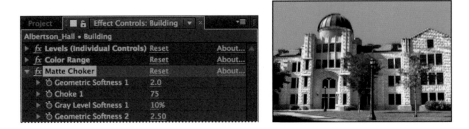

11 Hide the Matte Choker properties in the Effect Controls panel, and save your work so far.

Adding a new background

With the original sky keyed out, you're ready to add the clouds to the scene.

1 Click the Project tab to display the Project panel. Then drag the storm_clouds.jpg item from the Project panel to the Timeline panel, placing it below the Building layer.

2   Select the storm_clouds.jpg layer, press Enter or Return, rename the layer
    Clouds, and press Enter or Return again.

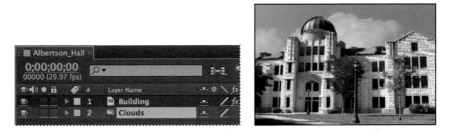

3   Click the Video switch (👁) for the Building layer to hide it.

Now you can fully see the storm clouds layer. You need to scale and reposition
the clouds to fit the sky area of the image.

4   With the Clouds layer selected in the Timeline panel, press the S key to display
    its Scale property.

5   Decrease the Scale values to **60, 60%**.

6   Make sure the Clouds layer is still selected in the Timeline panel, and press P to
    display its Position property.

7   Change the Position values to **360, 145**.

▶ **Tip:** If you're typing
the values, press Tab
to jump between
the fields.

8   Press P to hide the Position property.

Color-correcting the clouds

Although the storm clouds are dramatic, the contrast of the image and the color cast don't really match the building. You'll use the Auto Levels effect to correct that.

The Auto Levels effect automatically sets highlights and shadows by defining the lightest and darkest pixels in each color channel as white and black, and then redistributing intermediate pixel values proportionately. Because Auto Levels adjusts each color channel individually, it may remove or introduce a color cast. In this case, with the default settings applied, Auto Levels introduces a blue color cast that makes the clouds more intense.

1   With the Clouds layer selected in the Timeline panel, choose Effect > Color Correction > Auto Levels.

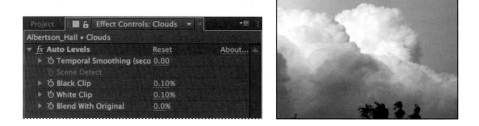

2   Turn on the Video switch (●) for the Building layer so you can see the building with the clouds.

3   Choose File > Save to save your work.

Removing unwanted elements

The color is looking great, but you're not quite done. The director wants you to remove the lamppost that appears directly in front of the doors to the building, as she believes it's distracting. You'll use the Clone Stamp tool to paint out this unwanted element of the scene. Cloning in After Effects is similar to cloning in Photoshop, but in After Effects, you can clone across the entire timeline, rather than in a single image.

Because the lamppost doesn't move, you can touch up a single frame and apply it to the entire movie.

1   Press the Home key or move the current-time indicator to the beginning of the time ruler.

2   Double-click the Building layer in the Timeline panel to open it in the Layer panel.

You can paint only on individual layers—not on the composition as a whole.

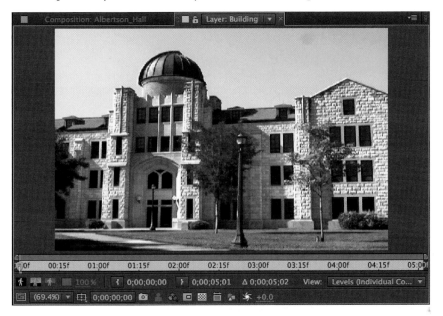

3 Zoom in to see the area around the doors clearly.

4 Select the Clone Stamp tool (⬇) in the Tools panel.

The Clone Stamp tool samples the pixels on a source layer and applies the sampled pixels to a target layer; the target layer can be the same layer or a different layer in the same composition.

When you select the Clone Stamp tool, After Effects opens the Brushes and Paint panels.

5 In the Brushes panel, select a hard, 5-pixel brush.

6 In the Paint panel, choose Constant from the Duration menu.

The Constant setting applies the Clone Stamp effect from the current time forward. Because you're starting at the beginning of the composition, the changes you make will affect every frame in the composition.

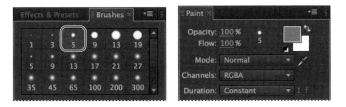

7   In the Layer panel, position the cursor to the right of the top of the lamp-post. Alt-click (Windows) or Option-click (Mac OS) to designate a source point for cloning.

▶ **Tip:** If you make a mistake, just press Ctrl+Z (Windows) or Command+Z (Mac OS) to undo the stroke, and then try again.

8   Click on the lamppost to clone an area, and then continue clicking to remove the entire lamppost.

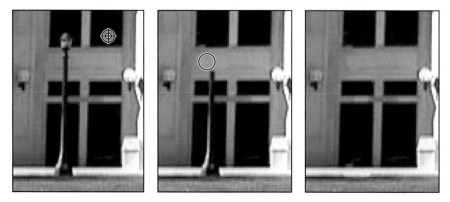

9   When the lamppost is gone, select the Selection tool, and then close the Layer panel, returning to the Composition panel.

10 Hide the Building layer properties in the Timeline panel.

Correcting a range of colors

● **Note:** Synthetic Aperture Color Finesse 3 is a powerful color-correction plug-in. Once you're familiar with it, you can use it to perform a wide variety of color corrections.

You've corrected the overall color for the scene, but you can also enhance a specific area as a secondary color correction. In this shot, the color correction caused the grass in front of the building to look like a mature bluegrass instead of a welcoming green lawn. To shift the grass to green, you will use the Synthetic Aperture Color Finesse 3 effect, a third-party plug-in that installs with After Effects and offers the capability to isolate a color range and adjust only those colors.

Color Finesse 3 applies its effect to the original layer, ignoring any effects. Because you've already performed some color correction, you'll precompose the layer to include the results of the effects you've already applied.

1   Select the Building layer in the Timeline panel, and then press Ctrl+D (Windows) or Command+D (Mac OS) to duplicate the layer.

2 With the duplicate layer (Building 2) selected, choose Layer > Pre-compose.

3 In the Pre-compose dialog box, name the new composition **Grass Enhance**, select Move All Attributes Into The New Composition, and click OK.

You've created the precomposed layer, so you'll retain the color-correction effects you've applied. However, to avoid any issues with the cloning you performed to remove the lamppost, you'll mask the grass area. The mask will ensure that only the grass is affected.

4 With the Grass Enhance layer selected in the Timeline panel, select the Pen tool (✎) in the Tools panel. Click around the grass area to create a mask.

5 With the Grass Enhance layer still selected in the Timeline panel, press the F key to display the Mask Feather property, and change the amount to **2,2** pixels. Feathering blends the layers more naturally.

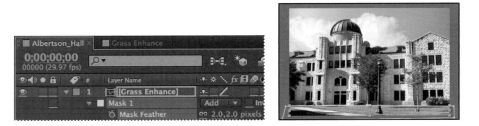

6 Press the F key again to hide the Mask Feather property.

Now you're ready to use Color Finesse 3.

7 With the Grass Enhance layer selected, choose Effect > Synthetic Aperture > SA Color Finesse 3.

Note: SA Color Finesse 3 may prompt you to register the effect. If you don't register, a Synthetic Aperture logo appears on your video where you've used the effect.

8 In the SA Color Finesse 3 area of the Effect Controls panel, click Full Interface.

SA Color Finesse 3 opens in its own window.

9 Check the box in the Secondary tab to activate secondary color correction and open its color-correction controls.

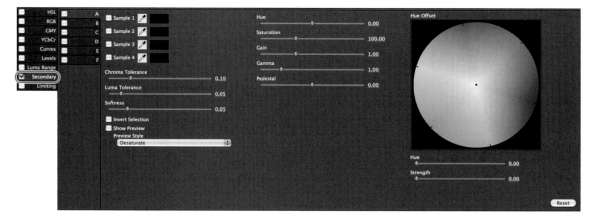

SA Color Finesse 3 enables you to perform up to six different secondary color-correction operations. You'll need only one for this project, however.

10 Check the box on the A tab, where you'll perform the color correction.

11 Using the four Sample eyedroppers, click to collect four color samples in the grass area. Try to sample various shades of green from light to dark; zoom in if necessary to help you select a range of hues.

Four samples don't encompass the entire contrast range of the grass, but SA Color Finesse 3 has controls to refine the color selection.

12 Still on the A tab, choose Mask from the Preview Style menu, and then select Show Preview.

Now you can see the areas that are selected and those that are masked (shaded in red).

13 Adjust the Chroma Tolerance, Luma Tolerance, and Softness sliders until all the grass is selected. It's okay if trees or shrubs are selected; the mask you applied earlier ensures that those adjustments will not appear in the final composition.

14 Increase the Saturation amount to **150**.

● **Note:** To learn more about SA Color Finesse 3, within the plug-in's interface, choose Help > View Color Finesse User's Guide or Help > View Color Finesse Online Knowledge Base.

15 Deselect Show Preview, and then click OK to apply the correction and to close the SA Color Finesse 3 window.

16 Choose File > Save to save your work.

Warming colors with the Photo Filter effect

Finally, you'll use the Photo Filter effect to warm up the entire shot and make it more inviting.

The Photo Filter effect mimics the technique of using a colored filter on a camera lens to adjust the color balance and color temperature of the light transmitted through the lens. You can choose a color preset to apply a hue adjustment to an image, or you can specify a custom color using the Color Picker or the eyedropper.

To apply the warming filter to all the elements in the shot, you'll apply the Photo Filter effect to an adjustment layer.

1 Click an empty area in the Timeline panel to deselect all layers.

2 Choose Layer > New > Adjustment Layer. The new adjustment layer should be the top layer in the layer stack.

3 With the Adjustment layer selected in the Timeline panel, choose Effect > Color Correction > Photo Filter.

4 In the Effect Controls panel, choose Warming Filter (81) from the Filter menu.

5 Choose File > Save.

If you'd like to output the composition, see Lesson 14, "Rendering and Outputting," for details.

Congratulations. You've transformed the color of this composition and removed a distracting element.

Review questions

1 Why would you need to color-correct a shot?

2 What does the SA Color Finesse 3 effect do?

3 What effect can you use to warm up the colors in an image?

4 How can you clone an area across an entire timeline?

Review answers

1 Color correction is performed to optimize the source material, to focus attention on a key element in the shot, to correct errors in white balance and exposure, to ensure color consistency from one shot to another, or to create a color palette to match the visual look the director prefers.

2 SA Color Finesse 3 is a third-party plug-in installed with After Effects CC. It performs a wide variety of color-correction effects, such as isolating a color range for enhancement. SA Color Finesse 3 affects the original layer, ignoring any effects that have already been applied to the layer.

3 You can use the Photo Filter color-correction effect to warm up the color of an image. The Photo Filter effect mimics the technique of using a colored filter over the lens of a camera to adjust the color balance and color temperature. Choose the Warming Filter in the Photo Filter Effect Controls panel to warm up the color of an image.

4 To ensure that cloning occurs across the entire timeline, move the current-time indicator to the beginning of the time ruler, and then choose Constant from the Duration menu in the Paint panel.

11 USING 3D FEATURES

Lesson overview

In this lesson, you'll learn how to do the following:

- Create a 3D environment in After Effects.

- Look at a 3D scene from multiple views.

- Create 3D text.

- Rotate and position layers along x, y, and z axes.

- Animate a camera layer.

- Add lights to create shadows and depth.

- Export an After Effects composition to use in Maxon Cinema 4D.

- Import a Cinema 4D scene into After Effects.

 This lesson will take approximately an hour to complete. Download the Lesson11 project files from the Lesson & Update Files tab on your Account page at www.peachpit.com, if you haven't already done so. As you work on this lesson, you'll preserve the start files. If you need to restore the start files, download them from your Account page.

PROJECT: TITLE CARD FOR A PRODUCTION COMPANY

By clicking a single switch in the Timeline panel in After Effects, you can turn a 2D layer into a 3D layer, opening up a whole new world of creative possibilities. Maxon Cinema 4D Lite, included with After Effects, gives you even greater flexibility.

Getting started

Adobe After Effects can work with layers in two dimensions (x, y) or in three dimensions (x, y, z). So far in this book, you've worked almost exclusively in two dimensions. When you specify a layer as three-dimensional (3D), After Effects adds the z axis, which provides control over the layer's depth. By combining this depth with a variety of lights and camera angles, you can create animated 3D projects that take advantage of the full range of natural motion, lighting and shadows, perspective, and focusing effects. In this lesson, you'll explore how to create and animate 3D layers. Then you'll use Maxon Cinema 4D Lite (installed with After Effects) to create high-end 3D text for a title card for a fictional production company.

First, you'll preview the final movie, and then set up the project.

1 Make sure the following files are in the AECC_CIB/Lessons/Lesson11 folder on your hard disk, or download them from your Account page at www.peachpit.com now:

   • In the Assets folder: Lunar.mp3, Space_Landscape.jpg

   • In the Sample_Movie folder: Lesson11.mov

2 Open and play the Lesson11.mov file to see what you will create in this lesson. When you are done, quit QuickTime Player. You may delete this sample movie from your hard disk if you have limited storage space.

When you begin this lesson, restore the default application settings for After Effects. See "Restoring default preferences" on page 2.

3 Start After Effects, and then immediately hold down Ctrl+Alt+Shift (Windows) or Command+Option+Shift (Mac OS). When prompted, click OK to delete your preferences. Click Close to close the Welcome screen.

After Effects opens to display an empty, untitled project.

4 Choose File > Save As > Save As.

5 In the Save Project As dialog box, navigate to the AECC_CIB/Lessons/Lesson11/Finished_Project folder. Name the project **Lesson11_Finished.aep**, and click Save.

6 Click the Create A New Composition button (■) at the bottom of the Project panel.

7   In the Composition Settings dialog box, do the following, and then click OK:

  - Name the composition **Lunar Landing Media**.

  - Choose HDTV 1080 24 from the Preset menu.

  - Enter **3:00** for the Duration.

  - Make sure the background color is black.

8   Choose File > Save.

Creating 3D Text

In order to move something in 3D space, you need to make it a 3D object. Initially, any layer is flat, with only x (width) and y (height) dimensions, and can be moved only along those axes. But all you have to do to move a layer in three dimensions in After Effects is to turn on its 3D layer switch, which lets you manipulate the object along its z axis (depth). You'll create text, and then make it 3D. This layer will serve as a placeholder for text you'll create later in Cinema 4D.

1   Click in the Timeline panel to make it active.

2   Select the Horizontal Type tool (T) in the Tools panel.

After Effects opens the Character and Paragraph panels.

3 In the Character panel, select the following settings:

- Font: Blackoak Std

- Fill color: Black

- Stroke color: White

- Font size: **70** px

- Leading: **70** px

- Tracking: **20** px

- Stroke width: **5** px

- Horizontal Scale: **65**%

4 Select All Caps, and then make sure Stroke Over Fill is chosen from the pop-up menu in the Character panel.

5 In the Paragraph panel, select the Center Text alignment option.

6 Click anywhere in the Composition panel and type **Lunar Landing Media**, with each word on its own line, as in the image below.

● **Note:** After Effects uses a different coordinate numbering convention than other 3D applications. In After Effects, the upper left corner of the composition is considered 0,0. In many 3D applications, including Maxon Cinema 4D, the center of the world (often the screen) is the origin, or 0, 0, 0 point.

7 Select the Selection tool (➤).

8 In the Timeline panel, expand the Transform properties for the Lunar Landing Media layer, and set the Position property to **960, 540**.

The text is centered in the composition.

9 In the Timeline panel, select the 3D Layer switch (⬡) for the Lunar Landing Media layer to give it three dimensions.

Three 3D Rotation properties appear in the Transform group for the layer, and properties that previously supported only two dimensions now display a third value for the z axis. In addition, a new property group named Material Options appears.

A color-coded 3D axis appears over the layer's anchor point in the Composition panel. The red arrow controls the x axis, the green arrow controls the y axis, and the blue arrow controls the z axis. At the moment, the z axis appears at the intersection of the x and y axes; it may be difficult to see against the black background. The letter x, y, or z appears when you position the Selection tool over the corresponding axis. When you move or rotate the layer while the pointer is over a particular axis, the layer's movement is restricted to that axis.

10 Hide the properties for the Lunar Landing Media layer.

Using 3D Views

Sometimes the appearance of 3D layers can be deceptive. For example, a layer might appear to be scaling smaller along its x and y axes when it's actually moving along the z axis. You can't always tell from the default view in the Composition panel. The Select View Layout pop-up menu at the bottom of the Composition panel lets you divide the panel into different views of a single frame, so you can see your work from multiple angles. You specify different views using the 3D View pop-up menu.

1   At the bottom of the Composition panel, click the Select View Layout pop-up menu, and choose 4 Views, if your screen is large enough to display them. Otherwise, choose 2 Views - Horizontal.

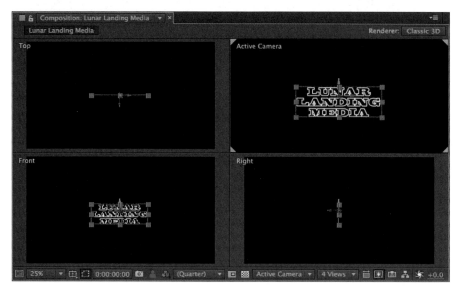

With 4 Views selected, the upper left quadrant displays the scene from the top (along the y axis). There, you can see the z axis, and it's clear that the text layer has no depth. The lower left quadrant shows the view from the front. The upper right quadrant displays what the camera sees, but because there is no camera in the scene, it's the same as the front view. The lower right quadrant shows the view from the right, as if you were observing it along the x axis.

With 2 Views - Horizontal selected, the left view shows the scene from the top, and the right shows the camera's view (currently the front view).

2   Click the Front view to make it active. (Orange corner tabs appear around the active view.) Then, from the 3D View pop-up menu, choose Custom View 1 to see the scene from a different perspective. (If your Composition window displays only two views, click the Top view, and choose Custom View 1 from the 3D View pop-up menu.)

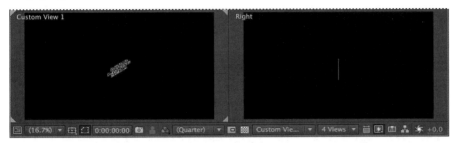

Viewing your 3D scene from different perspectives can help you align elements more accurately, view how layers are interacting with each other, and understand how objects, lights, and cameras are positioned in 3D space.

Importing a background

The text in your title card should appear to be moving in outer space. You'll import an image to use as a background.

1   Double-click an empty area of the Project panel to open the Import File dialog box.

2   Navigate to the Lesson11/Assets folder, and double-click the Space_Landscape.jpg file.

3   Drag the Space_Landscape.jpg item into the Timeline panel, placing it at the bottom of the layer stack.

4   Rename the Space_Landscape.jpg layer **Background**.

5   In the Timeline panel, select the Background layer, and then click the 3D Layer switch (⬡) to convert it to a 3D layer.

6   Make sure the Background layer is selected. Then, in the Right view in the Composition panel, drag the z-axis arrow (the blue arrow) to the right to move the Background layer further behind the text. Watch the other layers as you drag to see how the layer interacts with 3D space.

● **Note:** If you're displaying only two views, select the Active Camera view, and choose Right from the 3D View pop-up menu. Then complete step 6.

7   In the Timeline panel, press the P key to display the Position property for the Background layer. Change the Position to **960, 300, 150**.

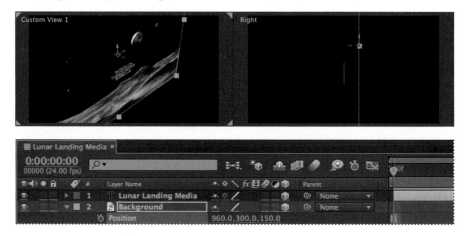

8   Choose File > Save to save your work so far.

Adding 3D Lights

You've created a 3D scene, but it doesn't yet look three-dimensional from the front. Adding light to a composition creates shadows that give depth to the scene. You'll create two new lights for your composition.

Creating a light layer

In After Effects, a *light* is a type of layer that shines light on other layers. You can choose from among four different types of lights—Parallel, Spot, Point, and Ambient—and modify them with various settings. Lights, by default, point to a point of interest, which is the focus area of the scene.

1   Press the Home key or move the current-time indicator to the beginning of the time ruler.

2   Choose Layer > New > Light.

3   In the Light Settings dialog box, do the following:

- Name the layer **Key Light**.

- Choose Spot from the Light
  Type menu.

- Set Color to a light orange
  (R=**255**, G=**235**, B=**195**).

- Make sure Intensity is set
  to **100%** and Cone Angle to
  90 degrees.

- Make sure Cone Feather is set
  to **50%**.

- Select the Casts Shadows option.

- Set Shadow Darkness to **50%** and
  Shadow Diffusion to **150** pixels.

- Click OK to create the light layer.

The light layer is represented by a light bulb icon (◉) in the Timeline panel, and the
point of interest appears in the Composition panel as a cross-hair icon (⊕).

Positioning the spotlight

The point of interest for this light is currently pointed at the center of the scene.
Because that's where the text layer is located, you don't need to adjust it. However,
you'll change the light position so the scene looks less bleak.

1   Select the Key Light layer in the Timeline panel, and press the P key to reveal
    the Position property for the light layer.

2   In the Timeline panel, type **955**, **–102**, **–2000** in the Position property.

The light is in front of and above the object, aiming down.

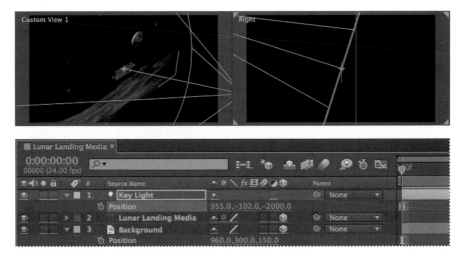

Creating and positioning the fill light

The key light gives the scene a moody look, but it's still very dark. You'll add a fill light to lighten the darker areas.

1   Choose Layer > New > Light.

2   In the Light Settings dialog box, do the following:

- Name the layer **Fill Light**.

- Choose Spot from the Light Type menu.

- Set the Color to a light blue (R=**205,** G= **238,** B=**251**).

- Set Intensity to **50%** and Cone Angle to **90** degrees.

- Make sure Cone Feather is set to **50%**.

- Deselect Casts Shadows.

- Click OK to create the light layer.

3   In the Timeline panel, select the Fill Light layer, and press the P key to reveal its Position property.

4   Change the position to **2624**, **370**, **–1125**.

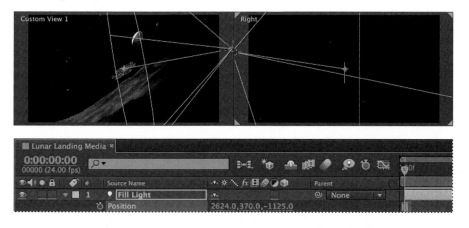

The text stroke, stars, and moon highlight are all much brighter now.

5   Hide the open properties for all layers.

6   Choose File > Save.

Casting shadows and setting material properties

The scene is looking better, with a mix of warm and cool colors. However, it still doesn't look three-dimensional. You'll change the Material Options properties to determine how the 3D layers interact with the lights and shadows.

1   Select the Lunar Landing Media layer in the Timeline panel, and press the A key twice (AA) to reveal the Material Options properties for the layer.

The Material Options property group lets you define the surface properties of the 3D layer. You can also set shadow and light transmission values.

2   For Casts Shadows, click the word *Off* to toggle the setting on. (Make sure it says *On*, not *Only*.)

The text layer now casts shadows based on the lights in the scene.

3   Change the Diffuse value to **60%** and the Specular Intensity to **60%** so that the text layer reflects more of the light in the scene.

4   Increase the Specular Shininess to **15%** to give the surface a more metallic shine.

5   Hide the properties for the Lunar Landing Media layer.

Adding a camera

You've already seen that you can view a 3D scene from different perspectives. You can also view 3D layers from various angles and distances using layers called *cameras*. When you set a camera view for your composition, you look at the layers as though you were looking through that camera. You can view a composition through the active camera or through a named, custom camera. If you have not created a custom camera, then the active camera is the same as the default composition view.

So far, you have been viewing this composition primarily from the Front, Right, and Custom View 1 angles. Currently, the Active Camera view doesn't let you see your composition from any specific angle. To see everything you want to see, you'll create a custom camera.

1   Chose Layer > New > Camera.

2   In the Camera Settings dialog box, choose 20mm from the Presets menu, and click OK.

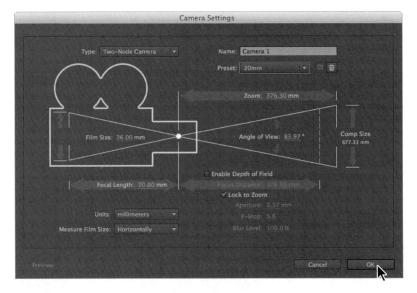

The Camera 1 layer appears at the top of the layer stack in the Timeline panel (with a camera icon next to the layer name), and the Composition panel updates to reflect the new camera layer's perspective. The view should change slightly because the 20mm preset shows a wider field of view than the default. If you didn't notice the scene change, toggle the visibility of the Camera 1 layer to see it, and then make sure it's visible.

3   Choose 2 Views - Horizontal from the Select View Layout pop-up menu at the bottom of the Composition panel. Change the view on the left to Right, and make sure the view on the right is set to Active Camera.

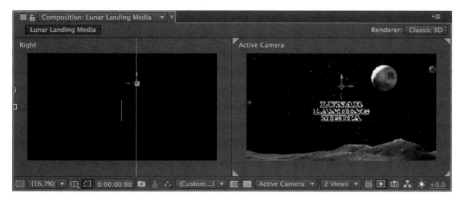

Like light layers, camera layers have a *point of interest* that can be used to determine what the camera looks at. By default, the camera's point of interest is the center of the composition. That's where your text currently is, so that point of interest works well.

4   Make sure the current-time indicator is at the beginning of the time ruler. With the Camera 1 layer selected, press the P key to reveal the Position property for the layer. Create an initial keyframe by clicking the stopwatch icon (⏱) next to the Position property.

5   Set the z-axis value to –**1000**.

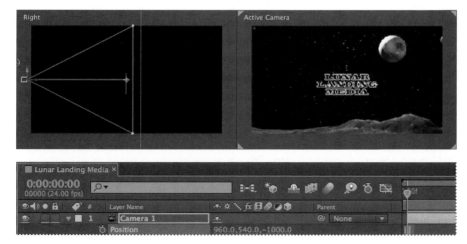

The camera moves slightly closer to the text.

6 Go to 1:00.

7 Change the z-axis value to **–500.**

The camera moves much closer to the text.

8 Right-click (Windows) or Control-click (Mac OS) the second Position keyframe, and choose Keyframe Assistant > Easy Ease In.

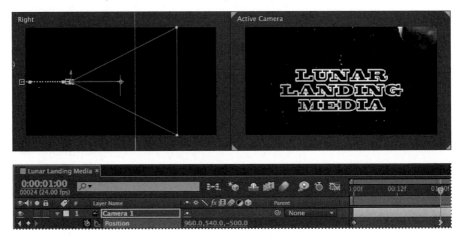

9 Manually scrub through the timeline to 1:00. As the camera moves through the scene, notice how the light reflects off the text layer, and how the overall image is influenced by the wider camera lens.

10 Hide the Position property for the Camera 1 layer, and choose File > Save.

Repositioning layers

At 1:00, the text sits low on the screen. You want to add text below it, so you'll need to make some adjustments. Also, now that the camera is in place, you'll reposition the background layer so that more of the moonscape is visible.

1 Press the Home key or move the current-time indicator to the beginning of the time ruler.

2 Select the Background layer in the Timeline panel, and press P to show its Position property. Then change the z-axis value for the Position property to **700**.

3 Select the Lunar Landing Media layer in the Timeline panel, and press P to see its Position property. Change the y-axis value for the Position property to **470**.

4   Hide the Position properties for the Background and Lunar Landing Media layers.

5   Click an empty area in the Timeline panel to deselect all layers.

Adding a text layer

Now that there's space below the text, you'll create a new text layer to go there.

1   Select the Horizontal Type Tool (T) in the Tools panel. In the Character panel, select the following settings:

- Font: Chaparral Pro
- Font Style: Regular
- Fill Color: White
- Font Size: **40** px
- Leading: **100** px
- Tracking Value: **0%**
- Stroke Width: **0** px
- Horizontal Scale: **100%**

2   Deselect All Caps in the Character panel.

3 In the Composition panel, click an insertion point, and type **A Space Pod LLC**.

4 Select the Selection tool (▸) in the Tools panel.

5 Click the 3D Layer switch for the A Space Pod LLC layer to convert it to 3D.

● **Note:** You can use the onscreen widget to position the layer if you prefer.

6 Press the P key to display the Position property for the layer. Then type **960, 675, 0** for the Position property to situate the new text below *Lunar Landing Media*. Press P to hide the Position property.

7 Move to 1:04 in the timeline. Expand the A Space Pod LLC layer, and choose Opacity from the Animate pop-up menu.

8 Change the Opacity value under Range Selector 1 to **0**%.

9 Expand Range Selector 1, and make sure the Start value is 0%. Then click the stopwatch icon (⏱) to create an initial keyframe for the Start value.

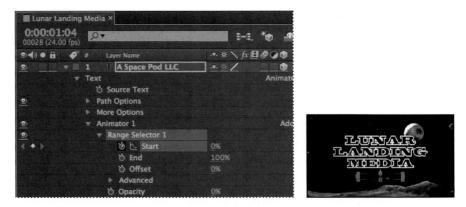

10 Move to 1:12 in the timeline, and change the Start value to **100**%.

11 Manually scrub through the timeline to 1:12 to preview the animation.

12 Hide all open properties, and choose File > Save to save your work.

Working with Cinema 4D Lite

After Effects CC installs a version of Maxon Cinema 4D that allows motion graphic artists and animators to insert 3D objects directly into an After Effects scene without pre-rendering passes and potentially complicated file exchanges. You can import, create, and edit 3D objects in a variety of formats.

You'll use Cinema 4D Lite to create extruded text, which you'll add to the After Effects scene.

Exporting a scene file

After Effects and Cinema 4D measure coordinates from different places in a scene. In After Effects, the 0,0,0 position is in the upper left corner of the scene; in Cinema 4D, the same coordinates are in the center. Keep this in mind when you move between the two applications. You can open an After Effects composition in Cinema 4D without a problem, but it's easier if you line everything up initially. You'll use a null object to do that.

1   Make sure the Timeline panel is active, and then choose Layer > New > Null Object.

A null object is an invisible layer that has all the properties of a visible layer, so that it can be a parent to any layer in the composition. You'll use a null object to reposition the scene to 0,0,0.

2   In the Timeline panel, select the Null 1 layer, and click the 3D switch (🔲) to make it a 3D layer.

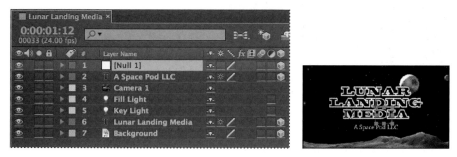

3   Select the A Space Pod LLC layer, and then Shift-click the Background layer to select all the layers except the Null 1 layer.

4 Choose Null 1 from the Parent pop-up menu for the Background layer.

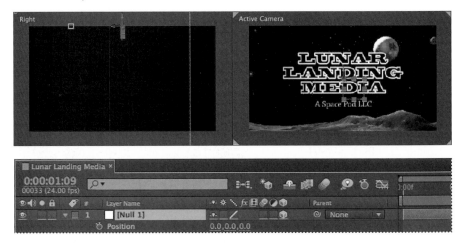

All the selected layers are parented to the Null 1 layer. Any changes to the null object affect them all.

5 Select the Null 1 layer, and press P to reveal its Position property. Then change the x and y values to **0**.

Nothing appears to happen in the Active Camera view in the Composition panel, but in the Right view, the contents of the scene appears to shift.

6 Choose File > Save.

7 Select the Lunar Landing Media composition in the Project panel, and then choose File > Export > Maxon Cinema 4D Exporter.

8 In the Save As dialog box, name the file **Lesson11.c4d**, and save it in the Lesson11 folder. Click Save to export the file.

The Cinema 4D exporter exports the lights, cameras, and certain layers from your After Effects scene into a Cinema 4D file. You can also import the resulting .c4d file directly into After Effects for compositing into an After Effects scene.

9 Choose File > Import > File, select the Lesson11.c4d file you just saved, and click Import or Open.

10 Drag the Lesson11.c4d file from the Project panel to the Timeline panel, placing it between the Lunar Landing Media and Key Light layers.

When you add a .c4d file to the Timeline panel, After Effects opens the Cineware effect. Cineware creates and manages the link between After Effects and Cinema 4D.

While you're working with a Cinema 4D file in After Effects, you should usually choose Software or Standard (Draft) from the Renderer menu in the Cineware effect. However, when you prepare to render your final project, choose Standard (Final) from the Renderer menu.

11 Choose Standard (Draft) from the Renderer menu in the Cineware effect in the Effect Controls panel.

The Software option creates a low-resolution version of the file. The Standard (Draft) option gives you a better view of what the Cinema 4D file looks like.

12 Choose Comp Camera from the Camera menu in the Effect Controls panel.

The Comp Camera option lets you use the After Effects camera you created earlier in this composition to make any refinements to your camera motion. Cineware will automatically adjust the 3D objects from the Cinema 4D scene.

Creating 3D Text in Cinema 4D

After Effects didn't export the text layer into Cinema 4D, but it did export the background solid object, the two lights you created, and the camera layer. You will use Cinema 4D Lite to create extruded text for this project.

1 In the Project panel, select the Lesson11.c4d file, and then choose Edit > Edit Original.

● **Note:** When you open Cinema 4D Lite, you may be prompted to update the application.

The Lesson11.c4d file opens in Cinema 4D Lite.

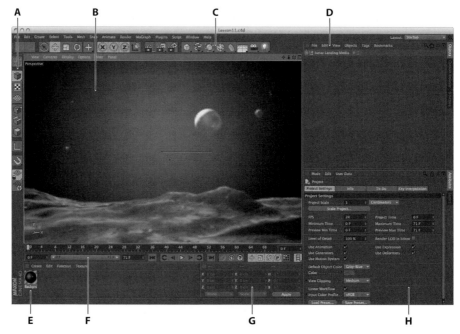

A. Modes Icon Palette B. Viewport C. Tools Icon Palette D. Object Manager E. Material Manager
F. Timeline G. Coordinates Manager H. Attribute Manager

2   In the Cinema 4D Timeline, change the clip length to **72** frames.

3   Make After Effects active. Then, right-click or Control-click the Lesson11.c4d
    layer in the Timeline panel, and choose Time > Time Stretch.

4   Type **3:00** for New Duration, make sure Layer In-Point is selected in the Hold
    In Place area of the Time Stretch dialog box, and then click OK.

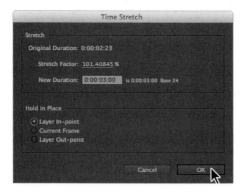

5   Still in After Effects, choose File > Save.

6 Switch back to Cinema 4D Lite.

7 In the Tools Icon Palette (below the menu bar), click and hold the triangle in the lower right corner of the Freehand icon (🖉) to display its menu, and then select the Text tool (T).

A basic text spline appears in the middle of the scene.

8 In the text box in the Attribute Manager, type **LUNAR LANDING MEDIA**, with each word on its own line.

9 In the Attribute Manager, change the text settings as follows:

   • Font: Blackoak Std

   • Height: **70** cm

   • Vertical Spacing: **–30** cm

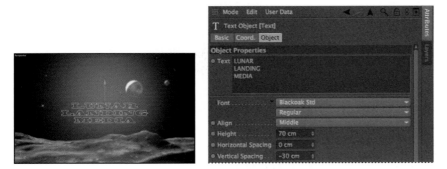

10 Drag the playhead in the Timeline to frame 24 (1:00).

The camera moves just as it did in After Effects. There's also a 3D axis in the Viewport similar to the one in the Composition panel in After Effects.

11 Click the y-axis arrow (the green one), and drag the text object until its position is similar to the one in the image. Your goal is to make sure there's room for the other text below it.

12 In the Tools Icons Palette, click and hold the triangle in the lower right corner of the HyperNURBS icon (🔵) to view its menu, and then select Extrude NURBS (🔷).

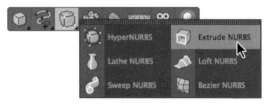

13 In the Object Manager, select the Text object, and then drag it to the middle column to the right of Extrude NURBS to parent it. You'll know you've positioned it correctly when the cursor becomes a box with an arrow pointing down (🔽).

In the Object Manager, the Text object appears nested below the Extrude NURBS object, indicating the parent relationship. In the Viewport, the text is now extruded.

14 In the Object Manager, click the Extrude NURBS object to make it active (it turns bright orange).

15 In the Attribute Manager, select the Object tab, and then change the z-axis Movement value to **70** cm.

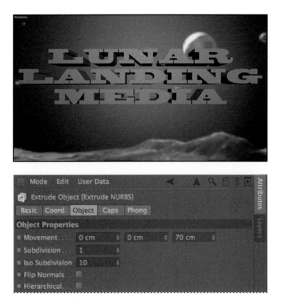

The extruded text looks much better. You'll enhance the text even further by beveling the edges and making some adjustments.

16 In the Attribute Manager, select the Caps tab, and do the following:

- Choose Fillet Cap from the Start menu.

- Increase the Steps value to **2**.

- Decrease the Radius value to **3** cm.

- Choose Concave from the Fillet Type menu.

The changes you made give the text an interesting edge.

Surfacing the Object

Cinema 4D Lite comes with a number of preset surfaces you can apply to 3D objects. You'll add a metallic surface to the text.

1　In the Materials Manager, click Create, and then choose Load Material Preset > Lite > Materials > Metal > Metal - Stainless Steel Brushed Radial.

2　In the Materials Manager, click the Metal surface you just added, and drag it onto the text in the Viewport.

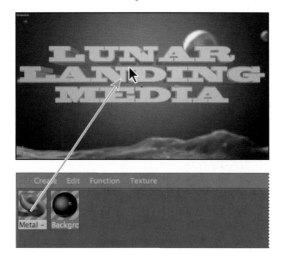

3　Choose File > Save.

Updating the project in After Effects

You've made all the changes you need to make in Cinema 4D Lite, so you can return to After Effects to see how it works in your project. As a final touch, you'll add an audio file for the title card.

1　Return to After Effects.

After Effects updates, and the Cinema 4D object appears in the Active Camera view in the Composition panel.

2　Choose 1 View from the Select View Layout pop-up menu at the bottom of the Composition panel. Choose Active Camera from the 3D View pop-up menu if it isn't already selected.

3   In the Timeline panel, deselect the Video switch for the Lunar Landing Media text layer to hide it.

The original text layer was a placeholder for the 3D text you created in Cinema 4D Lite. You don't need it in the final project.

4   If you need to reposition the text in the Cinema 4D file, return to Cinema 4D Lite, adjust the text, and choose File > Save. Then return to After Effects again.

You can move back and forth between After Effects and Cinema 4D Lite.

5   Double-click an empty area of the Project panel, and then navigate to the Lesson11/Assets folder. Double-click the Lunar.mp3 file to import it.

6   Drag the Lunar.mp3 file from the Project panel to the bottom of the layer stack in the Timeline panel.

7   Choose File > Save.

8   (Optional) Create a RAM Preview to view the project before you render. To create the RAM Preview faster, expand the properties for the Lesson11.c4d layer in the Timeline panel, and click CINEWARE under Effects. Then, in the Effect Controls panel, select both No Pre-calculation and Keep Textures In RAM.

You're ready to render the file.

9   Select the Lunar Landing Media composition in the Project panel, and choose Composition > Add To Render Queue.

10 In the Render Queue panel, click Best Settings to open the Render Settings dialog box. Then choose Half from the Resolution menu. (If your system is very slow, you may want to choose Quarter or Third.) Click OK.

11 Click the orange text next to Output To, and navigate to the Lesson11/Finished_ Project folder. Then click Save.

12 Click Render in the Render Queue panel.

13 When your project has rendered, open it in QuickTime to see your handiwork!

You've only just scratched the surface of what is possible when working with a 3D scene in After Effects, and what you can do with the workflow between Adobe After Effects and Maxon Cinema 4D Lite.

Extra credit

Extruding 3D text

Using the Ray-Traced 3D Renderer, you can extrude 3D text without leaving After Effects. Extruded text includes properties that give you greater control and flexibility.

1. Open a new project, and click the Create A New Composition button. In the Composition Settings dialog box, name the new composition **Extruded text**, deselect Lock Aspect Ratio, and then enter **800** px for the Width, **400** px for the Height, and **3:00** for the Duration. Set the background color to gray. Then click OK.

2. Click in the Timeline panel to make it active, and select the Horizontal Type tool. Then select the following settings in the Character panel:

   - Font: Blackoak Std
   - Fill color: White
   - Stroke: None
   - Font size: **70** px
   - Leading: **70** px
   - Tracking: **20** px
   - Horizontal Scale: **65**%
   - All Caps

3. In the Paragraph panel, select the Center Text alignment option. Then click anywhere in the Composition panel and type **Lunar Landing Media**, with each word on its own line.

4. Select the Selection tool. Select the Lunar Landing Media layer in the Timeline panel, and press P. Set its Position property to **400**, **225**. Then hide the Position property.

5. Make sure the Extruded Text composition is active in the Timeline panel, and choose Composition > Composition Settings.

6. In the Composition Settings dialog box, click the Advanced tab. Choose Ray-Traced 3D from the Renderer menu. Read the alert, and click OK. Click OK to close the Composition Settings dialog box.

Now that the Ray-Traced 3D Renderer is enabled, you can extrude the text.

7. Select the 3D Layer switch for the Lunar Landing Media layer, if it isn't already enabled.

8. Ctrl-click (Windows) or Command-click (Mac OS) the triangle in the Label column for the Lunar Landing Media layer to display all the properties for the layer.

9. Under Geometry Options, choose Convex from the Bevel Style menu, change the Bevel Depth to **3**, the Hole Bevel Depth to **20**%, and the Extrusion Depth to **60**.

10. Under Material Options, toggle Casts Shadows on, change Specular Shininess to **50**%, and change Metal to **50**%. Leave all other settings at their defaults. Then hide the properties for the layer.

continues on next page

Extra credit (continued)

These settings give you a very basic 3D object that you can work with. The Hole Depth Extrusion keeps the open spaces in the text from becoming too tight. When you extrude text, you may also need to adjust the kerning (the space between the letters) to keep the 3D letters from bumping into one another. Now you'll add light so you can see the extruded text more clearly.

11 Choose Layer > New > Light. In the Light Settings dialog box, do the following:
   - Name the light **Spotlight**.
   - Choose Spot from the Light Type menu.
   - Select a light yellow color (we used R=241, G=235, B=197).
   - Select Casts Shadows.
   - Change Shadow Diffusion to **25** pixels.
   - Click OK to add the spotlight.

12 Select the Spotlight layer in the Timeline panel, and expand its Transform properties. Then change its Point Of Interest to **528**, **238**, **−148** and its Position to **136**, **184**, **−300**.

13 Choose Layer > New > Light. In the Light Settings dialog box, do the following:
   - Name the light **Fill Light**.
   - Choose Point from the Light Type menu.
   - Select a light purple color (we used R=200, G=184, B=217).
   - Change Intensity to **100%**.
   - Leave everything else as it was in the previous light.
   - Click OK to add the fill light.

14 Select the Fill Light layer in the Timeline panel, and press P. Change the light's Position to **58**, **130**, **−350**.

Now just add the background, and you're done!

15 Double-click an empty area of the Project panel, and import the Space_Landscape.jpg file.

16 Drag the Space_Landscape.jpg file from the Project panel to the bottom of the Timeline panel. Expand its Transform properties, and then change its Position to **459**, **96** and its Scale to **35**%.

Review questions

1 What happens to a layer when you select its 3D Layer switch?

2 Why is it important to look at multiple views of a composition that contains 3D layers?

3 What is a camera layer?

4 What is a 3D light in After Effects?

Review answers

1 When you select a layer's 3D Layer switch in the Timeline panel, After Effects adds a third axis, the z axis, to the layer. You can then move and rotate the layer in three dimensions. In addition, the layer takes on new properties that are unique to 3D layers, such as the Materials Options property group.

2 The appearance of 3D layers can be deceptive, depending on the view in the Composition panel. By enabling 3D views, you can see the true position of a layer relative to other layers in the composition.

3 You can view After Effects 3D layers from any number of angles and distances using layers called *cameras*. When you set a camera view for your composition, you look at the layers as though you were looking through that camera. You can choose between viewing a composition through the active camera or through a named, custom camera. If you have not created a custom camera, then the active camera is the same as the default composition view.

4 In After Effects, a light is a type of layer that shines light on other layers. You can choose from among four different types of lights —Parallel, Spot, Point, and Ambient— and modify them with various settings.

12 WORKING WITH THE 3D CAMERA TRACKER

Lesson overview

In this lesson, you'll learn how to do the following:

- Track footage using the 3D Camera Tracker.

- Add camera and text elements to a tracked scene.

- Set a ground plane and origin.

- Create realistic shadows for new 3D elements.

- Lock elements to planes using null objects.

- Adjust camera settings to match real-world footage.

- Remove rolling shutter distortions from DSLR footage.

This lesson will take approximately 1½ hours to complete. Download the Lesson12 project files from the Lesson & Update Files tab on your Account page at www.peachpit.com, if you haven't already done so. As you work on this lesson, you'll preserve the start files. If you need to restore the start files, download them from your Account page.

PROJECT: OPENING SEQUENCE FOR TV SHOW

The 3D Camera Tracker effect analyzes two-
dimensional footage to create a virtual 3D camera
that matches the original. You can use this data
to add 3D objects that merge realistically with
your scene.

About the 3D Camera Tracker effect

The 3D Camera Tracker effect automatically analyzes the motion present in existing 2D footage, extracts the position and lens type of the real camera that shot the scene, and creates a new 3D camera in After Effects to match it. The effect also overlays 3D track points onto the 2D footage, so you can easily attach new 3D layers onto the original footage.

These new 3D layers have the same movement and perspective changes as the original footage. The 3D Camera Tracker effect even helps create "shadow catchers," so your new 3D layers can appear to cast realistic shadows and reflections onto the existing footage.

The 3D Camera Tracker performs its analysis in the background. Therefore, you can work on other compositions while the footage is being analyzed.

Getting started

In this lesson, you'll create the opening scene for a fictional reality show that estimates the value of everyday objects found on office desks. You'll begin by importing the footage and tracking it with the 3D Camera Tracker effect. Then you'll add 3D text elements that track precisely with the scene. Finally, you'll animate the text, add audio, and enhance the footage to complete the show's introduction.

First, you'll preview the final movie and set up your project.

1 Make sure the following files are in the AECC_CIB/Lessons/Lesson12 folder on your hard disk, or download them from your Account page at www.peachpit.com now:

   • In the Assets folder: DesktopC.mov, Treasures_Music.aif, Treasures_Title.psd

   • In the Sample_Movie folder: Lesson12.mov

2 Open and play the Lesson12.mov file to see what you will create in this lesson. When you're done, quit QuickTime Player. You may delete the sample movie from your hard disk if you have limited storage space.

When you begin this lesson, restore the default application settings for After Effects. See "Restoring default preferences" on page 2.

3 Start After Effects, and then immediately hold down Ctrl+Alt+Shift (Windows) or Command+Option+Shift (Mac OS). When prompted, click OK to delete your preferences. Click Close to close the Welcome screen.

After Effects opens to display an empty, untitled project.

4 Choose File > Save As > Save As.

5   In the Save As dialog box, navigate to the AECC_CIB/Lessons/Lesson12/ Finished_Project folder.

6   Name the project **Lesson12_Finished.aep**, and then click Save.

Importing the footage

You need to import three footage items for this lesson.

1   Choose File > Import > File.

2   Navigate to the AECC_CIB/Lessons/Lesson12/Assets folder, Shift-click to select the DesktopC.mov, Treasures_Music.aif, and Treasures_Title.psd files, and then click Import or Open.

3   Choose File > New > New Folder to create a new folder in the Project panel, or click the Create A New Folder button (■) at the bottom of the panel.

4   Type **Footage** to name the folder, press Enter or Return to accept the name, and then drag the DesktopC.mov and Treasures_Title.psd items into the Footage folder.

5   Create another new folder, and name it **Audio**. Then drag the Treasures_Music.aif item into the Audio folder.

6   Expand the folders so that you can see their contents.

Creating the composition

Now, you will create a new composition based on the aspect ratio and duration of the DesktopC.mov file.

1   Drag the DesktopC.mov item onto the Create A New Composition button (■) at the bottom of the Project panel. After Effects creates a new composition named DesktopC and displays it in the Composition and Timeline panels.

2 Drag the DesktopC composition to an empty area of the Project panel to move it out of the Footage folder.

3 Drag the current-time indicator across the time ruler to preview the shot.

The camera moves around a desktop so that you can see the objects on it. You'll add labels and dollar amounts, animated in time with background music.

4 Choose File > Save to save the file.

Repairing rolling shutter distortions

Digital cameras with CMOS sensors—including video-capable DSLRs, which are becoming increasingly popular for the creation of films, commercials, and television shows—typically have what is commonly known as a "rolling" shutter, which captures a frame of video one scan line at a time. Due to time lag between scan lines, not all parts of the image are recorded at exactly the same time, causing motion to ripple down the frame. If the camera or the subject is moving, the rolling shutter can cause distortions, such as leaning buildings and other skewed images.

The Rolling Shutter Repair effect attempts to correct this problem automatically. To use it, select the problem layer in the Timeline panel, and choose Effect > Distort > Rolling Shutter Repair.

Due to a rolling shutter distortion, the pillars of the building appear to be leaning.

After applying the effect, the building looks much more stable.

The default settings usually do the trick, but you may need to change the Scan Direction or the Method being used to analyze the footage.

If you plan to use the 3D Camera Tracker effect with footage on which you've used the Rolling Shutter Repair effect, precompose the footage first.

Tracking the footage

The 2D footage is in place. Now you'll let After Effects track it and interpolate where a 3D camera should be placed.

1   In the Timeline panel, click the Audio icon for the DesktopC.mov layer to mute the audio.

You'll add a soundtrack later, and you don't want any ambient noise from this clip.

2   Right-click (Windows) or Control-click (Mac OS) the DesktopC.mov layer in the Timeline panel, and choose Track Camera.

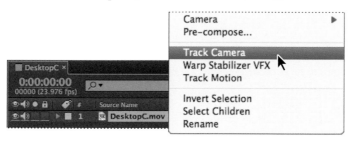

After Effects opens the Effect Controls panel and displays its progress as it analyzes the footage in the background. When the analysis is complete, many tracking points appear in the Composition panel. The size of a tracked point indicates its proximity to the virtual camera: Larger points are closer and smaller points are further away.

The default analysis of the footage often yields satisfactory results, but you can perform a more detailed analysis to better solve the camera position.

3   In the Effect Controls panel, expand the Advanced category, and then select Detailed Analysis.

After Effects analyzes the footage again. If you're working with a slower machine and you suspect you'll need a detailed analysis, you can save time by selecting Detailed Analysis while the 3D Camera Tracker is performing its initial analysis. The detailed analysis may take a few minutes, depending on your system. Because the analysis is performed in the background, you could work on other aspects of your project while it progresses.

4   When the analysis is complete, choose File > Save to save your work so far.

Creating a ground plane, a camera, and the initial text

● **Note:** You can also add a camera by clicking the Create Camera button in the Effect Controls panel.

You have a 3D scene, but it needs a 3D camera. You'll add a camera when you create the first text element, and then you'll add a second text element related to the first.

1   Press the Home key or move the current-time indicator to the beginning of the time ruler.

● **Note:** If the size of the target makes it difficult to see the plane, resize the target by pressing Alt or Option as you drag from the center of the target.

2   In the Composition panel, hover the cursor over the hole in the record on the desk until the displayed target is in line with the plane and the perspective matches. (If you don't see the track points and target, click the 3D Camera Tracker effect in the Effect Controls panel to make it active.)

When you hover the cursor between three or more neighboring track points that can define a plane, a semitransparent triangle appears between the points. Additionally, a red target shows the orientation of the plane in 3D space.

3   Right-click (Windows) or Control-click (Mac OS) the plane, and choose Set Ground Plane And Origin.

The ground plane and origin provide a reference point, setting a point where the coordinates are (0,0,0). Though nothing appears to change in the Composition panel using the Active Camera View, the ground plane and origin make it easier to change the camera's rotation and position.

4 Right-click (Windows) or Control-click (Mac OS) the same plane, and choose Create Text And Camera.

After Effects displays a large text item lying flat in the Composition panel. It also adds two layers to the Timeline panel: Text and 3D Tracker Camera. The 3D switch is enabled for the Text layer, but the DesktopC.mov layer remains 2D. Because the text elements are the only ones that need to be positioned in 3D space, there is no reason to make the background footage layer a 3D layer.

5 Move the current-time indicator along the time ruler. The text remains in position, tracking with the camera. Return the current-time indicator to the beginning of the time ruler.

6 Double-click the Text layer in the Timeline panel to open the Character and Paragraph panels.

7   In the Paragraph panel, select Center Text for the alignment. The text is centered over the record.

8   In the Character panel, change the font to a sans serif font such as Arial Narrow or Helvetica Light. Then change the font size to **20** px, the stroke width to **1** px, and the stroke type to Fill Over Stroke. Make sure the fill color is white and the stroke color is black (the default colors).

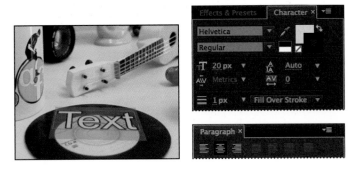

The text looks great, but you want it to stand on end. You'll change its location in space, and then replace it with the price of the object.

Note: Instead of entering values, you could use the Rotation tool to adjust the individual axes in the Composition panel.

9   With the Text layer selected in the Timeline panel, press the R key to display the Rotation property of the layer. Then change the Orientation values to **0, 350, 0** degrees.

Any new 3D layer you create uses the ground plane and origin to orient the layer in the scene. The Text layer was originally flat, with the Orientation of 270 degrees on the X axis. When you change that value to 0, the text becomes vertical.

10 Double-click the Text layer in the Timeline panel to make it active in the Composition panel.

When the text is editable, it appears to have a light red mask surrounding it.

11 With the text selected in the Composition panel, type **$35.00** to replace it.

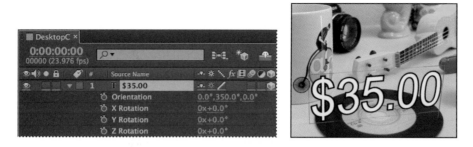

So far, so good. Next, you want to label the item, and the label needs to stay with the price as the camera moves. You'll duplicate the layer, modify it, and then parent one layer to another.

12 Select the $35.00 layer in the Timeline panel, and press Ctrl+D (Windows) or Command+D (Mac OS) to duplicate it.

13 Double-click the $35.2 layer, and type **HENDRIX 45 RPM** (in all capital letters) in the Composition panel.

The text is too large; it's the same size as the price text. You'll parent it to the $35.00 layer and then scale it.

14 Select the Hendrix 45 RPM layer in the Timeline panel, and press the P key to reveal the Position property for the layer. Drag the pick whip from the Hendrix layer to the $35.00 layer.

The Position value for the Hendrix layer changes to 0,0,0 because its position is in relationship to the parent layer. However, you want the Hendrix layer to appear above the $35.00 layer, not in front of it.

15 Change the y-axis position value to **−18** to move the Hendrix label above the price text.

16 With the Hendrix layer selected, press the S key to reveal the Scale property, and change the Scale values to **37.4, 37.4, 37.4%**.

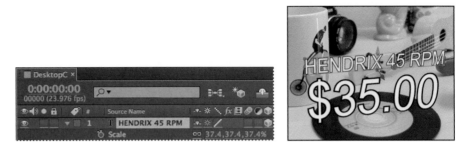

17 Close the open properties, and then choose File > Save to save your work so far.

Creating realistic shadows

You've set up your first text elements, but unlike 3D objects, they aren't casting any shadows. You'll create a shadow catcher and a light to add depth to your video.

1 Press the Home key or move the current-time indicator to the beginning of the time ruler.

● **Note:** Be sure to select the 3D Camera Tracker effect in the DesktopC.mov layer, not the 3D Tracker Camera layer.

2 Select the DesktopC.mov layer in the Timeline panel, press the E key to display the 3D Camera Tracker effect, and then select the 3D Camera Tracker effect.

3 Select the Selection tool (**⯭**) in the Tools panel. Then, in the Composition panel, hover until you find the same plane you used to create the text layer.

4 Right-click (Windows) or Control-click (Mac OS) the target, and choose Create Shadow Catcher And Light.

After Effects adds a light source to the scene. The default settings are applied, so a shadow appears in the Composition panel. However, you'll need to reposition the light to match the light in the source footage. The Shadow Catcher 1 layer that After Effects adds to the Timeline panel is a shape layer that has its material options set so that it accepts shadows only from the scene.

5 Select the Light 1 layer in the Timeline panel, and press the P key to reveal the Position property for the layer.

6 Enter the following values for the Position property to reposition the light: **1900, –2500, –375**.

7 Choose Layer > Light Settings.

You can change the intensity, color, and other attributes of the light in the Light Settings dialog box.

8 Name the light **Key Light**. Choose Point from the Light Type menu, and then select a slightly red color (we used R=232, G=214, B=213) to match the slight color cast in the room. Then change the Shadow Darkness to **15%** and the Shadow Diffusion to **100** px. Click OK.

▶ **Tip:** In a real-world project, it's ideal to work with the lighting plan that was used to shoot the original 2D scene. The goal is to have the new 3D lights match the original source lighting as closely as possible.

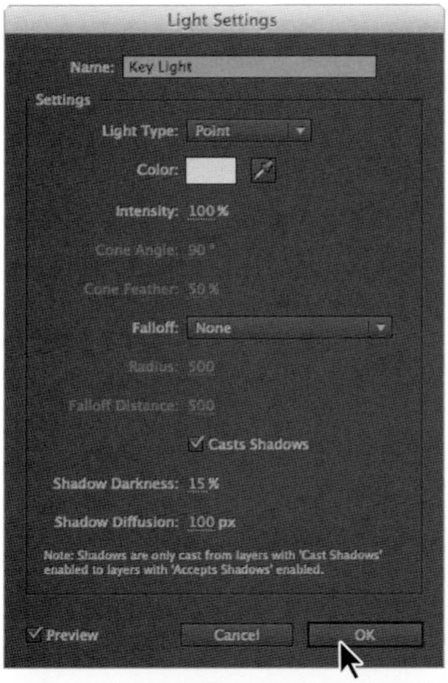

9   Select the Shadow Catcher 1 layer in the Timeline panel, and press the S key to reveal the Scale property.

10 Change the Scale value to **340%**.

Scaling the Shadow Catcher 1 layer changes the area in which shadows can appear for the light that was created with it.

Adding ambient light

The shadow looks better after the adjustments you made to the light, but it's now causing the text to appear black. You'll add ambient light to address this. Unlike a point light, ambient light creates a more diffuse light throughout the scene.

1   Choose Layer > New > Light.

2   Name the light **Ambient Light**, choose Ambient from the Light Type menu, and change its Intensity value to **80%**. The light color should be the same as the color you selected for the point light.

3   Click OK to add the light to the scene.

4   Hide the properties for all layers in the Timeline panel, except for the DesktopC.mov layer.

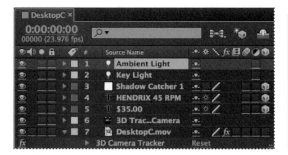

Creating additional text elements

You created the label for the Hendrix record. Now you need to perform the same tasks to create labels for the camera, gold statue, pocket knife, and ukulele. You'll use the same steps to create each label, but because the objects are in different places on the table, you'll need to use different orientation and scaling values, as listed in the following chart. You'll also find it easiest to attach the label for each to the correct plane at different points in the time ruler.

▶ **Tip:** If a 3D object should be obscured by an object in the background, duplicate the background layer, move it to the top of the layer stack, and then use the Mask tool to create masks around portions of the foreground elements. You will need to animate these masks over time, but if you do it carefully, you can create a seamless composition.

OBJECT	POSITION IN TIME RULER (STEP 1)	ORIENTATION (STEP 5)	PRICE (STEP 6)	PRICE SCALE (STEP 7)	LABEL (STEP 9)
camera	3:00	0, 310, 0	$298.00	3000	35MM CAMERA
statue	5:00	0, 325, 0	$612.00	2000	GOLD STATUE
knife	7:00	0, 340, 0	$75.00	2500	POCKET KNIFE
ukulele	9:00	0, 310, 0	$500.00	3000	1942 UKULELE

1 Move the current-time indicator to get a better view of the object.

2 In the Timeline panel, select the 3D Camera Tracker (under the DesktopC.mov layer) to make it active. (If you don't see the 3D Camera Tracker, press the E key to reveal it.)

3 Make sure the Selection tool is selected. Then, in the Composition panel, hover over an area so that the red target is parallel to the front of the object.

4 Right-click (Windows) or Control-click (Mac OS) the target, and choose Create Text.

5 Select the Text layer in the Timeline panel, and press the R key to reveal the Rotation values. Then change the Orientation values.

6 Double-click the Text layer to make it editable, and then type the price in the Composition panel.

7 Select the price layer in the Timeline panel, and press S to reveal the Scale property. Change the Scale value.

8 With the price layer selected, press Ctrl+D (Windows) or Command+D (Mac OS) to duplicate the layer.

9 Double-click the duplicate layer in the Timeline panel, and then type the label in the Composition panel.

● **Note:** Make sure you select the 3D Camera Tracker effect in the DesktopC.mov layer, not the 3D Tracker Camera layer.

Note: If you turn on Caps Lock to type the label, be sure to turn it off again. Otherwise, you'll get unexpected results, and After Effects won't be able to update the layer name.

10 Select the label layer in the Timeline panel, and press P to reveal its Position property. Then drag the pick whip from the label layer (e.g., 35MM CAMERA) to the price layer (e.g., $298.00).

11 Change the y value of the Position property for the label layer to **−18** to move the label above the price.

12 Select the label layer again, and press S to reveal the Scale property. Change its Scale values to **50, 50, 50%**.

13 Hide the properties for the layers you just created.

14 Repeat steps 1–13 to label the additional objects, using the values in the chart on the previous page.

The labels all look good, but they overlap in places that can make them hard to read. Adjust the labels for the ukulele and the statue.

15 Select the $500.00 layer in the Timeline panel, and press P. Then change the Position property to **2300, −580, 3500**.

16 Select the $612.00 layer in the Timeline panel, and press P. Then change the Position property to **1830, 54, 236**.

17 Choose File > Save to save your work so far.

Locking a layer to a plane with a null object

The title card for the show should be flat on the table, using the same plane you used to attach text to the record. You'll use a null object to attach the title card to that plane. The title card is an Adobe Photoshop file.

1   Press the Home key or move the current-time indicator to the beginning of the time ruler.

2   In the Timeline panel, select the 3D Camera Tracker (under the DesktopC.mov layer) to make it active. (If you don't see the 3D Camera Tracker, press the E key to reveal it.)

3   Select the Selection tool, and then move the cursor so that the target is lying flat over the record.

4   Right-click (Windows) or Control-click (Mac OS) the target, and choose Create Null.

After Effects adds a Track Null 1 layer to the top of the layer stack in the Timeline panel. Because we know that the record is on the same plane as the desktop, we can use this null object to position the title of the show in the open area of the desk, and still have it move correctly in relation to other elements and the camera in the scene.

5   Select the Track Null 1 layer in the Timeline panel, press Enter or Return, and change the name to **Desktop Null**. Press Enter or Return again to accept the name change.

6   From the Project panel, drag the Treasures_Title.psd asset to the Timeline panel, placing it directly above the Desktop Null layer.

▶ **Tip:** Instead of dragging the pick whip, you could choose 2.Desktop Null from the Parent menu in the Treasures_Title layer.

7 Drag the pick whip from the Treasures_Title layer to the Desktop Null layer to parent the layer.

8 Click the 3D switch for the Treasures_Title layer to make it a 3D layer.

Because you've parented the title layer to the null object, when it becomes a 3D layer it is automatically oriented to be flat on the desktop.

9 Move to the end of the time ruler so you can see how the title card is positioned.

You need to move the title to the empty area of the desktop, and then rotate it and resize it.

10 Select the Treasures_Title layer in the Timeline panel, and press R to reveal its Rotation property. Then change its Z Rotation value to **305** degrees.

11 Press the S key to reveal the Scale property, and change the Scale amount to **625%**.

12 With the Selection tool, move the title text into position, as in the image at the bottom of this page.

13 Click the Toggle Switches/Modes button at the bottom of the Timeline panel. Choose Luminosity from the Mode menu for the Treasures_Title layer.

14 Click the Toggle Switches/Modes button again to return to displaying switches.

15 Choose File > Save to save your work so far.

Animating the text

The 3D text elements, camera, and lighting are all complete, but you can make the introduction more interesting by animating the text to appear according to cues in the soundtrack. You'll add an audio track, and then animate the labels to appear when cash register sounds occur.

Animating the first text elements

You'll animate the record label and price to appear early in the intro, with the price cycling through characters until it arrives at the final text.

1   In the Project panel, drag the Treasures_Music.aif file from the Audio folder to the bottom of the layer stack in the Timeline panel.

2   Move the current-time indicator to the beginning of the timeline, and then create a RAM preview for the first few seconds of the composition.

Notice that the cash register sound occurs periodically. You'll animate the text to appear at those points.

3   Go to 1:00, and select the $35.00 layer. Press the S key to reveal the Scale property, and then change the Scale amount to **0%**. Click the stopwatch icon (⏱) to create an initial keyframe.

4   Go to 1:08, and change the Scale amount for the $35.00 layer to **3200%** so that the text is larger than its final size.

5   Go to 1:10, and change the Scale amount to **3000%**, the final value for the text.

6   Go to 1:00, and press S to hide the Scale property. Then click the arrow next to the $35.00 layer to reveal all its properties.

7   Next to the Text property, click the arrow next to Animate, and choose Character Offset from the pop-up menu.

8   Expand Range Selector 1 in the Animator 1 properties. Then click the stopwatch next to Offset to create an initial keyframe, and make sure the value is **0%**.

9   Create an initial keyframe for Character Offset (under Character Range), and make sure its value is **0**.

10 Go to 1:12, and change the Range Selector 1 Offset value to −**100%**.

11 Click the word *Offset* to select both keyframes, right-click (Windows) or Control-click (Mac OS) one of the keyframes, and then choose Keyframe Assistant > Easy Ease.

12 Go to 1:17, and change the Character Offset value to **20**.

13 Create a RAM preview to see the first 2 seconds of the composition.

The title of the record pops up as the text cycles through to the estimated price. The character offset values determine how the text cycles through characters to arrive at the final one.

Copying the animation to other text elements

Now that you've animated the text for the record, you can copy the animation for the other objects, placing the keyframes at the appropriate points in the time ruler.

1 Select the $35.00 layer, and press the U key to reveal only the properties that have keyframes.

2 In the time graph, drag a marquee around all the keyframes to select them.

3 Choose Edit > Copy to copy the keyframes and their values.

4 Go to 3:00, and select the $298.00 layer. Choose Edit > Paste to paste the keyframes and their values, beginning at the current time.

5 Go to 5:00, and select the $612.00 layer. Press Ctrl+V (Windows) or Command+V (Mac OS) to paste the keyframes and their values.

6 Go to 7:00, select the $75.00 layer, and press Ctrl+V (Windows) or Command+V (Mac OS).

7 Go to 9:00, select the $500.00 layer, and press Ctrl+V (Windows) or Command+V (Mac OS).

8 Hide the properties for all the layers, and then choose File > Save.

Adjusting the camera's depth of field

The intro is looking pretty good, but you can make the computer-generated elements more closely match the source footage if you adjust the depth of field for the 3D camera. You'll use the values that were used in the camera that shot the original footage, so the text that is further away from the camera appears to be more out of focus.

1   Select the 3D Tracker Camera layer in the Timeline panel.

2   Choose Layer > Camera Settings.

3   In the Camera Settings dialog box, do the following, and then click OK:

   • Select Enable Depth of Field.

   • Set the Focus Distance to **200** mm.

   • Change the F-Stop value to **5.6**.

   • Set the Focal Length to **27.2**.

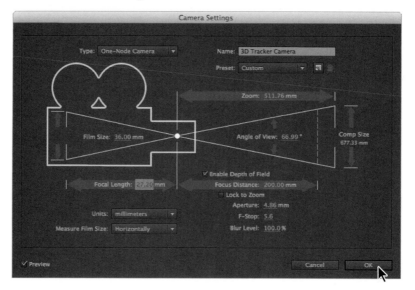

4   In the Timeline panel, select all of the layers except the audio layer. Then select the Motion Blur switch for one of the layers, applying it to all selected layers.

5   Select the Enable Motion Blur button (⊘) at the top of the Timeline panel to enable motion blur for all layers.

6   Choose File > Save to save your project.

Rendering the composition

You've done some complex work to create a scene that merges the added components with an existing tableau. To see the final results, you'll render the project. You'll learn more about rendering in Lesson 14, "Rendering and Outputting."

1 Choose Window > Render Queue to open the Render Queue panel.

2 Drag the DesktopC composition from the Project panel to the Render Queue panel.

3 Click the orange, underlined words next to Render Settings. Then, in the Render Settings dialog box, choose Half from the Resolution menu, and click OK.

4 Click the orange, underlined words next to Output Module. Then, in the Output Module Settings dialog box, choose QuickTime from the Format menu.

5 Click Format Options in the Output Module Settings dialog box. Then do the following in the QuickTime Options dialog box, and click OK:

   • Choose H.264 from the Video Codec menu.

   • Select Limit Data Rate To in the Bitrate Settings area.

   • Change the data rate limit to **8000** kbps.

6 In the Output Module Settings dialog box, make sure Audio Output Auto is chosen in the Audio Output pop-up menu. Then click OK.

When Audio Output Auto is selected, After Effects automatically detects active audio in the composition.

7 Click the orange, underlined text next to Output To, navigate to the Lesson12 folder, and click Save.

8 Click Render in the Render Queue panel to render the composition.

9 When After Effects has finished rendering the composition, play the QuickTime movie to admire your work!

Review questions

1 What does the 3D Camera Tracker effect do?

2 How can you make an added 3D element look like it is the same size as elements that are farther from the camera?

3 Can you use DSLR footage with the 3D Camera Tracker?

Review answers

1   The 3D Camera Tracker effect automatically analyzes the motion present in existing 2D footage, extracts the position and lens type of the real camera that shot the scene, and creates a new 3D camera in After Effects to match it. The effect also overlays 3D track points onto the 2D footage, so you can easily attach new 3D layers onto the original footage.

2   To make an added 3D element appear to recede, so that it looks like it's farther from the camera, adjust its Scale property. Adjusting the Scale property keeps its perspective locked with the rest of the composition.

3   Yes, you can use DSLR footage with the 3D Camera Tracker. However, if you're using DSLR footage, first evaluate the footage to identify any wobbling, skewing, or other artifacts from a rolling shutter. If there are any artifacts, correct the footage using the Rolling Shutter Repair effect before applying the 3D Camera Tracker effect.

13 ADVANCED EDITING TECHNIQUES

Lesson overview

In this lesson, you'll learn how to do the following:

- Stabilize a shaky camera shot.

- Use single-point motion tracking to track one object in a shot to another object in a shot.

- Perform multipoint tracking using perspective corner-pinning.

- Use Imagineer Systems mocha for After Effects to track motion.

- Create a particle system.

- Use the Timewarp effect to create slow-motion video.

This lesson will take approximately 2 hours to complete. Download the Lesson13 project files from the Lesson & Update Files tab on your Account page at www.peachpit.com, if you haven't already done so. As you work on this lesson, you'll preserve the start files. If you need to restore the start files, download them from your Account page.

PROJECT: SPECIAL EFFECTS AND EDITING TECHNIQUES

After Effects provides advanced motion stabilization, motion tracking, high-end effects, and other features for the most demanding production environments.

Getting started

In previous lessons, you've used many of the essential 2D and 3D tools you need for motion graphics design. But Adobe After Effects also offers motion stabilization, motion tracking, advanced keying tools, distortion effects, the capability to retime footage using the Timewarp effect, support for high dynamic range (HDR) color images, network rendering, and much more. In this lesson, you will learn how to use Warp Stabilizer VFX to stabilize a handheld camera shot, how to track one object to another in an image so that their motion is synchronized, and how to use corner-pinning to track an object with perspective. Finally, you will explore some of the high-end digital effects available in After Effects: a particle system generator and the Timewarp effect.

This lesson includes multiple projects. Take a peek at all of them before beginning.

1 Make sure the following files are in the AECC_CIB/Lessons/Lesson13 folder on your hard disk, or download them from your Account page at www.peachpit.com now:

   • In the Assets folder: flowers.mov, Group_Approach[DV].mov, majorspoilers. mov, metronome.mov, mocha_tracking.mov, multipoint_tracking.mov

   • In the Sample_Movies folder: Lesson13_Multipoint.mov, Lesson13_ Particles.mov, Lesson13_Stabilize.mov, Lesson13_Timewarp.mov, Lesson13_Tracking.mov

● **Note:** You can view these movies all at once or, if you don't plan to complete these exercises in one session, you can watch each sample movie just before you are ready to complete the associated exercise.

2 Open and play the sample movies in the Lesson13/Sample_Movies folder to see the projects you will create in this lesson.

3 When you're done, quit QuickTime Player. You may delete these sample movies from your hard disk if you have limited storage space.

Using Warp Stabilizer VFX

If you shoot footage using a handheld camera, you will probably end up with shaky shots. Unless this look is intentional, you'll want to stabilize your shots to eliminate unwanted motion.

Warp Stabilizer VFX in After Effects automatically removes extraneous jitters. When played back, the motion appears smooth, because the layer itself is scaled and moves incrementally to offset the unwanted movement.

Bicubic scaling

When you scale video footage or an image to a larger size, After Effects must sample data to add information where none existed before. You can choose which sampling method After Effects uses when scaling a layer. For details, see After Effects help.

In previous versions, After Effects has used only bilinear sampling. Bicubic sampling, new in After Effects CC, uses a more complex algorithm that typically provides better results when color transitions are more gradual, as in nearly all real-world photographic images. Bilinear scaling may be a better option for sharp-edged graphics.

To choose a sampling method for a layer, select the layer, and choose Layer > Quality > Bicubic or Bilinear. Bicubic and bilinear sampling are available only for layers that are set to Best quality. (To change a layer's quality setting to Best, choose Layer > Quality > Best.)

Setting up the project

As you start After Effects, restore the default application settings for After Effects. See "Restoring default preferences" on page 2.

1 Start After Effects, and then immediately hold down Ctrl+Alt+Shift (Windows) or Command+Option+Shift (Mac OS) to restore default preferences settings. When prompted, click OK to delete your preferences.

2 Click Close to close the Welcome screen.

After Effects opens to display a new, untitled project.

3 Choose File > Save As > Save As.

4 In the Save As dialog box, navigate to the AECC_CIB/Lessons/Lesson13/ Finished_Projects folder.

5 Name the project **Lesson13_Stabilize.aep**, and then click Save.

Importing the footage

You need to import one footage item to start this project.

1   Double-click an empty area of the Project panel to open the Import File dialog box.

2   Navigate to the AECC_CIB/ Lessons/Lesson13/Assets folder. Select the flowers.mov file, and then click Import or Open.

Creating the composition

You'll start by creating the composition.

1   Drag the flowers.mov clip in the Project panel onto the Create A New Composition button (🔳) at the bottom of the panel.

After Effects creates a new composition named Flowers with the same pixel size, aspect ratio, frame rate, and duration of the source clip.

2   Click the RAM Preview button in the Preview panel to preview the footage. Press the spacebar to stop the preview when you've seen the whole clip.

This clip was shot with a handheld camera in the late afternoon. A slight breeze rustles the vegetation, and the camera moves unsteadily.

Applying Warp Stabilizer VFX

Warp Stabilizer VFX starts analyzing footage as soon as you apply it. Stabilization is a background process, so you can work on other compositions while it finishes. How long it takes depends on your system. After Effects displays a blue banner while it analyzes the footage and an orange banner while it applies stabilization.

1   Select the flowers.mov layer in the Timeline panel, and choose Animation > Warp Stabilizer VFX. The blue banner appears immediately.

2   When Warp Stabilizer VFX has finished stabilizing, and the orange banner has disappeared, create another RAM preview to view the changes.

3   Press the spacebar to stop the preview.

The clip is still shaky, but it's smoother than it was initially. Warp Stabilizer VFX moved and repositioned the footage. To see how it applied changes, view the effects in the Effect Controls panel. For example, the clip's borders were scaled up (to about 103%) to hide black gaps that occur when the image is repositioned in the stabilization process. You'll adjust the settings that Warp Stabilizer VFX uses.

Adjusting the Warp Stabilizer VFX settings

You'll change the settings in the Effect Controls panel to make the shot smoother.

1   In the Effect Controls panel, increase the Smoothness amount to **75%**.

Warp Stabilizer VFX immediately begins stabilizing again. It doesn't need to analyze the footage, because the initial analysis data is stored in memory.

2   When Warp Stabilizer VFX has finished, create another RAM preview to view the changes.

3   Press the spacebar to stop playback when you're done.

It's better, but still a little rough. The Auto-scale setting in the Effect Controls panel now displays 103.7%; the effect moved the frames more dramatically, requiring more scaling to eliminate black gaps around the edges.

Rather than change the amount Warp Stabilizer VFX smooths the footage, now you'll change its goal.

4   In the Effect Controls panel, choose No Motion from the Result menu.

With this setting, Warp Stabilizer VFX attempts to lock the camera in position. This requires even more scaling. When No Motion is selected, the Smoothness option is dimmed.

5   When the orange banner disappears, create another RAM preview. Press the spacebar to stop the playback.

Now the camera stays in position, so that the movement you notice is the rustling of the flowers in the wind, not the shakiness of the camera. In order to achieve this effect, Warp Stabilizer VFX had to scale the clip to 112.4% of its original size.

Fine-tuning the results

The default analysis works well most of the time, but sometimes you may need to massage the end results even further. In this project, the clip skews subtly in a few places, most noticeably at about the five-second mark. Casual viewers may not notice the problem, but a keen producer will. You'll change the method that Warp Stabilizer VFX uses to remove the skew.

1   In the Effect Controls panel, choose Position, Scale, Rotation from the Method menu.

2   Choose Stabilize Only from the Framing menu.

3   Increase the Additional Scale to **114%**.

Note: Scaling a video layer up degrades the image. A good rule of thumb is to not increase the layer larger than 15% of the original source.

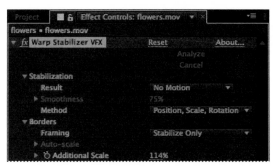

4   Create another RAM preview.

Now the shot looks rock-steady. The only movement is that caused by the wind rustling the flowers.

5   Press the spacebar to stop the playback when you're done.

6   Choose File > Save to save your work.

7   Choose File > Close Project.

As you have discovered, stabilizing a shot is not without its drawbacks. To compensate for the movement or rotation data applied to the layer, the frames must be scaled, which could ultimately degrade the footage. If you really need to use the shot in your production, this may be the best compromise.

▶ **Tip:** You can use Warp Stabilizer VFX advanced settings to achieve more complex effects, too. To learn more, see *Adobe After Effects CC Visual Effects and Compositing Studio Techniques*, available from Adobe Press.

Warp Stabilizer VFX settings

This is just a summary of the Warp Stabilizer VFX settings to help you get started. To learn more about the settings, and to read more tips for using the effect successfully, see After Effects Help.

- **Result** controls the intended result. Smooth Motion makes camera movement smoother, but doesn't eliminate it; use the Smoothness setting to control how smooth the movement becomes. No Motion attempts to remove all of the camera motion.

- **Method** specifies the most complex operation the Warp Stabilizer VFX performs on the footage to stabilize it: Position, which is based on position data only; Position, Scale, Rotation, which uses these three types of data; Perspective, which effectively corner-pins the entire frame; or Subspace Warp (the default), which attempts to warp various parts of the frame differently to stabilize the entire frame.

- **Borders** settings adjust how borders (the moving edges) are treated for footage that is stabilized. Framing controls how the edges appear in a stabilizing result, and determines whether the effect crops, scales, or synthesizes edges using material from other frames.

- **Auto-scale** displays the current auto-scale amount, and allows you to set limits on the amount of auto-scaling.

- **Advanced** settings give you even greater control over the actions of the Warp Stabilizer VFX effect.

Using single-point motion tracking

With the increase in the number of productions that incorporate digital elements into final shots, compositors need an easy way to synchronize computer-generated effects with film or video backgrounds. After Effects lets you do this with the capability to follow, or track, a defined area in the shot, and to apply that movement to other layers. These layers can contain text, effects, images, or other footage. The resulting visual effect precisely matches the original moving footage.

When you track motion in an After Effects composition that contains multiple layers, the default tracking type is Transform. This type of motion tracking tracks position and/or rotation to apply to another layer. When tracking position, this option creates one track point, and generates Position keyframes. When tracking rotation, this option creates two track points, and produces Rotation keyframes.

In this exercise, you will track a shape layer to the weighted arm of a metronome. This will be especially challenging, as the camera operator chose not to use a tripod.

Setting up the project

If you've just completed the first project, and After Effects is open, skip to step 3. Otherwise, restore the default application settings for After Effects. See "Restoring default preferences" on page 2.

1 Start After Effects, and then immediately hold down Ctrl+Alt+Shift (Windows) or Command+Option+Shift (Mac OS) to restore default preferences settings. When prompted, click OK to delete your preferences.

2 Click Close to close the Welcome screen.

After Effects opens to display a new, untitled project.

3 Choose File > Save As > Save As.

4 In the Save As dialog box, navigate to the AECC_CIB/Lessons/Lesson13/ Finished_Projects folder.

5 Name the project **Lesson13_Tracking.aep**, and then click Save.

Creating the composition

You need to import one footage item to start this project. You'll use it to create the composition.

1 Double-click an empty area of the Project panel to open the Import File dialog box.

2 Navigate to the AECC_CIB/Lessons/Lesson13/Assets folder. Select the metronome.mov file, and then click Import or Open.

3 In the Project panel, drag the metronome.mov clip onto the Create A New Composition button at the bottom of the panel.

After Effects creates a new composition named Metronome with the same pixel size, aspect ratio, frame rate, and duration of the source clip.

4 Drag the current-time indicator across the time ruler to manually preview the footage.

Creating a shape layer

You're going to attach a star to the end of the metronome. First, you need to create the star. You'll use a shape layer.

1 Press the Home key or move the current-time indicator to the beginning of the time ruler, and then click an empty area of the Timeline panel to deselect the layer.

2   Select the Star tool (☆), hidden behind the Rectangle tool in the Tools panel.

3   Click the Fill Color swatch, and select a light yellow such as R=**220**,
    G=**250**, B=**90**. Click the word *Stroke*, select None in the Stroke Options dialog
    box, and click OK.

4   In the Composition panel, draw a small star.

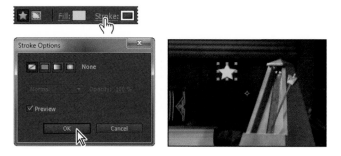

5   Use the Selection tool to position the star over the weighted end of the
    pendulum arm.

6   Select Shape Layer 1 to see the layer's anchor point. Use the Pan Behind (⊠) tool
    to move the anchor point to the center of the star shape, if it isn't already there.

Positioning the track point

After Effects tracks motion by matching pixels from a selected area in a frame
to pixels in each succeeding frame. You create tracking points to specify the area
to track. A track point contains a feature region, a search region, and an attach
point. After Effects displays the track point in the Layer panel as it tracks.

You will track the metronome weight (the rhombus at the end of its arm) by placing tracking regions around the area that you'll track another layer to. With the star shape added to the Tracking composition, you are ready to position the track point.

1   Select the metronome.mov layer in the Timeline panel.

2   Choose Animation > Track Motion.

The Tracker panel opens, and After Effects opens the selected layer in the Layer panel. A Track Point 1 indicator is in the center of the image.

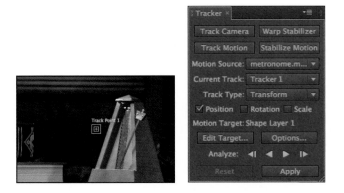

Notice the settings in the Tracker panel: Metronome.mov is selected in the Motion Source menu. The Current Track is Tracker 1, and the Motion Target is Shape Layer 1, because After Effects automatically sets the Motion Target to the layer immediately above the source layer.

Now, you'll position your track point.

3   Using the Selection tool (➤), move the Track Point 1 indicator (drag the empty portion of the feature region) in the Layer panel over the metronome weight.

4   Enlarge the search region (the outer box) to encompass the area around the pendulum. Then adjust the feature region (the inner box) within the weight.

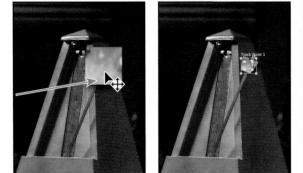

● **Note:** In this exercise, you want the star to move atop the metronome weight. However, if you wanted an object to move in relationship to the tracked area but not on top of it, you could reposition the attach point accordingly.

Moving and resizing the track points

In setting up motion tracking, it's often necessary to refine a track point by adjusting its feature region, search region, and attach point. You can resize or move these items independently or in groups by dragging with the Selection tool. The pointer icon changes to reflect one of many different activities.

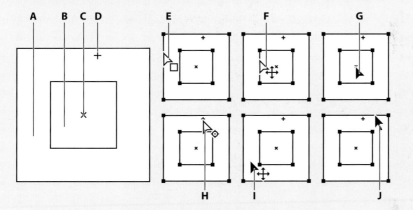

Track point components (left) and Selection tool pointer icons (right):
A. Search region **B.** Feature region **C.** Keyframe marker **D.** Attach point
E. Moves search region **F.** Moves both regions **G.** Moves entire track point
H. Moves attach point **I.** Moves entire track point **J.** Resizes region

- To turn feature region magnification on or off, choose Magnify Feature When Dragging from the Tracker panel menu. A check mark appears next to the option when it's on.

- To move only the search region, using the Selection tool, drag the edge of the search region; the Move Search Region pointer (⮫) appears (E, above).

- To move just the feature and search regions together, Alt-drag (Windows) or Option-drag (Mac OS) with the Selection tool inside the feature or search region; the Move Both Regions pointer (⮫) appears (F, above).

- To move only the attach point, using the Selection tool, drag the attach point; the Move Attach Point pointer (⮫) appears (H, above).

- To resize the feature or search region, drag a corner handle (J, above).

- To move the feature region, search region, and attach point together, drag with the Selection tool inside the track point area (avoiding the region edges and the attach point); the Move Track Point pointer (⮫) appears.

For more information about track points, see After Effects Help.

Analyzing and applying tracking

Now that the search and feature regions are defined, you can apply the tracker.

Note: The tracking analysis may take quite a while. The larger the search and feature regions, the longer After Effects takes to analyze tracking.

1 Click the Analyze Forward button (▶) in the Tracker panel. Watch the analysis to ensure the track point stays with the metronome weight. If it doesn't, press the spacebar to stop the analysis, and reposition the feature region. (See the sidebar "Checking for drift.")

2 When the analysis is complete, click the Apply button.

3 In the Motion Tracker Apply Options dialog box, click OK to apply the tracking to the x and y dimensions.

Checking for drift

As an image moves in a shot, the lighting, surrounding objects, and angle of the object can all change, making a once-distinct feature no longer identifiable at the subpixel level. It takes time to develop an eye for choosing a trackable feature. Even with careful planning and practice, you may often find that the feature region drifts away from the desired feature. Readjusting the feature and search regions, changing the tracking options, and trying again are all standard parts of digital tracking. When you notice drifting occurring, try the following:

1 Immediately stop the analysis by pressing the spacebar.

2 Move the current-time indicator back to the last good tracked point. You can see this in the Layer panel.

3 Reposition and/or resize the feature and search regions, being careful to not accidentally move the attach point. Moving the attach point will cause a noticeable jump in your tracked layer.

4 Click the Analyze Forward button to resume tracking.

The motion-tracking data is added to the Timeline panel, where you can see that the track data is in the metronome layer, but the results are applied to the Position property of the Shape Layer 1 layer.

4 Watch a RAM preview. The star not only follows the pendulum; it moves with the camera's movement.

5 When you're ready, press the spacebar to stop playback.

6 Hide the properties for both layers in the Timeline panel, choose File > Save, and then choose File > Close Project.

Motion tracking an element onto background footage can be fun. As long as you have a stable feature to track, single-point motion tracking can be quite easy.

Using multipoint tracking

After Effects also offers two more advanced types of tracking that use multiple tracking points: parallel corner-pinning and perspective corner-pinning.

When you track using parallel corner-pinning, you simultaneously track three points in the source footage. After Effects calculates the position of a fourth point to keep the lines between the points parallel. When the movement of the points is applied to the target layer, the Corner Pin effect distorts the layer to simulate skew, scale, and rotation, but not perspective. Parallel lines remain parallel, and relative distances are preserved.

When you track using perspective corner-pinning, you simultaneously track four points in the source footage. When applied to the target footage, the Corner Pin effect uses the movement of the four points to distort the layer, simulating changes in perspective.

You'll attach an animation to a computer monitor using perspective corner-pinning. If you haven't already watched the sample movie for this exercise, do so now.

Setting up the project

Start by launching After Effects and creating a new project.

1   If it's not already open, start After Effects, and then immediately hold down Ctrl+Alt+Shift (Windows) or Command+Option+Shift (Mac OS) to restore default preferences settings. When prompted, click OK to delete your preferences, and click Close to close the Welcome screen.

After Effects opens to display an empty, untitled project.

2   Choose File > Save As > Save As.

3   In the Save As dialog box, navigate to the AECC_CIB/Lessons/Lesson13/ Finished_Projects folder.

4   Name the project **Lesson13_Multipoint.aep,** and then click Save.

5   Double-click an empty area of the Project panel to open the Import File dialog box, and then navigate to the AECC_CIB/Lessons/Lesson13/Assets folder.

6   Ctrl-click (Windows) or Command-click (Mac OS) to select both the majorspoilers.mov and multipoint_tracking.mov files, and then click Import or Open.

7   Press Ctrl+N (Windows) or Command+N (Mac OS) to create a new composition.

8   In the Composition Settings dialog box, do the following, and then click OK:

- Type **Multipoint_Tracking** in the Composition Name field.

- Make sure the Preset pop-up menu is set to NTSC DV.

- Set the Duration to **7:05**, the length of the majorspoilers.mov file.

9 Drag the multipoint_tracking.mov item from the Project panel to the Timeline panel. Manually preview the footage, which is shaky because it was shot with a handheld camera.

Because you're positioning the majorspoilers.mov layer on the computer monitor, it will be fairly easy to place tracking markers on the flat plane. By default, the tracker tracks by luminance, so you will use the areas around the screen that have high contrast differences for tracking.

10 Press the Home key or move the current-time indicator to the beginning of the time ruler.

11 Drag the majorspoilers.mov footage item from the Project panel to the Timeline panel, placing it at the top of the layer stack.

12 To make it easier to see the underlying movie as you place the tracking points, turn off the Video switch for the majorspoilers.mov layer in the Timeline panel.

Positioning the track points

You're ready to add the track points to the multipoint_tracking.mov layer.

1 Select the multipoint_tracking.mov layer in the Timeline panel.

2 Choose Window > Tracker to open the Tracker panel if it isn't open.

3 In the Tracker panel, choose multipoint_tracking.mov from the Motion Source menu.

4 Select the multipoint_tracking.mov layer again, and then click Track Motion.

The desk scene opens in the Layer panel, with a track point indicator in the center of the image. However, you will be tracking four points in order to attach the animated movie to the computer screen.

5   Choose Perspective Corner Pin from the Track Type menu.

Three more track point indicators appear in the Layer panel.

▶ Tip: Refer to the sidebar "Moving and resizing the track points" for help moving the track point regions.

6   Drag the track points to four different high-contrast areas of the image. The four corners of the computer screen provide excellent contrast. Use the following image as a guide. (Because the areas of high contrast are also where you want to attach the majorspoilers layer, you don't need to move the attach points.)

▶ Tip: It may be helpful to zoom in when placing and adjusting the track points. Zoom out again when you have finished.

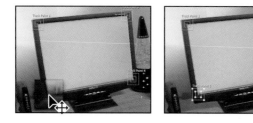

Applying the multipoint tracker

You're ready to analyze the data and apply the tracker.

1   Click the Analyze Forward button (▶) in the Tracker panel. When the analysis is complete, click the Apply button to calculate the tracking.

● Note: If the composition doesn't appear in the Composition panel, click in the Timeline window to move the current-time indicator and refresh the display.

2   Notice the results in the Timeline panel: You can see the Corner Pin and Position property keyframes for the majorspoilers layer and the track point data for the motion_tracking layer.

3   Make the majorspoilers layer visible again, move the current-time indicator to the beginning of the timeline, and watch a RAM preview to see the results of the tracker.

4   When you're done watching the preview, press the spacebar to stop playback.

If you don't like the results, return to the Tracker panel, click the Reset button, and try again. With practice, you will become adept at identifying good feature regions.

5   Hide the layer properties to keep the Timeline panel neat, and choose File > Save to save your work.

6   Choose File > Close Project.

mocha for After Effects

In most cases, you'll get better and more accurate tracking results using mocha from Imagineer Systems to track points in video. A version of mocha is included with After Effects. To track using mocha, choose Animation > Track In Mocha AE.

One advantage of mocha for After Effects is that you don't have to accurately place tracking points to obtain a perfect track. Rather than using tracking points, mocha for After Effects uses a planar tracker, which attempts to track an object's translation, rotation, and scaling data based on the movement of a user-defined plane. Planes provide more detail to the computer than is possible with single-point and multipoint tracking tools.

When you work with mocha for After Effects, you need to identify planes in a clip that coincide with movement you want to track. Planes don't have to be tabletops or walls. For example, if someone is waving goodbye, you can use their upper and lower limbs as two planes. After you track the planes, you can export the tracking data for use in After Effects.

mocha for After Effects uses two different spline technologies for tracking: X splines and Bezier splines. X splines may work better for tracking, especially with perspective motion, but Bezier splines work well, too, and are the industry standard.

To learn more about mocha for After Effects, choose Help > Online Help or Help > Offline Help in mocha.

We've saved some tracking data for the computer monitor in mocha for After Effects, so that you can apply it in After Effects if you'd like. To apply the data, follow these steps:

1   Create a new project in After Effects, and import the majorspoilers.mov and mocha_tracking.mov files from the Lesson13/Assets folder. Create a new composition from the mocha_tracking.mov file, and then drag the majorspoilers.mov file to the top of the layer stack in the Timeline panel.

2   Open the mocha_data.txt file (in the Lesson13/Optional_Mocha_Tutorial folder) in a text editor such as WordPad or TextEdit. (Don't use Notepad on Windows. It doesn't retain the mocha formatting, so After Effects doesn't recognize its content on the clipboard.) Choose Edit > Select All, and then Edit > Copy to copy all the data.

3   Select the majorspoilers.mov layer in the Timeline panel, and choose Edit > Paste. All the data is applied to the layer.

4   Watch a RAM preview to see the results.

Creating a particle simulation

After Effects includes several effects that do an excellent job of creating particle simulations. Two of them—CC Particle Systems II and CC Particle World—are based on the same engine. The major difference between the two is that Particle World enables you to move the particles in 3D space, rather than in a 2D layer.

In this exercise, you'll learn how to use the CC Particle Systems II effect to create a supernova that could be used as the opening of a science program or as a motion background. If you haven't already watched the sample movie for this exercise, do so now before continuing.

Setting up the project

Start by launching After Effects and creating a new composition.

1   If it's not already open, start After Effects, and then immediately hold down Ctrl+Alt+Shift (Windows) or Command+Option+Shift (Mac OS) to restore default preferences settings. When prompted, click OK to delete your preferences, and click Close to close the Welcome screen.

After Effects opens to display an empty, untitled project.

2   Choose File > Save As > Save As.

3   In the Save As dialog box, navigate to the AECC_CIB/Lessons/Lesson13/ Finished_Projects folder.

4   Name the project **Lesson13_Particles.aep**, and then click Save.

You don't need to import any footage items for this exercise. However, you do need to create the composition.

5   In After Effects, press Ctrl+N (Windows) or Command+N (Mac OS).

6   In the Composition Settings dialog box, do the following, and then click OK:

   • Type **Supernova** in the Composition Name field.

   • Choose NTSC D1 from the Preset pop-up menu.

   • Set the Duration to **10:00**.

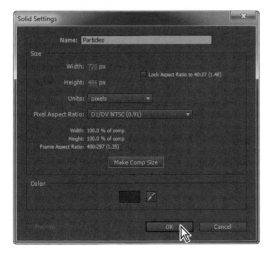

Creating a particle system

You will build the particle system from a solid layer, so you'll create that next.

1 Choose Layer > New > Solid to create a new solid layer.

2 In the Solid Settings dialog box, type **Particles** in the Name box.

3 Click Make Comp Size to make the layer the same size as the composition. Then click OK.

4   With the Particles layer selected in the Timeline panel, choose Effect > Simulation > CC Particle Systems II.

5   Go to 4:00 to see the particle system.

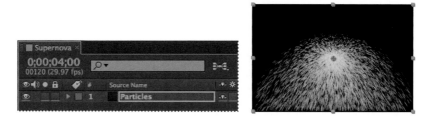

A large stream of yellow particles appears in the Composition panel.

Customizing the particle effect

You will turn this stream of particles into a supernova by customizing the settings in the Effect Controls panel.

1   Expand the Physics property group in the Effect Controls panel. The Explosive Animation setting works fine for this project, but instead of the particles falling down, you want them to flow out in all directions, so change the Gravity value to **0.0**.

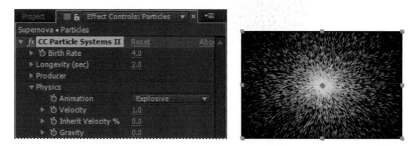

2   Hide the Physics property group, and expand the Particle property group. Then choose Faded Sphere from the Particle Type menu.

Now the particles look intergalactic. Don't stop there, though.

3   Change the Death Size to **1.50**, and increase the Size Variation to **100%**.

This allows the particles to change birth size randomly.

4   Reduce the Max Opacity to **55%** to make the particles semitransparent.

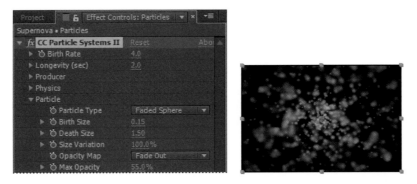

5   Click the Birth Color swatch, and change the color to R=**255**, G=**200**, B=**50** to give the particles a yellow hue at birth.

6   Click the Death Color swatch, and change the color to R=**180**, G=**180**, B=**180** to give the particles a light gray hue as they fade out.

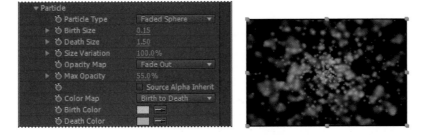

7   To keep the particles from staying onscreen too long, decrease the Longevity value to **0.8** seconds.

● **Note:** Even though they're at the top of the Effect Controls panel, it is often easier to adjust the Longevity and Birth Rate settings after you have set the other particle properties.

The Faded Sphere particle type softens the look, but the particle shapes are still too sharply defined. You will fix that by blurring the layer to blend the particles with one another.

Understanding Particle Systems II properties

Particle systems have a unique vocabulary. Some of the key settings are explained here for your reference. They're listed in the order in which they appear (top to bottom) in the Effect Controls panel.

Birth Rate Controls the number of particles generated per second. The value itself is arbitrary and does not equal the actual number of particles being generated. However, the higher the number, the more densely packed the particles become.

Longevity Determines how long the particles are visible.

Producer Position Controls the center point or origin of the particle system. The position is set based on the x, y coordinates. All particles emanate from this single point. You can control the size of the producer by making adjustments to the x and y radius settings. The higher these values, the larger the producer point will be. A high x value and a y value of zero (0) result in a line.

Velocity Controls the speed of particles. The higher the number, the faster the particles move.

Inherent Velocity % Determines how much of the velocity is passed along to the particles when the Producer Position is animated. A negative value causes the particles to move in the opposite direction.

Gravity Determines how fast particles fall. The higher the value, the faster the particles fall. A negative value causes particles to rise.

Resistance Simulates particles interacting with air or water, slowing over time.

Direction Determines which directions the particles flow. Use with the Direction Animation type.

Extra Introduces randomness into the movement of the particles.

Birth/Death Size Determines the size of the particles when they are created and when they expire.

Opacity Map Controls opacity changes for the particle over its lifetime.

Color Map Use with the Birth and Death colors to shade the particles over time.

8   Hide the CC Particle Systems II effect properties.

9   Choose Effect > Blur & Sharpen > Fast Blur.

10 In the Fast Blur area of the Effect Controls panel, increase the Blurriness value to **10**. Then select Repeat Edge Pixels to keep the particles from being cropped at the edge of the frame.

Creating the sun

You will now create a bright halo of light that will go behind the particles.

1   Go to 0:07.

2   Press Ctrl+Y (Windows) or Command+Y (Mac OS) to create a new solid layer.

3   In the Solid Settings dialog box, do the following:

•   Type **Sun** in the Name box.

•   Click Make Comp Size to make the layer the same size as the composition.

•   Click the color swatch to make the layer the same yellow as the Birth Color of the particles (**255, 200, 50**).

•   Click OK to close the Solid Settings dialog box.

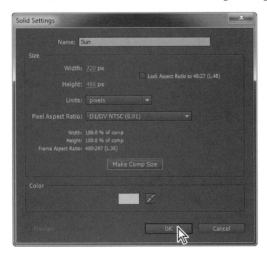

4 Drag the Sun layer below the Particles layer in the Timeline panel.

5 Select the Ellipse tool (◯), which is hidden behind the Rectangle tool (▢) or the Star tool (☆) in the Tools panel, and Shift-drag in the Composition panel to draw a circle with a radius of roughly 100 pixels, or one-fourth the width of the composition.

6 Using the Selection tool (▶), drag the mask shape to the center of the Composition panel.

7 With the Sun layer selected in the Timeline panel, press the F key to reveal its Mask Feather property. Increase the Mask Feather amount to **100, 100** pixels.

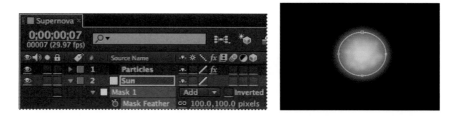

8 Press Alt+[(Window) or Option+[(Mac OS) to set the In point of the layer to the current time.

9 Hide the properties for the Sun layer.

Lighting the darkness

Since the sun is bright, it should illuminate the surrounding darkness.

1 Make sure the current-time indicator is still at 0:07.

2 Press Ctrl+Y (Windows) or Command+Y (Mac OS) to create a new solid layer.

3 In the Solid Settings dialog box, name the layer **Background**, click the Make Comp Size button to make the layer the same size as the composition, and then click OK to create the layer.

4 In the Timeline panel, drag the Background layer to the bottom position in the layer stack.

5 With the Background layer selected in the Timeline panel, choose Effect > Generate > Gradient Ramp.

The Gradient Ramp effect creates a color gradient, blending it with the original image. You can create linear ramps or radial ramps, and vary the position and colors of the ramp over time. Use the Start Of Ramp and End Of Ramp settings to specify the start and end positions. Use the Ramp Scatter setting to disperse the ramp colors and eliminate banding.

6 In the Gradient Ramp area of the Effect Controls panel, do the following:

- Change Start Of Ramp to **360, 240** and End Of Ramp to **360, 525**.

- Choose Radial Ramp from the Ramp Shape menu.

- Click the Start Color swatch, and set the start color to dark blue (R=**0**, G=**25**, B=**135**).

- Set the End Color to black (R=**0**, G=**0**, B=**0**).

7 Press Alt+[(Windows) or Option+[(Mac OS) to set the In point of the layer to the current time.

Adding a lens flare

To tie all the elements together, you'll add a lens flare to simulate an explosion.

1 Press the Home key or move the current-time indicator to the beginning of the time ruler.

2 Press Ctrl+Y (Windows) or Command+Y (Mac OS) to create a new solid layer.

3 In the Solid Settings dialog box, name the layer **Nova**, click the Make Comp Size button to make the layer the same size as the composition, set the Color to black (R=**0**, G=**0**, B=**0**), and then click OK. The Nova layer should be at the top of the layer stack in the Timeline panel.

4 With the Nova layer selected in the Timeline panel, choose Effect > Generate > Lens Flare.

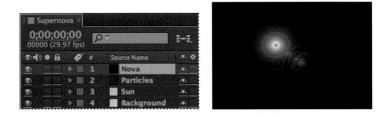

5 In the Lens Flare area of the Effect Controls panel, do the following:

- Change Flare Center to **360, 240**.

- Choose 50–300mm Zoom from the Lens Type menu.

- Decrease Flare Brightness to **0%**, and then click the Flare Brightness stopwatch icon (⏱) to create an initial keyframe.

6 Go to 0:10.

7 Increase the Flare Brightness to **240%**.

8 Go to 1:04, and decrease the Flare Brightness to **100%**.

9   With the Nova layer selected in the Timeline panel, press the U key to see the animated Lens Flare property.

10 Right-click (Windows) or Control-click (Mac OS) the ending Flare Brightness keyframe, and choose Keyframe Assistant > Easy Ease In.

11 Right-click (Windows) or Control-click (Mac OS) the beginning Flare Brightness keyframe, and choose Keyframe Assistant > Easy Ease Out.

Finally, you need to make the layers under the Nova layer visible in the composition.

12 Press F2 to deselect all layers, and choose Columns > Modes from the Timeline panel menu. Then choose Screen from the Mode menu for the Nova layer.

13 Watch a RAM preview. When you're done, press the spacebar to stop the preview.

14 Choose File > Save, and then choose File > Close Project.

About high dynamic range (HDR) footage

After Effects also supports high dynamic range (HDR) color.

The dynamic range (ratio between dark and bright regions) in the physical world far exceeds the range of human vision and of images that are printed or displayed on a monitor. But while human eyes can adapt to very different brightness levels, most cameras and computer monitors can capture and reproduce only a limited dynamic range. Photographers, motion-picture artists, and others working with digital images must be selective about what's important in a scene, because they're working with a limited dynamic range.

HDR footage opens up a world of possibilities, because it can represent a very wide dynamic range through the use of 32-bit floating-point numeric values. Floating-point numeric representations allow the same number of bits to describe a much larger range of values than integer (fixed-point) values. HDR values can contain brightness levels, including objects as bright as a candle flame or the sun, that far exceed those in 8-bit-per-channel (bpc) or 16-bpc (non-floating-point) mode. Lower dynamic range 8-bpc and 16-bpc modes can represent RGB levels only from black to white, which represents an extremely small segment of the dynamic range in the real world.

Currently, HDR images are used mostly in motion pictures, special effects, 3D work, and some high-end photography. After Effects supports HDR images in a variety of ways. For example, you can create 32-bpc projects to work with HDR footage, and you can adjust the exposure, or the amount of light captured in an image, when working with HDR images in After Effects. For more information about support in After Effects for HDR images, see After Effects Help.

Retiming playback using the Timewarp effect

The Timewarp effect in After Effects gives you precise control over a wide range of parameters when changing the playback speed of a layer, including interpolation methods, motion blur, and source cropping to eliminate unwanted artifacts.

In this exercise, you will use the Timewarp effect to change the speed of a clip for a dramatic slow-motion playback. If you haven't already watched the sample movie for this exercise, do so now.

Setting up the project

Start by launching After Effects and creating a new project.

1   If After Effects isn't open, start it, and then immediately hold down Ctrl+Alt+Shift (Windows) or Command+Option+Shift (Mac OS) to restore default preferences settings. When prompted, click OK to delete your preferences, and click Close to close the Welcome screen.

After Effects opens to display an empty, untitled project.

2   Choose File > Save As > Save As.

3   In the Save As dialog box, navigate to the AECC_CIB/Lessons/Lesson13/Finished_Projects folder.

4   Name the project **Lesson13_Timewarp.aep**, and then click Save.

5   Double-click an empty area of the Project panel to open the Import File dialog box. Then navigate to the AECC_CIB/Lessons/Lesson13/Assets folder on your hard disk, select the Group_Approach[DV].mov, and click Import or Open.

6   Click OK in the Interpret Footage dialog box.

Now, you'll create a new composition based on the footage item's aspect ratio and its duration.

7   Drag the Group_Approach[DV].mov file onto the Create A New Composition button (■) at the bottom of the Project panel.

After Effects creates a new composition named for the source file, and displays it in the Composition and Timeline panels.

8   Choose File > Save to save your work.

Using Timewarp

In the source footage, a group of young people approaches the camera at a steady pace. At around 2 seconds, the director would like the motion to begin to slow down to 10%, and then ramp back up to full speed at 7:00.

1 With the Group_Approach [DV] layer selected in the Timeline panel, choose Effect > Time > Timewarp.

2 In the Timewarp area of the Effect Controls panel, choose Pixel Motion from the Method menu and Speed from the Adjust Time By menu.

With Pixel Motion selected, Timewarp creates new frames by analyzing the pixel movement in nearby frames and creating motion vectors. The Speed option controls the time adjustment by percentage rather than by a specific frame.

3 Go to 2:00.

4 In the Effect Controls panel, set the Speed to **100**, and click the stopwatch (⏱) to set a keyframe.

This tells Timewarp to keep the speed of the clip at 100% until the 2-second mark.

5 Go to 5:00, and change the Speed to **10**. After Effects adds a keyframe.

6 Go to 7:00, and set the Speed to **100**. After Effects adds a keyframe.

● **Note:** Be patient. The RAM preview might take some time to calculate, but it will provide a more accurate playback than a spacebar preview.

7 Press the Home key or move the current-time indicator to the beginning of the time ruler, and then watch a RAM preview of the effect.

The speed adjustments are rather abrupt—not the smooth, slow-motion curve you would expect to see in a professional effect. This is because the keyframes are linear instead of curved. You'll fix that next.

8 Press the spacebar to stop playback when you're ready.

9 With the Group_Approach[DV] layer selected in the Timeline panel, press the U key to see the animated Timewarp Speed property.

10 Click the Graph Editor button () in the Timeline panel so you can see the Graph Editor instead of the layer bars. Make sure the Speed property name for the Group_Approach[DV] layer is selected. The Graph Editor displays its graph.

11 Click to select the first Speed keyframe (at 2:00), and then click the Easy Ease icon (𝌠) at the bottom of the Graph Editor.

This adjusts the influence into and out of the keyframe to smooth out sudden changes.

12 Repeat step 11 for the other two Speed keyframes in the motion graph, at 5:00 and 7:00.

▶ **Tip:** Close columns in the Timeline panel to see more icons in the Graph Editor. You can also apply an Easy Ease adjustment by pressing the F9 key.

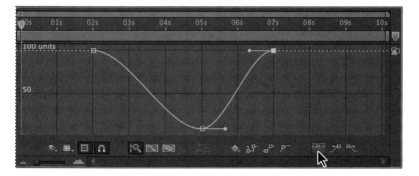

The motion graph is now smoother, but you can tweak it even more by dragging the Bezier handles.

Note: If you need a refresher on using Bezier handles, see Lesson 7, "Working with Masks."

13 Using the Bezier handles for the keyframes at 2:00 and 5:00, adjust the curve so that it resembles the following image.

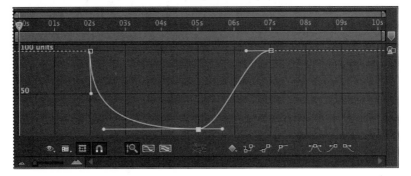

14 Watch another RAM preview. This time, the slow-motion Timewarp effect looks professional.

15 Choose File > Save to save the project, and then choose File > Close Project.

You've now experimented with some of the advanced features in After Effects, including motion stabilization, motion tracking, particle systems, and the Timewarp effect. To render and export any or all of the projects you completed in this lesson, see Lesson 14, "Rendering and Outputting," for instructions.

Review questions

1 What is Warp Stabilizer VFX, and when do you need to use it?

2 Why might drifting occur when you're tracking an image?

3 What is the birth rate in a particle effect?

4 What does the Timewarp effect do?

Review answers

1 Shooting footage using a handheld camera typically results in shaky shots. Unless this look is intentional, you will want to stabilize the shots to eliminate unwanted motion. Warp Stabilizer VFX in After Effects analyzes the movement and rotation of the target layer, and then makes adjustments to it. When played back, the motion appears smooth, because the layer itself moves incrementally to offset the unwanted motion. You can change the way Warp Stabilizer VFX crops, scales, and performs other adjustments by modifying settings for the effect.

2 Drifting occurs when the feature region loses the feature that's being tracked. As an image moves in a shot, the lighting, surrounding objects, and angle of the object can change, making a once-distinct feature unidentifiable at the subpixel level. Even with careful planning and practice, the feature region often drifts away from the desired feature. Readjusting the feature and search regions, changing the tracking options, and trying again are all standard procedures in digital tracking.

3 The birth rate in a particle effect determines how often new particles are created.

4 The Timewarp effect gives you precise control over a wide range of parameters to change the playback speed of a layer, including interpolation methods, motion blur, and source cropping to eliminate unwanted artifacts.

14

RENDERING AND OUTPUTTING

Lesson overview

In this lesson, you'll learn how to do the following:

- Create render-settings templates for the Render Queue.

- Create output-module templates for the Render Queue.

- Output movies using Adobe Media Encoder.

- Select the appropriate compressor for your delivery format.

- Use pixel aspect ratio correction.

- Output the final composition for NTSC broadcast video.

- Produce a test version of a composition.

- Create custom presets in Adobe Media Encoder.

- Render and output a web version of the final composition.

 The total amount of time required to complete this lesson depends in part on the speed of your processor and the amount of RAM available for rendering. The amount of hands-on time required is less than an hour. Download the Lesson14 project files from the Lesson & Update Files tab on your Account page at www.peachpit.com, if you haven't already done so. As you work on this lesson, you'll preserve the start files. If you need to restore the start files, download them from your Account page.

WEB

BROADCAST

The success of any project depends on your ability to deliver it in the format you need, whether it's for the web or broadcast output. Using Adobe After Effects and Adobe Media Encoder, you can render and export a final composition in a variety of formats and resolutions.

Getting started

This lesson continues from the point at which all preceding lessons end: when you're ready to output the final composition. In order to produce several versions of the animation for this lesson, you'll explore options available within the Render Queue panel and Adobe Media Encoder. For this lesson, we provide you with a starting project file that is essentially the final composition from Lesson 12 of this book.

1 Make sure the following files are in the AECC_CIB/Lessons/Lesson14 folder on your hard disk, or download them from your Account page at www.peachpit.com now:

- In the Assets folder: DesktopC.mov, Treasures_Music.aif, Treasures_Title.psd

- In the Start_Project_File folder: Lesson14_Start.aep

- In the Sample_Movies folder: Lesson14_Final_360p_Web.mp4, Lesson14_Final_1080p.mp4, Lesson14_Final_lowres_Web.mp4, Lesson14_Final_MPEG4.mov, Lesson14_HD_test_1080p.mp4

● **Note:** The Lesson14_HD_test_1080p.mp4 file includes only the first five seconds of the movie.

2 Open and play the sample movies for Lesson 14, which represent different final versions of the movie—rendered with different quality settings—that you created in Lesson 12. When you're done viewing the sample movies, quit QuickTime Player. You may delete the sample movies from your hard disk if you have limited storage space.

As always, when you begin the lesson, restore the default application settings for After Effects. See "Restoring default preferences" on page 2.

3 Start After Effects, and then immediately hold down Ctrl+Alt+Shift (Windows) or Command+Option+Shift (Mac OS). When prompted, click OK to delete your preferences. Click Close to close the Welcome screen.

4 Choose File > Open Project.

● **Note:** If you receive an error message about missing layer dependencies (Arial Narrow Regular), click OK.

5 Navigate to the AECC_CIB/Lessons/Lesson14/Start_Project_File folder, select the Lesson14_Start.aep file, and click Open.

6   Choose File > Save As > Save As.

7   In the Save As dialog box, navigate to the AECC_CIB/Lessons/Lesson14/ Finished_Project folder.

8   Name the project **Lesson14_Finished.aep**, and then click Save.

9   Choose Window > Render Queue to open the Render Queue panel.

Creating templates for the Render Queue

In previous lessons, you selected individual render and output-module settings on those occasions when you output your compositions. In this lesson, you'll create templates for both render settings and output-module settings. These templates are presets that you can use to streamline the setup process when you render items for the same type of delivery format. After you define templates, they appear in the Render Queue panel on the appropriate pop-up menu (Render Settings or Output Module). Then, when you're ready to process a job, you can simply select the template that is appropriate for the delivery format that your job requires, and the template applies all the settings.

Creating a render-settings template for test renderings

You'll create a render-settings template, selecting settings appropriate for rendering a test version of your final movie. A test version is smaller—and therefore renders faster—than a full-resolution movie. When you work with complex compositions that take relatively long times to render, it is a good practice to render a small test version first. This helps you find any final tweaks or blunders that you want to adjust before you take the time to render the final movie.

1   Choose Edit > Templates > Render Settings. The Render Settings Templates dialog box appears.

2   In the Settings area, click New to create a new template.

3 In the Render Settings area of the Render Settings dialog box, do the following:

- Leave Quality at Best.

- For Resolution, choose Third, which reduces the linear dimension of the composition to one-third.

4 In the Time Sampling area, do the following:

- For Frame Blending, choose Current Settings.

- For Motion Blur, choose Current Settings.

- For Time Span, choose Length Of Comp.

5 In the Frame Rate area, select Use This Frame Rate, and type **12** (fps). Then click OK to return to the Render Settings Templates dialog box.

6 For Settings Name, type **Test_lowres** (for *low resolution*).

7   Examine your settings, which now appear in the lower half of the dialog box.
    If you need to make any changes, click Edit to adjust the settings. Then click OK.

The Test_lowres option will be available on the Render Settings pop-up menu
in the Render Queue panel.

Creating templates for output modules

Using processes similar to those in the previous section, you'll create a template
to use for output-module settings. Each output-module template includes unique
combinations of settings that are appropriate for a specific type of output. You'll
create one that is appropriate for a low-resolution test version of the movie, or for
a web version of the movie.

1   Choose Edit > Templates > Output Module to open the Output Module Templates
    dialog box.

2   In the Settings area, click New to create a new template.

3   In the Output Module Settings dialog box, make sure the Format is QuickTime.

4 For Post-Render Action, choose Import.

5 In the Video Output area, click Format Options.

6 Select the following settings in the QuickTime Options dialog box:

- For Video Codec, choose MPEG-4 Video. This compressor automatically determines the color depth.

- Set the Quality slider to **80**.

- In the Advanced Settings area, select Key Frame Every, and then type **30** (frames).

- In the Bitrate Settings area, select Limit Data Rate To, and type **150** (kbps).

● **Note:** The IMA 4:1 compressor is commonly used when compressing audio for web or desktop playback.

7 Select the Audio tab, and choose IMA 4:1 from the Audio Codec menu.

8   Click OK to close the QuickTime Options dialog box and return to the Output Module Settings dialog box.

9   Choose Audio Output On from the pop-up menu at the bottom of the dialog box. Then choose the following audio settings, from left to right:

    • Rate: 22.050 kHz.

    • Use: Stereo.

10 Click OK to close the Output Module Settings dialog box.

11 In the lower half of the Output Module Templates dialog box, examine your settings, and click Edit if you need to make any changes.

12 For Settings Name, type **Test_MPEG4**, and then click OK. Now this output template will be available on the Output Module pop-up menu in the Render Queue panel.

As you might expect, greater compression and lower audio sample rates create smaller file sizes, but they also reduce the quality of the output. However, this low-resolution template is fine for creating test movies or movies for the web.

Exporting using the Render Queue

Now that you have created templates for your render settings and output modules, you can use them to export the test version of your movie.

About compression

Compression is essential to reduce the size of movies so that they can be stored, transmitted, and played back effectively. When exporting or rendering a movie file for playback on a specific type of device at a certain bandwidth, you choose a compressor/decompressor (also known as an encoder/decoder), or *codec*, to compress the information and generate a file that is readable by that type of device at that bandwidth.

A wide range of codecs is available; no single codec is the best for all situations. For example, the best codec for compressing cartoon animation is generally not efficient for compressing live-action video. When compressing a movie file, you can fine-tune it for the best-quality playback on a computer, video playback device, the web, or from a DVD player. Depending on which encoder you use, you may be able to reduce the size of compressed files by removing artifacts that interfere with compression, such as random camera motion and excessive film grain.

The codec you use must be available to your entire audience. For instance, if you use a hardware codec on a capture card, your audience must have the same capture card installed, or a software codec that emulates it.

For more about compression and codecs, see After Effects Help.

► **Tip:** Alternatively, you can drag the composition from the Project panel onto the Render Queue panel.

1 Select the DesktopC composition in the Project panel, and choose Composition > Add To Render Queue.

In the Render Queue panel, note the default settings in the Render Settings and Output Module pop-up menus. You'll change those settings to your low-resolution templates.

2 Choose Test_lowres from the Render Settings menu.

3 Choose Test_MPEG4 from the Output Module menu.

4 Click the orange, underlined words next to Output To.

5 In the Output Movie To dialog box, locate the AECC_CIB/Lessons/Lesson14 folder, and create a new folder called **Final_Movies**:

- In Windows, click the Create New Folder icon, and then type a name for the folder.

- In Mac OS, click the New Folder button, name the folder, and click Create.

6 Open the Final_Movies folder.

7 Name the file **Final_MPEG4.mov**, and then click Save to return to the Render Queue panel.

8 Choose File > Save to save your work.

● **Note:** You do not need to render a movie multiple times to export it to multiple formats with the same render settings. You can export multiple versions of the same rendered movie by adding output modules to a render item in the Render Queue panel.

9   Click the Render button in the Render Queue panel. After Effects renders the movie. If there were additional movies—or the same movie with different settings—in the queue, After Effects would render those, too.

When the processing is complete, the Final_MPEG4 movie appears in the Project panel.

To preview the movie, double-click it in the Project panel, and then create a RAM preview.

If you need to make any final changes to the movie, reopen the composition and make those adjustments now. Remember to save your work when you finish, and then output the test movie again using the appropriate settings. After examining the test movie and making any necessary changes, you'll proceed with outputting the movie for full-resolution broadcast.

Preparing movies for mobile devices

You can create movies in After Effects for playback on mobile devices, such as the Apple iPad and mobile phones. To render your movie, add the composition to the Adobe Media Encoder encoding queue, and choose an appropriate device-specific encoding preset.

For the best results, consider the limitations of mobile devices as you shoot footage and work with After Effects. For a small screen size, pay careful attention to lighting, and use a lower frame rate. See After Effects Help for more tips.

Rendering movies with Adobe Media Encoder

Your movie is ready for final output. Adobe Media Encoder, which is included with After Effects, lets you easily render your movie in multiple high-quality formats.

Rendering a broadcast-quality movie

First, you'll select settings to render your movie in a quality suitable for broadcast.

1   In the Project panel, select the DesktopC composition, and choose Composition > Add To Adobe Media Encoder Queue.

After Effects opens Adobe Media Encoder, and adds your composition with default render settings. Your default settings may vary from ours.

2   Click the orange link in the Preset column.

Adobe Media Encoder connects to the Dynamic Link server.

● **Note:** If you don't need to change anything else in the Export Settings dialog box, you can change the preset using the Preset pop-up menu in the Queue panel.

3   When the Export Settings dialog box appears, choose HD 1080p 23.976 from the Preset menu.

Rendering the full movie with the HD 1080p 23.976 preset may take several minutes. You'll change the settings to render only the first five seconds of the movie so that you can preview the quality. You can change the range rendered using the time ruler at the bottom of the Export Settings dialog box.

4   Move the current time indicator to 5:00, and then click the Set Out Point button (◣) to the left of the Select Zoom Level pop-up menu.

5   Click OK to close the Export Settings dialog box.

6 Click the orange link in the Output File column. Name the movie **HD-test_1080p.mp4**, and specify the AECC_CIB/ Lessons/Lesson14/Final_Movies folder. Then click OK or Save.

You're ready to output this movie, but you'll set up a few additional movie options in the queue before you render it.

Adding another output preset to the queue

▶ **Tip:** If you render files frequently, consider setting up a "watch folder." When you place a file in the watch folder, Adobe Media Encoder automatically outputs it using the settings you've specified in the Watch Folders panel.

Adobe Media Encoder comes with dozens of built-in presets, suitable for output for traditional broadcast, mobile devices, and the web. You'll output a version of your composition ready for posting to YouTube.

1 In the Preset Browser panel, navigate to Web Video > YouTube > YouTube SD 360p Widescreen 23.976.

Preset Name	Format	Frame Size	Frame Rate	Target Rate	Comment
▼ ⊙ **DVD & Blu-ray**					
▶ Blu-ray					
▶ DVD					
▼ ▦ **Image Sequence**					
▶ DPX					
▶ JPEG					
▶ PNG					
▶ Targa					
▶ TIFF					
▢ Other					
▼ ⊕ **Web Video**					
▶ DG Fast Channel					
▶ Flash					
▶ Vimeo					
▼ YouTube					
YouTube HD 720p 23.976	H.264	1280x720	23.976 fps	5 Mbps	1280x7:
YouTube HD 720p 25	H.264	1280x720	25 fps	5 Mbps	1280x7:
YouTube HD 720p 29.97	H.264	1280x720	29.97 fps	5 Mbps	1280x7:
YouTube HD 1080p 23.976	H.264	1920x1080	23.976 fps	8 Mbps	1920x1:
YouTube HD 1080p 25	H.264	1920x1080	25 fps	8 Mbps	1920x1:
YouTube HD 1080p 29.97	H.264	1920x1080	29.97 fps	8 Mbps	1920x1:
YouTube SD 360p Widescreen 23.976	H.264	640x360	23.976 fps	1 Mbps	640x36:
YouTube SD 360p Widescreen 25	H.264	640x360	25 fps	1 Mbps	640x36:

2 Drag the YouTube SD 360p Widescreen 23.976 preset onto the DesktopC composition in the Queue panel.

Adobe Media Encoder adds another output item to the queue.

3   Click the orange link in the Output File column for the item you just added. Then
    name the file **Final_Web.mp4**, and specify the AECC_CIB/Lessons/Lesson14/
    Final_Movies folder.

Rendering movies

You've set up two versions of your movie in the queue. Now you'll render and view
them. Rendering is resource-intensive, and it can take a while, depending on your
system, the complexity and length of the composition, and the settings you use.

1   Click the green Start Queue button (▶) in the upper right corner of the Queue panel.

Adobe Media Encoder encodes the movies in the queue simultaneously, displaying
a status bar, and reporting the estimated time remaining.

Depending
on your system,
this may take
a while.

▶ Tip: If you forget where you saved your encoded movies, click the orange link in the Output File column next to the finished movie. Adobe Media Encoder opens a window to show you where your files were saved.

2   When Adobe Media Encoder has finished, navigate to the Final_Movies folder in the Finder or Explorer, and double-click your files to play them.

Preparing a movie for broadcast output

The project you're rendering in this lesson is already high-resolution and appropriate for broadcast output. However, you may need to adjust other compositions for your intended delivery format.

To change the composition size, create a new composition with the appropriate settings for your final format. Then drag the project composition into the new composition.

If you converted the composition from a square pixel aspect ratio to a nonsquare pixel aspect ratio, which is used in broadcasting, items in the Composition panel may appear wider than before. To view the video accurately, enable *pixel aspect ratio correction*. Pixel aspect ratio correction squeezes the view of the composition slightly to display the image as it will appear on a video monitor. By default, this feature is turned off, but you can easily turn it on by clicking the Toggle Pixel Aspect Ratio Correction button (▤) at the bottom of the Composition panel. The quality of the pixel aspect ratio correction for previews is affected by the Zoom Quality preference in the Previews category of the Preferences dialog box.

Creating custom presets for Adobe Media Encoder

In most cases, one of the default Adobe Media Encoder presets will be appropriate for your project. However, you can create your own presets if you have specialized needs. In this case, you'll create a preset that renders a lower-resolution file for YouTube more quickly than the one you just encoded.

1   Click the Create New Preset Group button (🗁) at the top of the Preset Browser panel, and give the group a unique name, such as your name.

2   Click the Create New Preset button (✚).

3 Do the following in the Preset Settings dialog box, and then click OK:

- Name the preset **Low-res_YouTube**.

- Make sure H.264 is chosen from the Format menu.

- Choose YouTube SD 360p Widescreen 23.976 from the Based On Preset menu.

- Choose 12 from the Frame Rate menu.

- Choose Baseline from the Profile menu.

- Make sure 3.0 is chosen from the Level menu.

- Choose VBR, 1 Pass from the Bitrate Encoding menu. (You may need to scroll down to see it.)

- Click the Audio tab, and choose 44100 Hz from the Sample Rate menu and Medium from the Audio Quality menu.

4 Drag the Low_res_YouTube preset onto the DesktopC composition in the Queue panel.

5 Click the orange link in the Output File column. Then name the file **Lowres_YouTube**, and specify the AECC_CIB/Lessons/Lesson14/Final_Movies folder.

6 Click the Start Queue button.

With the settings in your new preset, the movie encodes more quickly. However, the quality isn't as high.

7 When Adobe Media Encoder has finished, navigate to the Final_Movies folder in Explorer or the Finder, and double-click the Lowres_YouTube movie to view it.

You have created both a web version and a broadcast version of the final composition.

Congratulations! You have completed all the lessons in *Adobe After Effects CC Classroom in a Book*.

While this book is intended to give you a good foundation for working with After Effects, it can't cover everything. To continue learning about After Effects, check out the resources described in the Getting Started section at the beginning of the book.

Review questions

1   Name two types of templates you can create for the Render Queue panel, and explain when and why to use them.

2   What is compression, and what are some things you should consider when compressing files?

3   How can you output a movie using Adobe Media Encoder?

Review answers

1   In After Effects, you can create templates for both render settings and output-module settings. These templates are presets that you can use to streamline the setup process when you render items for the same type of delivery format. After you define these templates, they appear in the Render Queue panel on the appropriate pop-up menu (Render Settings or Output Module). Then, when you're ready to render a job, you can simply select the template that is appropriate for the delivery format that your job requires, and the template applies all the settings.

2   Compression is essential to reduce the size of movies so that they can be stored, transmitted, and played back effectively. When exporting or rendering a movie file for playback on a specific type of device at a certain bandwidth, you choose a compressor/decompressor, or codec, to compress the information and generate a file readable by that type of device at that bandwidth. A wide range of codecs is available; no single codec is the best for all situations. For example, the best codec for compressing cartoon animation is generally not efficient for compressing live-action video. When compressing a movie file, you can fine-tune it for the best-quality playback on a computer, video playback device, the web, or from a DVD player. Depending on which encoder you use, you may be able to reduce the size of compressed files by removing artifacts that interfere with compression, such as random camera motion and excessive film grain.

3   To output a movie using Adobe Media Encoder, select the composition in the Project panel in After Effects, and then choose Composition > Add To Adobe Media Encoder Queue. In Adobe Media Encoder, select a preset and any other settings, name the output file, and click the Start Queue button.

INDEX

K

keyframes

about 28

adding to current time 219

copying from one layer to another 140

creating from audio amplitude 119

roving 222

keyframing motion paths 134

keying 228, 254–255

L

layer features, used when snapping 109

layers

about 14, 16

adjustment layers 263

animating 154, 157

animating to match audio 119

audio 111

child 70, 71

converting to 3D layers 273

copying keyframes from 140

deselecting 17

duplicating 18

expanding in the Timeline panel 22

fitting to compositions 44

importing in Photoshop files 157

light, 3D 274–276

making visible in the Timeline panel 31

modifying the In values for 142

naming in Photoshop 158

naming text layers 47

nesting 50

null 311

parent 70, 71

precomposing 50, 168

rearranging in the Timeline panel 17

renaming 18, 73

scaling 212

shape 90, 94

snapping 106

solid 107, 141

soloing 161

text 62

transforming properties 22

trimming 128

video 111

viewing multiple properties 221

layer styles 159

Layer switches in the Timeline panel 25

learning resources for Adobe After Effects CC 5

Lens Flare effect 174, 346

lesson files, downloading 3

Levels (Individual Controls) effect 252

lighting, simulating changes in 160

lights

adding to a 3D scene 274–276

ambient 308

point 307

Q

QuickTime 2

R

Radial Blur effect 19

Radial Gradient option 95

Radio Waves effect 143

Ramp effect 345

RAM previews 32

Ray-Traced 3D Renderer 293

Rectangle tool 94, 205

red overlay in matte preview 233

Reduce Chatter value 238

Refine Edge tool 238–239

Refine Hard Matte effect 239

Refine Soft Matte effect 239

remap-time marker in the Source Time ruler 179

removing unwanted elements 258–260

renaming layers 18

Renderer options in the Cineware effect 285

rendering 317

    compositions 53

    for mobile devices 364

    movies 354

    templates 357

    test movies 361

    using compression in 362

    using the Render Queue panel 244, 362

    with Adobe Media Encoder 365–370

Render Queue panel 54, 177, 244, 357–364

    adding compositions to 54

    opening 54

Render Settings options 54

render-settings templates 357

Repeaters 99, 104

replacing content using a mask 197

resizing layers 212

resources for using After Effects 36

restoring default preferences 10, 40, 60

retiming

    compositions 178

    playback 348

rolling shutter distortions, repairing 300

rotating

    3D layers 198

    shapes 101, 105

Rotation property, animating 101

Roto Brush & Refine Edge effect 237

Roto Brush tool 226–245

    creating background strokes with 232–233

    creating foreground strokes with 231–232

    freezing results 239

    refining a segmentation boundary 234

rotoscoping 228

Roving keyframes 222

S

V

vector shapes, masking with 130

vertices

    converting 193

    in a mask 188

video layers 111

Video Preview 250

Video switch 31, 52

views, 3D 272

vignette, applying 204

W

walking cycle, animating 218

Warp Stabilizer VFX 322–327

    settings 325, 327

work area

    brackets 25, 66

    trimming 112

workflow 10

workspaces

    customizing 11

    in Adobe Bridge 42

    predefined 34

    saving custom 35

X

x axis 20

    in the 3D axis 271

Y

y axis 20

    in the 3D axis 271

Z

z axis 269

    in the 3D axis 271

Zoom-Bubble effect 27

Production Notes

Adobe After Effects CC Classroom in a Book was created electronically using Adobe InDesign CS6. Art was produced using Adobe InDesign, Adobe Illustrator, and Adobe Photoshop.

References to company names in the lessons are for demonstration purposes only and are not intended to refer to any actual organization or person.

Typefaces used

Adobe Myriad Pro and Adobe Warnock Pro as well as other Adobe typefaces are used throughout thelessons. For more information about OpenType and Adobe fonts, visit www.adobe.com/type/opentype.

Team credits

The following individuals contributed to the development of *Adobe After Effects CC Classroom in a Book*:

- **Project Manager:** Elaine Gruenke
- **Writer:** Brie Gyncild
- **Illustrator and Compositor:** Lisa Fridsma
- **Copyeditor and Proofreader**: Wendy Katz
- **Indexer:** Brie Gyncild
- **Cover design:** Eddie Yuen
- **Interior design:** Mimi Heft
- **Art Director:** Andrew Faulkner
- **Designers:** Elaine Gruenke, Megan Lee
- **Adobe Press Executive Editor:** Victor Gavenda
- **Adobe Press Project Editor:** Connie Jeung-Mills
- **Adobe Press Production Editor:** David Van Ness

Contributors

Mark Christiansen—Author of *After Effects CS4 Visual Effects and Compositing Studio Techniques* (Adobe Press), Mark has created visual effects and animations for feature films, network television, computer games, and an array of high-technology companies. Recent clients include *The Orphanage* (Dimension Films), *Telling Pictures* (The History Channel), and the Couturie Company (HBO), as well as Seagate, Sun, Intel, and Medtronic. Feature credits include *The Day After Tomorrow* and films by Robert Rodriguez.

Takeshi Hiraoka—Plucked out of paradise, Hiraoka moved to chilly San Francisco from Honolulu, Hawaii, one cold winter day in 2002. In San Francisco, he attended the Academy of Art University, graduating in May 2004. This is where Hiraoka met Sheldon Callahan, with whom he directed and produced the feature-length, DV film *Origin*. In addition to being a DV producer, Hiraoka is also a 2D and 3D animator.

Stephen Schleicher—Travelling from Kansas to Georgia to California, Stephen has worked as an editor, graphic designer, videographer, director, and producer on a variety of small and large video productions. Currently, Stephen teaches media and web development at Fort Hays State University. He also works on video and independent projects for state and local agencies and organizations, as well as his own works. Stephen is a regular contributor to Digital Media Net (www.digitalmedianet.com).

Anna Ullrich—Anna is a pale but fine digital artist based in Seattle, Washington, although her heart resides in Minnesota, where her spry and brilliant Democratic grandmother lives. Anna earned a BFA from the University of Washington in Seattle and an MFA from the University of Notre Dame in Indiana (both in photography).

Special Thanks

We offer our sincere thanks to Todd Kopriva, Stephen Schleicher, and Christine Yarrow for their support and help with this project. We couldn't have done it without you!

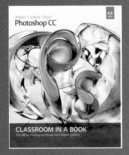
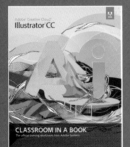

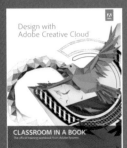